WJEC
CBAC

C000000549

WITHDRAWN

WJEC

ICT

for GCSE

Student's Book

■ Peter Vickers
■ Ian Paget

HODDER
EDUCATION
AN HACHETTE UK COMPANY

The Publishers would like to thank the following for permission to reproduce copyright material:

Photo credits
p.4 © Graça Victoria/Fotolia; **p.5** © GreenGate Publishing Services; **p.8** © Monkey Business/Fotolia; **p.10** © Ian Paget; **p.11** *T–B* © Agb/Fotolia; © TeamCrucillo/Fotolia; © GaToR-GFX/Fotolia; © C Barhorst/Fotolia; © Viktor Gmyria/Fotolia; © Viktor Gmyria/Fotolia; **p.14** © PSL Images/Alamy; **p.16** © edgecreative/Fotolia; **p.18** © Franz Pfluegl/Fotolia; **p.21** © masterpiece/Fotolia; **p.35** © Najlah Feanny/Corbis; **p.38** © Art Directors & TRIP/Alamy; **p.44** © NASA/Alamy; **p.44** © eddie toro/Fotolia; **p.45** © cristimatei/Fotolia; **p.49** *Top* © anubis3211/Fotolia; *Bottom* © Pindyurin Vasily/Shutterstock; **p.50** © Tomasz Trojanowski/Shutterstock; **p.55** © Paul Doyle/Alamy; **p.71** © Ian Paget; **p.87** © GreenGate Publishing Services; **p.97** © GreenGate Publishing Services; **p.113** © GreenGate Publishing Services; **p.127** © Alan Ward/Fotolia; **p.129** *L–R* © Ian Paget; **p.131** *L–R* © Ian Paget; **p.133** *L–R* © Ian Paget; **p.163** © Mike Paget; **p.164** *L–R* © GaToR-GFX/ Fotolia; © C Barhorst/Fotolia; © Agb/Fotolia; **p.174** © manipulateur/Fotolia; **p.177** © alphaspirit/Fotolia; **p.179** © imagebroker/Alamy; **p.181** © Rebel/Fotolia; **p.183** © diego cervo/Fotolia; **p.195** © Dennis MacDonald/Alamy; **p.196** © John Bavosi/Science Photo Library; **p.200** © Chris Cooper-Smith/Alamy; **p.206** © John Joannides/Alamy; **p.207** © Evgeny Tyzhinov/Fotolia; **p.208** *Top* © Gleam/Fotolia; *Bottom* © Amy Walter/Fotolia; **p.215** © Daisy Daisy/Fotolia; **p.216** © Andrejs Pidjass/Fotolia; **p.218** © Andrejs Pidjass/Fotolia; **p.219** © Ed Young/Science Photo Library; **p.220** © Vasily Smirnov/Shutterstock; **p.221** © John Henderson/Alamy; **p.222** © Al Teich/Fotolia; **p.224** © Andrei Merkulov/Shutterstock; **p.228** © endostock/Fotolia; **p.236** *Top* © D200/Fotolia; *Bottom* © Susan Montgomery/Fotolia

Acknowledgements
Brand names mentioned in this book are protected by their respective trademarks and are acknowledged: Amazon, screenshots of online shopping and logo; Card Watch, screenshot from www.cardwatch.org.uk; ClamWin, screenshot from www.clamwin.com/content/view/23/55; Jim Crawford, 'Fun With Rollovers' screenshot from www.crawforddirect.com; eBay, screenshot of site map; Google, screenshots of search engines and Google Mail; Halfords, screenshot of online reservation form; New Modellers Shop, screenshot of online catalogue; Raleigh, screenshot of online shop; Ticketmaster, online booking screenshots.

Adobe product screenshots reprinted with permission from Adobe Systems Incorporated.

Microsoft product screenshots reprinted with permission from Microsoft Corporation.

Every effort has been made to trace all copyright holders, but if any have been inadvertently overlooked the Publishers will be pleased to make the necessary arrangements at the first opportunity.

Although every effort has been made to ensure that website addresses are correct at time of going to press, Hodder Education cannot be held responsible for the content of any website mentioned in this book. It is sometimes possible to find a relocated web page by typing in the address of the home page for a website in the URL window of your browser.

Hachette UK's policy is to use papers that are natural, renewable and recyclable products and made from wood grown in sustainable forests. The logging and manufacturing processes are expected to conform to the environmental regulations of the country of origin.

Orders: please contact Bookpoint Ltd, 130 Milton Park, Abingdon, Oxon OX14 4SB. Telephone: (44) 01235 827720. Fax: (44) 01235 400454. Lines are open 9.00–5.00, Monday to Saturday, with a 24-hour message answering service. Visit our website at www.hoddereducation.co.uk

For files that support the activities please visit www.ict4wjecgcse.co.uk

© Peter Vickers, Ian Paget 2010

First published in 2010 by

Hodder Education,
An Hachette UK Company
338 Euston Road
London NW1 3BH

Impression number   5 4 3 2 1

Year   2015 2014 2013 2012 2011 2010

Cover photo © Klaus Tiedge/Corbis

Illustrations by GreenGate Publishing Services and Alex Machin

Typeset in Minion 12pt by GreenGate Publishing Services, Tonbridge, Kent

Printed in Italy

A catalogue record for this title is available from the British Library

ISBN: 978 1444 109580

Contents

CONTROLLED ASSESSMENT

Unit 2 Solving problems with ICT

Unit 4 Developing multimedia ICT solutions

Chapter 1

Data and quality of data

ICT: Information and Communication Technology is the study of how data is collected, stored, processed and distributed.

In this chapter, you will learn about data, information and knowledge and how they are related. You will find out how to check that data has been entered into the computer correctly and is sensible.

ICT, which stands for Information and Communication Technology, is the study of the ways in which data is collected, how it is stored, what processing can be done on it and the different methods by which the data can be sent between computer users. It is also a study of how the information produced from the data is used in the workplace or at home.

Data and information

Data consists of raw facts and figures. Here is an example of data:

17   17   18   20   20   21   22   22   23

These are just numbers in a sequence and have no apparent meaning. If we are told that they are readings in °C taken at hourly intervals from a temperature sensor in a classroom, then the data becomes information. If the data above was presented in the table below, it would represent information.

Temperature in room 37 on 20 May 2010

Time	8am	9am	10am	11am	12am	1pm	2pm	3pm	4pm
Temperature (°C)	17	17	18	20	20	21	22	22	23

Computers process data to produce information.

Data + Meaning = Information

Knowledge is the way that we can understand and use the information that we have.

Data given a meaning and context can become information. Information given understanding can be knowledge. Knowledge can be deduced from the information. We know from the table of information above that the room has become warmer; over the eight-hour period, the increase in temperature has been 6°C. So knowledge is obtained by applying rules to information.

Here is another example:

Data	3, 5
Information	The score in the football game was 3–5
Knowledge	The home team lost

◯ Processing data

Computers process data. People used to call computers "number crunchers". When data is input to a computer, it processes the data and gives back information. This data processing may involve organising the data, sorting it in some way or performing calculations on it.

Numbers are just one type of data. Data can be of other types such as words, pictures, videos or sounds. A computer can process any of these types just as easily.

If the information produced by computers is going to be useful, then the data that is used must be good quality data. A lot of time and effort is spent in making sure that no incorrect data gets into a computer system. There is a saying among computer users: garbage in, garbage out (GIGO). This means that if you give a computer incorrect data then it will produce incorrect results. Many problems that arise with the use of computers are not caused by the computer but by the data that is used. People tend to blame computers for mistakes but it is usually the fault of the person who collected or entered the data.

GIGO: Garbage in, garbage out.

Wow! A Quadrillion-Dollar Credit Card Bill

A Texas man has a 17-figure credit card statement after a bank glitch resulted in an eye-popping charge.

Figure 1.1 Garbage in, garbage out

○ Quality of data

For data to be useful, it must be:

- fit for purpose
- accurate
- non-biased
- up to date
- valid.

Suppose a customer orders a new bicycle from a company using an online order form, part of which is shown in Figure 1.2.

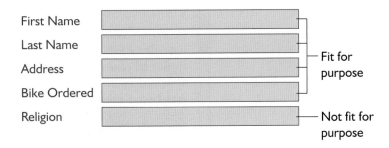

Figure 1.2 Online order form

The order form is **fit for purpose** because it asks for data that is needed to ensure the correct bike is delivered to the correct address. Asking for a customer's religion is **not** fit for this purpose.

If the data provided on the order form is not **accurate** either the wrong item will be delivered or the item will be delivered to the wrong address.

Data collected from a random sample is **non-biased**. If data is collected from a non-random sample it could be biased depending on the sample. For instance, if a survey was taken about the popularity of a particular band, it would not be much use only asking members of the fan club.

The data also needs to be **up to date**. If the customer gives an address and then moves house or uses an out-of-date credit card number to pay, they may never get their bike.

To be **valid**, the data needs to be sensible and within acceptable boundaries. We will be looking at a number of ways of making sure that data is valid later in this chapter. If, for instance, a customer ordered three chicken pizzas in the "bike ordered" field on the order form in Figure 1.2, the data would not be sensible and is therefore not valid.

Data validation

Organisations spend a lot of time trying to minimise the possibility of incorrect data getting into their computer systems.

Almost every business that uses ICT stores some data. It may be data about the items they sell, details of their customers or their sales figures for the last year. Whatever the data is, it is vital that there are no errors in it. Mistakes in the data may result in inappropriate decision-making or loss of sales.

Activity

Internet search

In March 2003, a person in Huddersfield failed to pay his electricity bill so he was sent another one, together with a threat to take him to court if he did not pay it. He was rather shocked when he opened the bill to discover the amount he was being asked to pay!

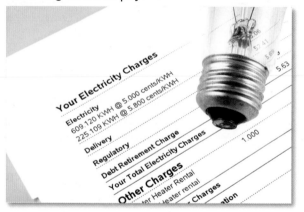

Figure 1.3

1 Use the internet (suggested search: +"electricity bill" +Huddersfield +2003) to find:
   ● the amount of his shocking electricity bill
   ● the amount of his original bill.
2 Do you think the problem was caused by the computer or was it incorrect data that was input?
3 Can you find any other cases where the use of computers has led to ridiculous situations?

Incorrect data becomes even more critical in systems that store personal data. How would a customer feel if a bank told them they had less money in their account than there actually was? What might happen if a patient in a hospital was given the wrong treatment on the basis of incorrect data? A person may be refused employment on the grounds of an incorrect criminal record.

Types of error

There are many different types of error that may occur when storing data. A business runs the risk of losing its customers if the customers lose confidence in the way the business holds information about them. A number of different methods are used to try to ensure the data is not corrupted and we discuss them in the next few sections.

Errors may occur at a number of different stages in the data's existence:

- Data might be collected and recorded wrongly.
- Data might be entered into the computer incorrectly.
- Processing of the data may cause errors.
- Stored data may be deliberately or accidentally changed by unauthorised people.
- Data transmitted from one computer to another could become corrupted.

Figure 1.4 Using a data capture form to collect data while conducting a street survey

Data capture forms and **questionnaires** must be carefully designed to minimise the chance of errors being recorded on them.

Possible error	Solution
When data is first collected, it may be recorded on a special data capture form or a questionnaire. The person who records the data may make a mistake and write down the wrong data.	Data capture forms and questionnaires must be designed in such a way that errors are minimised. The questions must be unambiguous – there must be no doubt in the mind of the person filling it in as to what they are meant to enter. Boxes might be used on the form to make sure that data is entered neatly and not scribbled down so quickly that the writing is illegible.

Data **verification** checks for transcription errors (errors made when the data is typed in).

After the data capture forms have been completed, they are then given to a computer operator who transcribes the data. This means that the operator types the data into the computer, probably using a keyboard. There are other methods of getting the data into the computer, such as using a scanner, which we shall study later in this book.

Possible error	Solution
Transcription errors may occur. The person typing the data into the computer may make a mistake and enter incorrect data.	Methods of data verification are studied in more detail in Chapter 14 but the data must be carefully checked by eye, or even double-keyed (entered twice into the computer) and only accepted if the two versions are identical.

> Data **validation** is used to check that data is sensible before it is processed. Typical validation checks are range checks, presence checks, format checks and the use of check digits.

Before data is processed, it is checked again to see if it is sensible data. This process is called data validation and makes sure that no unsuitable readings are processed by the computer. Most database and spreadsheet programs allow the user to set validation rules so the data is checked when it is entered.

There are many different methods of data validation and we look at a few here.

Possible error	Solution
Invalid data is entered. This may have been caused by incorrect data being collected or by a transcription error.	Data validation methods may be used to check that the data is sensible data.
Data is recorded which is outside a range, for instance: ● a mark of 11 given for a test out of 10 ● the month part of a date being given as 13 ● a child's height entered as 16.3 m.	**Range check:** Numerical data is checked to see if the value lies within an acceptable range of numbers.
Data may be missing, such as failing to record the size of an item of clothing ordered online.	**Presence check:** A check to see that data is not missing.
A postcode must be two letters followed by a number, a space, a number and two letters. Getting the order wrong would cause an error.	**Format check:** A check that the data is in the correct format (laid out in the agreed manner).
Digits in a number may be entered in the wrong order (**transposition error**).	**Check digit:** A calculation is carried out on the digits of a number to create an extra digit, which is then appended to the end of the number. The computer checks when the data is entered that the check digit is correct. You can find a check digit on the ISBN of this book.

Summary

S

- Data consists of raw facts and figures.
- To be useful, data needs to be:
  - fit for purpose
  - accurate
  - non-biased
  - up to date
  - valid.
- Computers process data to produce information.
- People use information to produce knowledge.
- GIGO – if you give a computer incorrect data, it will provide incorrect information.
- ICT stands for Information and Communication Technology. It is the study of how data is collected, processed, stored and distributed.
- ICT methods require less human effort and produce faster and more reliable results than traditional methods. It is easier to keep information secure.
- There are many different types of error that can occur. Businesses make great efforts to minimise the chance of errors occurring.
- Careful design of data capture forms cuts down on data collection errors.
- Data verification methods are used to minimise the risk of transcription errors.
- Data validation checks are made to make sure the data is sensible. Typical validation checks are:
  - range checks (making sure data falls within an acceptable range)
  - presence checks (making sure no data is missing)
  - format checks (making sure data is the correct type and format)
  - check digits (extra calculated digits added to numerical data).

Practice questions 1

P

1 Complete the following sentences:

(a) Data consists of _____. [1]

(b) Data + meaning = _____. [1]

(c) Knowledge is gained from information by _____. [1]

2 When a new pupil joins a school, a form is filled in with all the details. The school secretary then enters the data into the computer system.

(a) Describe **two** possible sources of error that could occur. [2]

(b) How could each of these errors be prevented? [2]

3 Explain what GIGO stands for and what it means. [2]

4 (a) What does data verification check for? [1]

(b) What does data validation check for? [1]

5 What are the four methods of data validation mentioned in this chapter and what does each method check? [8]

Chapter

2

Home entertainment

In this chapter, you will learn about ways that computers can be used in the home. You will look at examples of using the computer for gaming, social networking, interactive TV, music and phones. You will also learn how to be careful when using the internet.

Every home has some ICT devices in it and most people use some form of ICT every day, such as playing computer games, taking digital photographs or using a mobile phone.

When an ICT system is used, data has to be **input** to make it work and something must be **output**, such as a picture, words or sounds, to make it useful. Often data, such as the high score for a game, is **stored**. The devices that are used for input, output and storage are known collectively as **hardware** and the computer programs that help to make these devices work are known as **software**.

Figure 2.1 Input and output devices

○ Interactive TV

In 2008, changes to the way television was broadcast were introduced. Between 2008 and 2012, everyone with an analogue TV must change to digital TV if they want to continue to receive broadcasts and in 2012 all analogue broadcasts will end. This will mean better picture and sound quality but another, more significant, change is that the digital broadcasts are interactive. This means that you have a say in what you watch and you can participate in quiz shows or questionnaires, surveys or games.

Interactive television services provided by some television broadcasters include:

- interactive games
- voting in simple surveys and displaying the current results
- interactive shopping
- pay-to-view movies (you watch the films when you choose and the cost is added to your monthly bill)
- sports channels (you select from a number of different cameras or look at game statistics)
- news channels (you select a video from a choice of news stories)
- holiday advertising (you can make a booking directly)
- betting services
- email.

Caution should be taken as some of the services have costs that may not always be apparent.

Services offered by the internet are available through our televisions and it is possible to send emails or buy items using some TV sets.

Many homes have a cable connection for television and this can also be used to connect to the internet. It is possible to watch TV programmes on your computer, using services such as BBC iPlayer. In fact, the distinctions between the use of a computer and a television in the home are becoming blurred.

> Interactive systems have a two-way communication between user and machine. Interactive television is television that allows the viewer to actively participate in a number of activities.

> Services available over the internet are now being offered on interactive television channels.

Advantages of interactive digital TV

- The user is an active rather than a passive user of the system.
- A number of different activities can be carried out on one system.
- The pictures are of better quality.
- The viewer has a choice of languages.
- There are possibilities for interactive learning using TV.

Disadvantages of interactive digital TV

- There can be arguments over which vote to give or which camera angle to look at.
- There is more reliance on a system which requires little or no exercise.
- There is expense involved in buying new systems.

Interactive TV input and output devices

Input devices	Output devices
Remote control unit	TV screen
Keypad or keyboard	Speakers

Gaming

Figure 2.2 A computer games shop

Computer games have become very complex, using realistic videos and sound clips. The main reason for this is the rapid increase in the power of computers. The processors have become faster, which means that graphics can be displayed in greater detail, and digitally recorded sound gives a greater sense of realism. High-quality graphics cards and sound cards help speed up the processing and increase the performance of the game.

Special dedicated consoles can be bought which, because they only play games and do very little else, produce a better quality of video and sound. Games are usually bought on CD-ROM or DVD-ROM but some websites are dedicated to interactive game-playing.

> Interactive games use the internet to link competing players in a real-time game.

Advantages of using computers for playing games

- Many games are educational and people learn while they play.
- Games can also be simulations and real-life situations can be mimicked, such as great historic battles or learning to fly.
- Many games are collaborative and involve team work with other players.
- Quick thinking and good hand–eye coordination is developed.
- Games that normally need more than one player, such as chess, can be played alone.
- Games are fun!

Disadvantages of using computers for playing games

- Many people are concerned about the time that children and some adults spend playing computer games and they see it as a form of addiction.
- Solitary activity (playing alone) can prevent normal social interaction with others and limits the development of social skills.
- Children are becoming unfit as they are not getting enough exercise.

> Advice: Limit the time you spend on any computer activity … especially playing games!

Gaming input and output devices

Input devices	
	A **keyboard** is useful for typing words, numbers and special symbols into the computer. A keyboard can often have a number pad and function keys.
	A **gamepad** has special controls for playing games.
	A **joystick** is used mainly for playing games or for simulation programs, such as a flight simulator. It may also be used to control the movement of robotic devices.
	A **mouse** has a number of buttons which can be clicked to enable certain actions. As the mouse is moved it controls a pointer on the screen.
Output devices	
	A **monitor** or screen is used to display information. The size of a monitor is measured diagonally from corner to corner.
	**Speakers** allow sounds produced by the computer to be heard. These can range from the sound part of a DVD to beeps and clicks produced by the computer.

The resolution of a monitor is a measure of the number of pixels that can be displayed. (A pixel – short for picture element – is the smallest amount of information that can be displayed graphically on a screen, a single coloured dot.) Modern monitors can display millions of different colours.

○ Digital photography

Digital photography is when pictures are taken and recorded without the need for photographic film. Anyone can use a digital camera to take photographs and publish their pictures on the internet or display them using electronic picture frames or albums. Family photos can be placed on websites for relatives or friends to be able to see from anywhere in the world.

Photographs can be downloaded from digital cameras and stored on a computer's hard drive, where they can be organised into albums and viewed on the monitor. Since pictures can use up a large amount of storage space, they are often saved onto a CD or DVD. Selected photos can be printed using a colour printer. This is much faster than the conventional way of waiting for a film to be developed, but the quality of printed pictures depends on the quality of the printer.

Some digital cameras allow short movies to be taken and these videos can also be downloaded and stored, or published on a website. Using publishing software, catalogues can be produced of all the photographs that have been stored.

Digital camera

When photos are taken they are stored as digital files using a memory chip, so they can be downloaded directly into a computer and saved on a backing store such as hard disk or DVD or CD. The chips are removable and blank chips can be inserted to store more images.

Digital cameras have different maximum image resolutions. The more expensive cameras have higher resolutions. The resolution of the images can be set. More photos can be stored in the camera if a lower resolution is selected, but the quality is not as good as with a high-resolution setting.

Digital video camera

Similar to a digital camera, a digital video camera stores video clips as digital files, which can later be downloaded directly to a computer. Many video cameras also take still photos. To take high definition (HD) movies, an HD camera is needed.

Blu-ray recorders allow disks to be recorded that can contain HD pictures and movies. Although Blu-ray disks are the same physical size and shape as DVDs they can hold much more data.

Input: lens and microphone

Output: screen and speaker

There may be other input devices, such as a light-level sensor. Cameras can be connected to output devices, such as printers.

Figure 2.3 A digital video camera

Digital photography input and output devices

Input devices	Output devices
Digital camera	Screen on the camera
Microphone	Speakers
	Printer

Webcam services

A webcam is a camera often used to feed pictures at regular intervals to web pages.

> A webcam can feed pictures to a website.

A webcam is a digital video camera connected directly to a computer and set up in a fixed position. The webcam can be used to feed a stream of video or still pictures at regular intervals to a website. There are many thousands of web pages with webcam images on them and it is possible to view real-time images of places all over the world. Webcams are often set up to monitor conditions such as the weather, the skiing conditions on mountains or the traffic on congested roads. Webcams are often found as part of a monitor or in the lid of a laptop computer.

Webcams are also used in teleconferencing to allow two computer users in different places to communicate through video and audio links.

Figure 2.4 Various companies offer to help you broadcast your webcam pictures

Advantages of a webcam

- A webcam can be set up to monitor the security of your home so that you can view it while you are on holiday.
- A webcam can be set up in the baby's room so that it is possible to check on the welfare of the baby while working or carrying on with daily life.
- Pictures of you and your family can be sent directly to friends or relatives abroad.
- Remote sites can be monitored without a human presence, such as watching penguins in the Antarctic.

Disadvantages of a webcam

- You might not be aware that a webcam is taking pictures of you, which might lead to you being embarrassed.
- You could be tempted to do something foolish that you regret after it has been broadcast to the world.
- Your privacy could be compromised.

Webcam services input and output devices

Input devices	Output devices
Webcam	Monitor
Microphone	Speakers

Social networking

Figure 2.5 Signing up to a social networking site involves giving away personal information

There are many social networking sites. Well-known ones are Facebook, Friends Reunited, MSN, Bebo, MySpace and Twitter. New ones spring up all the time. To join a social networking site, you have to give certain personal information. You should think very carefully about how much personal information you give away when you sign up.

Every care should be taken when using social networking sites. Remember, people do not always tell the truth on these sites. Who you think is young may be old, a man may pretend to be a boy and so on. You can never tell.

Advantages of social networking

- The sites are usually free.
- They allow members to communicate with people who have similar ideas and interests.
- They provide an easy way of showing off your photos, achievements and so on.
- They provide an easy way to make friends online and keep in touch.
- Long-lost friends and family members can be traced.

Beware! Chat rooms and other social networking sites can be dangerous places as well as harmless fun.

Disadvantages of social networking

- People may not be who they say they are, and you should never give anybody personal information such as your name, address, email or telephone number.
- It is tempting to reveal something, such as an embarrassing photograph, which at the time you think is funny but you later regret.
- Online bullying can take place.
- Sometimes employers check social networking sites before offering a job, which can be a disadvantage if you have posted a silly picture of yourself or written something nasty about a previous employer.

Social networking input and output devices

Input devices	Output devices
Webcam	Monitor
Keypad or keyboard	Speakers
Mobile phone	

○ Chat

It is possible for users of the internet to log in to special chat websites and hold a real-time typed conversation with others. To manage this and make it easier for different people to find each other, there are special "chat rooms" where users can arrange to "meet".

Users of chat rooms sometimes use special abbreviations to save time when typing, for example, BCNU is short for "Be Seeing You". Similar abbreviations are often used when sending text messages on mobile phones.

> You should exercise extreme caution when using a chat room or any social networking site. It is never a good idea to arrange to meet somebody you have only chatted to online. If anything at all makes you feel uncomfortable or worries you, then tell somebody about it – preferably a parent or teacher.

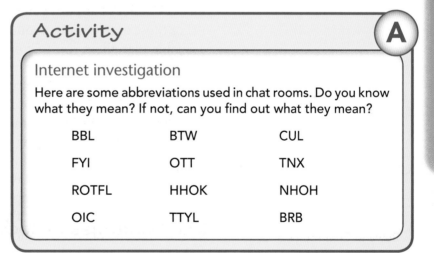

Activity **A**

Internet investigation

Here are some abbreviations used in chat rooms. Do you know what they mean? If not, can you find out what they mean?

BBL	BTW	CUL
FYI	OTT	TNX
ROTFL	HHOK	NHOH
OIC	TTYL	BRB

○ Radio, video and music

ICT allows access to all kinds of music on digital TV and digital audio broadcasting (DAB) radios, the internet, CDs and so on. You can tune to a radio station from almost anywhere in the world and listen to their live broadcast.

The speed of your internet connection is an important factor when listening to radio or viewing video broadcasts on a computer, as a slow connection can frequently cause the sound to stop for a few seconds. This is because the feed is being played at a faster speed than the signal is being received. Without a reasonably fast broadband service it may be impossible to receive broadcasts.

DVD and Blu-ray films

Because of the large storage capacity of a DVD and the even larger capacity of Blu-ray disks, it is possible to save the whole of a movie on one of them. This can then be played on a computer and viewed on an ordinary monitor. Many film DVDs also include extra material such as still photos, behind-the-scenes stories or a short documentary on the making of the film and special effects used.

Music and sound

Ripping is the process of copying the contents of CDs or DVDs on to the hard disk.

If you have speakers attached to your computer you can use programs such as Microsoft Media Player or Real Player to play music. Music tracks can be obtained from the internet in a special compressed format called MP3, which makes the files smaller and faster to download, though there is some loss of quality compared with a CD. Music files can also be ripped from CDs and stored in MP3 format.

Music companies allow some free downloading of sample music, but most charge for each track. The downloaded files can be saved on a computer's hard drive and then copied onto an MP3 player.

Musical instruments need a Musical Instrument Digital Interface (MIDI) to connect to a computer.

For those more serious about music, there are software packages available that allow you to connect musical instruments such as keyboards, drums and guitars to a computer. You can then record the music you play, or even compose pieces of music and play them back through the instruments. A number of different soundtracks can be recorded and then combined and edited using a program called a sequencer: a recording studio in your own home!

Microphones can be used to "sample" sounds. This means that a recording of the sound is taken at regular intervals and stored digitally. The greater the sampling rate, the better quality of the sound but the larger the file. The sound can be edited, saved and used in multimedia presentations.

Advantages of using ICT for music and sound

- Huge numbers of songs and videos can be stored in a very small space allowing us to take all our favourites with us wherever we go.

- Almost any kind of music can be found on the internet.

- Sounds and movies can be recorded while we are listening to music or watching something else.

Figure 2.6 ICT makes it easy to access music

- Music can be composed without needing to write down the notes. The computer software will do it for us.

Disadvantages of using ICT for music and sound

● Music may be illegally copied onto our systems.

● Record companies may lose business or fail because too many people copy the music digitally instead of buying the track.

● Music produced electronically may not sound the same as listening to live music.

Music and sound input and output devices

Input devices	Output devices
Remote control unit	TV screen
Keypad or keyboard	Speakers
Microphone	Monitor

> ## Activity **A**
>
> ### Sound
>
> 1 Download the file **noises.wav** from the activities website shown at the beginning of this book.
>
> 2 Play the file and you will hear sounds made by five different objects. The initial letters of these objects spell a word we use often in ICT.
>
> 3 Can you name the objects and discover the hidden word?

○ Mobile phones

Almost everyone has a mobile phone. They have become very complex and versatile. Some mobile phones allow you to browse internet pages or view small versions of web pages using Wireless Application Protocol (WAP). The pages need to be small because the screens on mobile phones are small but information on news, weather, sports events, share prices and other areas of interest are readily available. It may also be possible to create your own pages.

Owners of WAP mobile phones are also able to:

● send and receive text messages

● send and receive emails

Figure 2.7 A mobile phone

- play games
- listen to music or to the radio
- take photographs and send the images to another person
- capture short video clips
- download different ring tones
- use an installed memory chip for storing data.

Advantages of mobile phones

- Staying in touch is easy: children can phone home to be collected; people whose vehicle has broken down can phone for assistance, and so on.
- A mobile phone is very compact and can save carrying around a diary, camera and so on, as they are all in one device.
- You can access the internet (if you have a WAP phone).
- People who are constantly on the move can be contacted by their base.
- It can avoid the need to make expensive calls from phones in hotels.
- You can send and receive email.
- You can send and receive text messages.

Disadvantages of mobile phones

- Mobile phones can be an intrusive nuisance to others when used in public places (restaurants, bars, trains, etc.).
- Mobile phones can be expensive if used excessively or abroad.
- Health problems may occur with over-use or if living too near to a mobile phone mast.
- Mobile phones do not always work, for example if they are out of range of a transmitter–receiver.
- People can be contacted at any time, even when it is inconvenient.
- People use mobile phones in cars without hands-free kits, which is illegal, very dangerous and can lead to accidents.
- Mobile phones can interfere with the signals used in aeroplanes when taking off and landing.

Summary S

- An **input device**, e.g. a keyboard, sends data into a computer system.
- An **output device**, e.g. a monitor, produces results from the system.
- A **storage device**, e.g. a hard drive, records the data produced by the system.
- **Hardware** is the name given to input, output and storage devices as well as the processor itself.
- The computer programs that help to make these devices work are known as **software**.
- **Interactive systems** have two-way communication between user and machine.
- **Interactive television** allows the viewer to actively participate in a number of activities.
- Services previously only available over the internet are now offered on interactive television channels.
- Interactive games use the internet to link competing players in a real-time game.
- A **pixel** – short for picture element – is the smallest amount of information displayed graphically on a screen, a single coloured dot.
- Modern monitors can display millions of different colours.
- Digital photos are taken with a digital camera and stored as digital files using a memory chip.
- **Blu-ray disks** can contain high-definition (HD) pictures and movies and hold many times more data than traditional DVDs.
- **HD** televisions are capable of showing very good quality digital pictures.
- A **webcam** is a camera often used to feed pictures at regular intervals to web pages.
- Social networking involves people getting together to communicate and discuss matters of common interest. Social networking sites, such as Facebook, allow you to do this online.
- Chat is where users can log in to special websites and hold a real-time typed conversation with others using a computer.
- Rules for being online and when using social networking sites are:
  - Stay safe by not revealing too much personal information.
  - Never meet someone you have met online without clearing it with a responsible adult.
  - Don't accept messages or pictures from someone you do not know.
  - Remember, everything online is not necessarily reliable.
  - Tell a responsible adult if anything worries you when you are online.
- Music tracks can be obtained from the internet in a special compressed format called MP3.
- Musical instruments need a Musical Instrument Digital Interface (MIDI) to connect to a computer.
- Some mobile phones allow you to browse internet pages or view small versions of web pages using Wireless Application Protocol (WAP).

Practice questions 2 P

1 Tom uses a WAP mobile phone to access the internet.

   (a) Give **two** problems that may arise when using a mobile phone. [2]

   (b) Give **one** advantage of using a mobile phone over a standard landline phone. [1]

   (c) Give **two** other services Tom may be able to access with his mobile phone. [2]

2 Computer games are often played by pupils at home.

   (a) Give **two** reasons why playing a computer game may be a good thing. [2]

   (b) Give **two** reasons why playing a computer game may be a bad thing. [2]

3 (a) Describe what is meant by a social networking site. [2]

   (b) Explain the dangers involved in using a social networking site. [4]

Chapter

Home and personal communication systems

In this chapter, you will learn about devices and methods used to access the internet.

The internet

There has been no invention in recent years that has had more impact on the way we live than the **internet**. It has changed the way we work, the way we perform daily tasks, such as shopping or banking, and it has even had an effect on the ways in which we spend our leisure time. Some people have found it easy to make changes but there are many who have not yet been able to adapt to using the internet or are changing their ways only very slowly. The internet has made our lives easier in many ways. Tasks can now be performed from home that used to require travelling to shops, post offices, banks or other places of work, but it has also caused new problems.

The internet has created new types of criminal, who use the internet for theft, damage or fraud. We now have to protect our computers from viruses and hackers, as well as our houses from thieves and burglars.

> The internet is a global network of computers. All computers on the internet can communicate with each other (i.e. send or receive data).
>
> To use the internet you must subscribe to an internet service provider (ISP). The ISP has servers that are permanently connected to the internet.

Internet hardware and software

Any computer can be connected to the internet if it has the appropriate hardware and software installed but you will need to use the services of an internet service provider (ISP). An ISP has powerful computers called servers that are permanently connected to the internet. Examples of ISPs are TalkTalk, Orange, AOL and O_2.

There are a number of competing ISPs available and some of them are free but most charge for use of their services. This charge may be a set monthly fee or it may be based on how much you use the internet. The free ISPs are financed by advertising. An ISP will provide you with software to be installed on your computer.

When you want to use the internet, your computer connects to one of the ISP's computers. You probably then need to enter a username and a password. If it is accepted, the ISP links your computer to their server, which then provides a link to the internet.

The other software you need to install on your computer is an internet browser, such as Microsoft Internet Explorer or Mozilla Firefox.

Computers can be connected to the internet in a number of ways:

- dial-up
- broadband
- cable
- satellite
- mobile communications.

Dial-up

To link a computer to the telephone system, you need a modem. This is a device that makes sure that the digital signals the computer uses are compatible with those of the telephone lines. The computer is connected to the modem which is then connected to a telephone socket, although sometimes the modem is internal and hidden inside the computer. You may be able to hear the modem dialling and connecting to the ISP's computer.

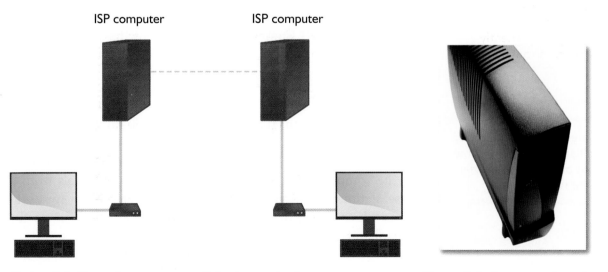

Figure 3.1 Two microcomputers linked over the internet

Figure 3.2 An external modem

The speed at which a modem sends and receives data is measured in kilobits per second (Kbps) or megabits per second (Mbps). The greater the speed of the connection, the faster you can browse websites on the internet or download data from them.

○ Broadband

Broadband is a term used to describe fast internet connections such as ISDN and ADSL. Integrated Services Digital Network (ISDN) is a faster method of connecting to the internet than dial-up but is quite old-fashioned. It has generally been replaced by Asymmetric Digital Subscriber Line (ADSL), which uses a nationwide network of digital connections. The system uses digital signals (already compatible with the computer signals), so there is no need for a modem.

ISDN, ADSL and cable are fast methods of connecting to the internet.

ADSL uses the existing telephone lines to connect to the internet. The technology allows very fast connection speeds. Downloading data is much faster than uploading, which makes this very suitable for applications such as web browsing.

ADSL links can be left permanently connected to the internet, which improves the speed of access to websites and allows email messages to be delivered as soon as they arrive. Some web pages are automatically refreshed after a given time interval and this allows users to access the scores from football games or other pages where the information is constantly changing.

○ Cable

Cable connections use fibre-optic cables to provide homes with broadband as well as television and telephone services. Unlike normal telephone connections, the signals do not get weaker the further you are from the origin, and upload and download speeds are generally faster than ADSL.

○ Satellite

A satellite in geostationary orbit stays above the same point on the Earth's surface all the time.

Using satellites means that expensive cables do not have to be laid to the home of the receiver. A satellite in geostationary orbit is contacted and signals are sent to and from an aerial connected to the computer. The satellite sends and receives signals from a base station somewhere on Earth. This is very useful for rural areas which may not have the necessary cable connections for broadband.

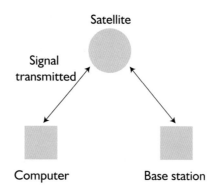

Figure 3.3 Satellite in geostationary orbit

Mobile communications

Mobile phone

Many mobile phones allow you to connect to the internet.

Wireless laptop

Most laptop computers have built in wireless technology. This means that you can access the internet wherever you are without physically plugging the laptop into an access point. Provided there is a "hot spot" broadcasting nearby and you have permission to use it, you can use a laptop to connect to the internet in an airport, hotel, school, home or anywhere. You can communicate with your email, social networking sites, online games and so on.

Dongle

A dongle is a USB attachment that you fit to your computer to allow you to connect wirelessly to the internet using an ISP. This is usually a mobile phone company. The dongle is very useful if you are out and about with your computer as you do not need to buy time on public WiFi points; the calls you make are paid for with your mobile phone bill.

Bluetooth

Bluetooth is a wireless technology that allows all kinds of gadgets, such as personal digital assistants (PDAs), mobile phones, laptop computers, wireless mice and keyboards and MP3 players, to share information.

It is possible to share:

● voice

● music, for example, using the car radio system to play music from your MP3 player

● videos and pictures, such as printing pictures directly from your mobile phone.

Bluetooth works wirelessly but only in a very small space, known as a "personal area network" (PAN). It usually works for a distance of up to 10 metres. For devices to communicate using Bluetooth, they must contain Bluetooth technology.

○ Comparison of communication methods

Method	Advantages	Disadvantages
Dial-up	● Most residential phone lines are capable of supporting dial up so it can be used in areas where broadband is not available ● Users can dial up from different locations	● Slow download speeds ● Blocks the phone line while using the internet ● Difficult or impossible to view videos ● Difficult to download multimedia and files (e.g. essential virus protection and software updates)
Broadband	● Fast download speeds ● Does not block the phone line ● Internet connection is always on – no need to dial up ● Several computers can run from the same connection including a wireless home network	● Speeds vary according to other local usage and distance from exchange ● Greater risk of hacking because it's "always on"
Cable	● Constant high speed link ● Can also be used for television ● Very reliable	● Expense of laying cables ● Access depends on where you live – cable does not reach everyone's home
Satellite	● No need for expensive cables ● Ideal for remote places where there is no telephone line	● Relies on line-of-sight to satellite ● Interactive games can be difficult to use because of signal lag owing to the long distances the signal travels
Mobile	● No need for cables ● Allows mobility of use	● Distance from source of transmission is limited ● Not all areas have mobile coverage

Geographical information systems

A geographical information system (GIS) uses a combination of hardware, software and data to manage, analyse and display all kinds of geographical data. This can be shown in the form of maps, charts or reports.

Summary **S**

- The internet is a global network of computers.
- To use the internet you must subscribe to an internet service provider (ISP).
- An internet browser is software that helps you explore the internet.
- There are several ways of connecting to the internet:
  - dial-up
  - broadband
  - cable
  - satellite
  - mobile communications.
- A satellite in geostationary orbit stays above the same point on the Earth's surface all the time.
- Bluetooth is a wireless technology that allows all kinds of gadgets to share information.

Practice questions 3 **P**

1 Give **two** benefits of using the internet. [2]

2 Computers can be connected to the internet in a number of ways. Name **four** different methods for connecting to the internet. [4]

3 Copy and complete the following table: [4]

Method of connection	Advantage
Dial-up	
Broadband	
Satellite	
Cable	

Chapter

Home business

4

In this chapter, you will learn about the ways that a computer can be used at home to carry out activities such as shopping, booking a cinema or theatre ticket online and browsing the internet for information.

○ Using the internet

There are now very few businesses in this country that are not linked to the internet and most homes are also connected to it as people see the benefits of being part of the biggest network in the world.

The types of network you find on the internet include:

- commercial networks: shops, banks, broadcasting services
- government networks: parliamentary departments, local government
- educational networks: universities, schools
- private networks: owned by individuals.

One of the main uses of the internet is for finding information. There is a huge amount of information to be found on websites from news stories to share prices, from sports results to weather information and almost every other topic imaginable. But care must be taken! Some of the information to be found on the internet is not always accurate and can often be out of date. It is better to check out several different sources of information and go to reputable websites.

Every website on the internet has a unique uniform resource locator (URL). This is the address where the website is to be found and can be entered into the address box of a browser. For example, www.bbc.co.uk is the URL of the BBC website.

A complete URL has a prefix that shows the type of internet resource you wish to use. If you do not use this, the browser assumes

Because of the danger of using banking and other personal details online, special secure web pages use **https://**.

you wish to view a website and places **http://** at the beginning of the address. There are other types of page that can be displayed such as **ftp://** (which is a resource that allows you to transfer files across the internet).

Each page of a website has hyperlinks that allow you to navigate from one page to another. The hyperlink might be placed on a word or a picture and clicking the hyperlink with a mouse causes the browser to display a different web page.

If you do not know the address of the website you want to display, there are powerful search engines which can help you, such as Google, Yahoo!, Ask Jeeves and many others. If you go to the website of a search engine and type in keywords (i.e. what you are looking for), it will list a large number of links which might be useful. Just click on any of these to navigate to the website. It is better to be specific about what you are searching for otherwise you are going to be given a list of links that is too large.

Web browsers offer other facilities:

- If you find a website that you wish to use frequently, then you can add it to a list of **favourites** for easy access.

- A **history** of recently visited websites is recorded and can be used to display them again.

- A **back** button lets you go back to the website or web page you have just visited.

- The **home page** is the web page that is displayed when the browser is first opened. You can set it to whichever page you prefer. A button on the browser will return the display to that of the home page.

- It is usually possible to **print** a web page.

Online shopping

Shopping can be done from the comfort of your own home using the internet.

Most businesses now operate websites on the internet, which act like shop windows allowing them to display details of the company and the goods they have for sale. **E-commerce** is the term used for buying or selling goods or services over the internet.

A buyer can navigate to the website of a business, browse the items offered for sale by looking at pictures and descriptions, and add the items they want to buy to a "shopping basket". When all items have been selected, the buyer then proceeds to a "check out" page where the details of the purchase are confirmed and the method of payment is chosen. This usually involves giving details of credit or debit cards and information about the address where the goods are to be delivered. The goods are then sent, usually within a few days, and delivered to the buyer's home. Most companies add a charge for delivery, or postage and packing.

Figure 4.1 An online shopping page

It is possible to buy almost any item over the internet these days, from books, CDs and DVDs to plants, insurance, computer equipment and even items you may buy at the chemist. The list is very large and increasing all the time as more and more companies set up e-commerce websites.

Advantages of shopping online

- The range of goods available is very large. Almost any item can be found for sale on an e-commerce site using a search engine. Gone are the days when you might travel some distance to a shop to find that it does not stock the particular item you want.

- Shopping can be done from home, avoiding the need for the time and expense of travelling to the shops.

- Goods are delivered directly to the doorstep. Some items can be large, heavy or difficult to carry, so having them delivered is helpful.

- A business operating an e-commerce website does not have to pay for premises such as an office or a shop.

- Businesses can easily expand their market to anywhere in the world. Any person with access to the internet can order an item from a website and have it sent to them.

- Buyers can read customer or magazine reviews to get independent opinions before buying an item.

- The wide range of goods on offer is a benefit particularly to those in rural areas.

Disadvantages of shopping online

- Sometimes there can be a wait of several days or weeks before an item purchased from an e-commerce site arrives. If you buy from a shop, you can have it immediately.

> When you use a **credit card**, the credit card company lends you money to buy the item and you pay the money back at a later date. When you use a **debit card**, the shop takes the money from your bank straight away.

- You cannot touch the goods. For example, it is sometimes not apparent from a picture what an item of clothing feels like (e.g. how soft or how heavy it is). Fresh food bought over the internet may not be exactly the same as the picture displayed and it would be impossible to feel how fresh an item of fruit is.

- You cannot smell the goods. There is no way of telling what a bottle of perfume or a bar of soap smells like.

- Some people are worried about giving their credit card details over the internet even though extensive precautions are taken by e-commerce companies to make sure the details are not intercepted. The details are usually encrypted (coded) before they are sent so they are meaningless to anyone else.

○ Searching for products on websites

Looking for a product online can be a difficult business. Suppose your parents want to buy you a new bicycle for your birthday and want to find a good, reliable and cheap bicycle. If they go to Google and type in "bicycle", they will get millions of "hits".

Search

Results

About 39 million hits for "bicycle"

Figure 4.2 Search results in Google

Search engines such as Google help to find websites, but you need to be specific with your search.

The search needs to be refined. There are a number of ways to refine or narrow down the research and reduce the number of hits:

- Choose pages from the UK. This limits the area of the search. It would probably not be realistic to go to another country to buy a bicycle and it would be expensive to have it sent from abroad.

- Choose a particular bike and put the search criteria in quotes. A search for *Mountain Bike for 15 year old boy* would produce hits with all the words. However, a search within the UK for "*Mountain Bike for 15 year old boy*" would give no hits at all as the search is too refined.

● Put in separate phrases and use linking words, such as AND, OR and NOT. However, *"Mountain Bike"* AND *"15 year old boy"* gives lots of news stories. *"Mountain Bike for sale"* AND *"male"* gives the required results.

Once a website has been found there are still opportunities to search for the required goods.

Menu —————

Search

Rollover

Figure 4.3 Online shop selling bicycles

Once an item is chosen, it has to be purchased. An online reservation form is used. The customer can pay straight away online or agree to pay in the shop when collecting the item.

Figure 4.4 Online reservation form

○ Online bookings

Whether booking a holiday in a Spanish villa, a flight to Paris, or a seat in a theatre, the chances are that a computerised booking system is used to make the reservation. Many booking systems are web-based and bookings can be made through the internet. A theatre may have information about its performances on a website where you can check if seats are available and what their prices are.

Some websites can look for seats in a number of different theatres, so if you cannot find what you want in one theatre, it may be available in another.

Theatregoers can reserve seats for performances of shows either by telephoning the theatre or by using an online website. They can check whether seats are available on a particular day and where in the theatre they can sit. If suitable seats are available then they can be booked. Payment is usually made by credit or debit card.

> A booking system is a large database which stores bookings. Searches can be made to find out if seats are available.

> Many event booking agencies have websites where available seats can be searched for and bookings can be made online.

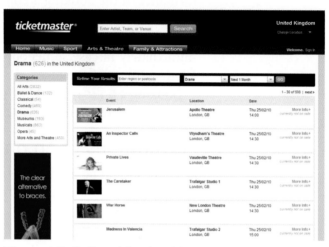

Figure 4.5 Online ticket bookings

The person booking the seats needs to input data about:

- the number of seats they want to reserve
- the time and date of the performance
- their details (e.g. name, address, telephone number, etc.)
- their card details for payment.

> Notice in Figure 4.6 that the email address has to be entered twice. This process is known as **verification**, where the data input is checked to see that it has been entered the same both times.

Figure 4.6 Online ticket booking form

Tickets for the show can be mailed to the customer or the customer can print off their own ticket at home with a unique barcode to prevent forgery. The system will also need to cater for people who turn up on the day of the performance and buy tickets at the door.

Theatres may offer a service where customers can input their email addresses and have information sent to them about shows being performed in the future.

A large database needs to be stored on the theatre's computer, which has details about every seat in the theatre for every performance of every show that takes place. When a customer contacts the theatre and wants to make a booking, the database is searched to find seats that are available for the requested performance. If the booking is confirmed, then the customer's details are entered into the record and those seats are shown as being no longer available and the record is saved. This needs to be done immediately in case somebody else wants to book the same seat for the same performance.

Booking a holiday would be done in a similar way to booking a seat in a theatre as detailed above.

Advantages of an online booking system

- There should be no double-booking of seats, where two people book the same seat at the same performance on the same date.

- It provides fast response to queries about seat availability from customers.

- Seats can be booked at any time of day or any day of the year, even when box offices are closed.

- It may be cheaper to book online.

- Since you are entering your own personal data there is less chance of error.

- Links to reviews of shows and other customers' experiences can be read.

Disadvantages of an online booking system

- Initial costs of buying and installing the system will be high.

- Booking agencies and travel agencies may close down because the customers are buying online and not visiting the agencies.

- People create their own tours so package holiday firms have to close through lack of customers.

- Not everyone has the facilities or the knowledge to book online.

- You must have a credit or debit card or use a service such as PayPal for most online bookings.

Summary

- The internet is a global network of computers that can communicate with each other.
- A computer network is a number of computers that are connected together by cable or the telephone network.
- A uniform resource locator (URL) is a unique address where a website can be found.
- A hyperlink allows you to jump from one web page to another or to another part of a web page.
- Online shopping is an example of e-commerce.
- Looking at websites and searching the internet for goods or information is known as "browsing".
- A search engine is a computer program that helps you browse the internet or search a website.
- Many event booking and holiday agencies have websites where available places can be searched for and bookings can be made online.

Practice questions 4

1 (a) State the meaning of the letters URL. [1]

   (b) Describe the use of a URL. [1]

2 (a) Give **two** advantages of shopping online. [2]

   (b) Give **two** disadvantages of shopping online. [2]

3 (a) Give **two** advantages of booking a holiday online. [2]

   (b) Give **two** disadvantages of booking a holiday online. [2]

4 Complete the table below using the following prefixes: [3]

http://   **ftp://**   **https://**

Description	Prefix
Placed at the beginning of a web address, usually followed by **www**	
Used for secure websites such as banks	
Used for transferring files on the internet	

Chapter 5

Organisations: School, home, environment

In this chapter, you will learn about ICT in education. You will look at a number of ways that ICT helps you to learn your lessons and also how schools use ICT to make the administration of schools more efficient. You will also learn how ICT can be used in data logging and weather forecasting.

ICT in education

There are many ways that ICT can be used in the school environment, not only to help with the administration but also to help with learning. ICT helps to make education more interesting. It is possible to use videoconferencing to join in with lessons from other schools or even schools in other countries, giving the pupils better motivation, so that the whole learning process has wider boundaries and is a more enjoyable experience. If a pupil is motivated and wants to learn, then this will improve their attention span and help them concentrate better. You learn more from an interesting lesson than a boring one!

Computers can help make the learning process more interactive, which means that pupils actively take part in their education. It is always more interesting to be doing something rather than just listening.

Interactive whiteboards (IWBs) are large white screens that can be seen by the whole class. They are connected to a computer and can be used like a large monitor. During a demonstration, a special pen is used like a mouse pointer to click on the IWB. Pupils can use interactive software to learn about a particular subject. For example, a computer-aided learning (CAL) program can be used to help you learn a foreign language. A pupil can learn new words, hear them spoken, repeat them and be tested on how much progress has been made.

ICT in the classroom interests, motivates and helps make learning more enjoyable. It's true!

Computer-aided learning (CAL): A way to learn a skill using a computer and interactive software on CD or DVD or by using the internet. Using CAL programs can be a more enjoyable way to learn than traditional methods.

If a computer is connected to a network, pupils can exchange ideas or discuss and debate online. The internet is a valuable resource and also provides other facilities, such as email and discussion groups.

Figure 5.1 An Interactive whiteboard

Coursework

Coursework is an essential part of school studies and ICT can help you with it.

There are many subjects for which pupils have to present coursework. Teachers provide guidance, but mainly you have to do the work on your own. This is where ICT can be of great help to you. The internet can help with research and pages on the web can be used to find information. Search engines can find relevant pages for you, but you have to be careful that the page is up to date and reliable. Wikipedia is an example of an online encyclopaedia which is produced and edited by the people who read it. If you find something incorrectly reported on Wikipedia or you have extra information to add, you can do it and so benefit others who come to read it after you. There are also many well-known commercial encyclopaedias that have websites, such as the Encyclopaedia Britannica, and these often provide sound or video clips to illustrate topics.

Always remember to check anything you find on the web by cross-referencing it with another source.

A discussion group on the internet (often called a bulletin board or a forum) can be helpful for getting ideas. A message can be posted and anyone who sees it can respond with their thoughts and ideas.

Email can provide contact with pupils in other schools in this country and abroad, and allow an exchange of ideas and help you to find out information from a current source. If you are learning French, corresponding with a pupil in a French school would be of great help in learning the language and it would also help them improve their English!

Desktop publishing (DTP) programs can help with the presentation of coursework. Publications can easily be produced

35

with a professional-looking layout, an important factor when it comes to impressing the examiner.

Spreadsheets and charts can help organise numerical data for mathematical or science coursework. Tables of data can be copied and pasted into a document and graphs and charts can help to illustrate points.

Databases can be used to store data, sort it and produce reports by searching through the data in different ways. For example, research into family sizes in different sociological groups can be stored in a database. Reports can then be produced about whether the size of the family is related to the circumstances they live in.

Your coursework can be a large piece of work. You need to make a back-up of your work at frequent intervals, and preferably in different places, in case the file gets lost or damaged in any way. If there is an up-to-date back-up of your work, then there will be no crisis if one copy gets corrupted.

> Always keep an up-to-date back-up of your coursework in case of computer problems.

Distance learning

> Distance learning is a means of studying for a qualification, such as a degree, at home, in your own time and at your own speed.

It is possible to carry out studies from home or anywhere in the world using distance learning. This involves signing up for a course on the internet and learning online, using web pages and other resources, and then taking online examinations and gaining a qualification.

There are many colleges that now offer distance-learning degree courses and you are not limited to colleges in this country if an overseas one is offering the course you want to study.

Care needs to be taken to select a course from a reputable college, but there are great benefits to learning this way as you can select the time and place for learning and proceed at your own speed. There are many courses offered online and it may be easier to find one that suits your needs, rather than try to find a college that offers that course.

The advantages of distance learning are that:

- You can learn from anywhere (no travelling to evening classes).
- Learning can be done in your own time and at your own speed.
- There are often online chat rooms or discussion forums where others who are learning the same subject can exchange ideas or discuss problems.
- There is a wide range of learning courses available.

The disadvantages of distance learning are that:

- Problems may not easily be solved, as there is no tutor to discuss them with.
- Students may feel somewhat isolated.
- There may be a lack of motivation if the student can select the frequency and times when learning takes place.

A computer, attached to a network or the internet, allows us to have access to a great range of educational services for distance learning, including:

● Online tutorials: Clicking a link provides a tutorial which may be animated and interactive.

● Online assessment: Questions are presented on the computer screen, the student answers on screen and often the mark and/or the corrections appear at once.

● Virtual learning environments (VLE): A complete educational course is provided online without a teacher needing to be present. A VLE provides a set of tools that allows a teacher to set up learning material, links and feedback to teach a particular topic. Working at a computer, a student can proceed through a lesson or series of lessons at their own pace.

	Advantages	Disadvantages
Online tutorial	● Readily available ● No teacher required ● Common questions quickly answered with on-screen demonstrations	● Cannot ask questions ● Cannot usually skip bits you know ● Often proceeds at a steady speed which may not suit you
Online assessment	● Test can be taken any time ● No wastage of paper and other resources ● Results are available immediately or very quickly ● Records of mistakes, marks and time taken on questions allows detailed statistics to be produced	● An impersonal way of testing ● Expensive and difficult to set the questions ● Very hard to mark subjective answers, such as essays ● Takes a lot of organisation and may need a lot of computers for a large class
VLE	● Learning can take place at any time ● A teacher does not need to be present ● A variety of text, graphics, audio and visual sources can be used	● Answers to questions may take a long time to arrive ● Material may become out of date ● Training to use the VLE could use up valuable learning time ● Equipment can fail leaving the student without a lesson

School events

ICT can help in the organising of school events. For example, your school may be performing a musical show at the end of term, involving the school orchestra and pupils who are actors or dancers. Here is a list of some of the different ways that ICT can help:

● A database can be used to store details of all the pupils taking part, including the forms they are in and whether they are actors, dancers or musicians. This will make it easier to contact pupils.

● A spreadsheet can be created and used to help in the financial planning. The expected costs of the show can be entered and this can then be used to set the prices of the tickets and the programmes to make sure that the show makes an overall profit.

● DTP software can be used to design posters to advertise the show, the tickets and the programmes.

● A word-processing program can be used to produce weekly rehearsal sheets showing the times of the rehearsals and which pupils are involved.

● After the show has taken place, a website can be created including pictures from the performance and a description of the development of the show, cast lists and any notable events that happened. This can be placed on the school intranet for all pupils to see.

● MIDI (see page 134) can be used with musical instruments.

● Computer-controlled lighting boards and sound systems can be used to run pre-programmed sequences of lighting effects or pre-recorded sounds.

> An **intranet** is a website that is under the control of an organisation such as a school. The pages of the intranet are available only to authorised users. Parts of a school's intranet may be available to sudents but other pages can only be accessed by staff or parents or governors.

School registration systems

Every school takes a register of pupils, usually twice a day, and the attendance record is stored on the computer system. It should make it easier to determine whether any pupil is absent from school and whether there are abnormal patterns of absence that need to be investigated. Some schools use a swipe card system of registration or an optical mark reader (OMR) to input attendance register information from sheets marked by the teachers. Others use laptops which are connected wirelessly to the school network to register the pupils electronically as they come to class. This way a teacher can see immediately if a pupil is legitimately absent and what the reason is for the absence. Also the school office staff know exactly where each pupil is at any time in case they are needed urgently.

Statistics (such as total number of attendances, truancies, absences and so on) are needed as it is a legal requirement for the school to keep such records. When the data is recorded electronically, it is much easier, quicker and more accurate to let the computer work out the statistics.

> Many schools have computerised systems of registration.

Figure 5.2 An optical mark reader for inputting National Lottery numbers

Management information systems

Computers in schools are not only found in classrooms. The school office probably has several and they are used for a wide range of administrative tasks.

There will be a database of all pupil details stored on the school computer system. The details stored on this database will be:

- pupil personal details (name, date of birth, nationality, religion, etc.)

- home details (address, telephone number, etc.)

- contact details (name and telephone number of person to contact in case of emergency)

- school details (date of joining school, form, form tutor, etc.)

Other fields may include details about how the pupil travels to school, school dinners, and any medical problems the pupil may have.

An administrative database can be searched to produce class lists or to quickly find the contact details for any specific pupil. These kinds of databases are part of a management information system (MIS).

A school MIS may also store the results of assessments and exams in each subject. This enables the monitoring of pupil progress. Pupils who are failing to make progress can be identified and the reasons investigated.

Computers are also now widely used by school administrators for creating timetables, the schedule of lessons and which teachers and rooms are assigned to them. Creating a school timetable is a complex exercise and a computer is programmed to identify when problems occur (e.g. if a teacher is assigned to take two classes at the same time).

Here is a list of school administration tasks that could be done on the school computer system:

- Spreadsheets could be used to plan the school budget. Allocation of money could be made, keeping the total expenditure within fixed limits.

- A word-processing program could be used to prepare circulars or letters to parents.

- Orders and invoices can be tracked by recording them on a computer database.

- In secondary schools, the process of administering pupil entries for exams is complex but is made simpler by using a computer database.

- In many schools, the library is administered using computers. A database of all titles kept in the school library helps pupils to find books quickly and the computer system also records book loans.

Computer databases in schools allow important information to be found quickly.

Using a computer to create the school timetable means it will be done more quickly and there will be fewer mistakes.

- An inventory of all items the school has bought can be kept up to date using a database. This may be important for insurance purposes.
- A school intranet may have a number of useful web pages for pupils.

The benefit of using computers in school administration is mainly that jobs can be completed faster and in an organised manner, and the results can be stored in such a way as to be useful later on.

Data logging systems

Data logging allows you to record a series of measurements taken by sensors during an experiment or investigation. Sensors are devices that measure quantities such as temperature, light or sound. Some sensors detect when an object moves in front of them and accurate clocks measure defined time intervals. A sensor can measure whatever is being investigated. That measurement can be recorded to be later used by a computer. You can also log data manually using a keyboard, mouse or microphone.

When the data has been recorded, it can be processed by the system. The software in the computer carries out an analysis or produces graphs with the data provided by the input from the sensors. These results can be printed off, displayed on a monitor or saved in the computer memory for use another time or as comparisons in another investigation.

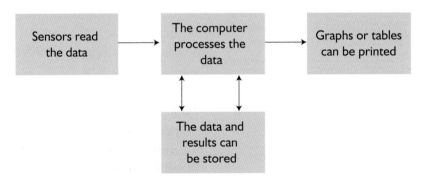

Figure 5.3 Data logging

Computers can be used to collect data automatically from a number of sensors using data logging. The frequency of the readings and the total length of time for which readings are to be taken can be set; once started the system does not need to be attended to.

An example of data logging may occur in a science lesson, when readings from an experiment might need to be taken every 10 seconds over a total time of 20 minutes. These readings can then be processed to produce a graph to illustrate the experiment. Another example may be the automatic collection of weather data from a

Data logging describes the automatic collection of data from a number of sensors.

school weather station. Readings may be taken at hourly intervals of the temperature, air pressure and wind speed and collected by a computer, stored and processed to produce statistics and graphs of local weather patterns.

Advantages of using a data logging system

- Data collection is automatic. No intervention is necessary.
- Readings can be taken continuously over long periods and through the night if necessary.
- There is no chance of somebody forgetting to take a reading. Scientific experiments may be useless if a reading is missed out.
- The readings will be more accurate if a computer takes them, as there is no chance of human error.
- Sensors can be placed in situations where it is dangerous for humans to go. For example, wind speed sensors (anemometers) may be placed on the roof of the school.
- If needed, readings can be taken very quickly. For some scientific experiments, it may be necessary to do several readings every second from a number of different sensors; humans could not achieve this.

Disadvantage of using a data logging system

If there is a fault, it may go unnoticed for a long time.

Control systems

Another use for computers in schools and homes is for controlling systems such as heating or alarm systems. These are examples of control systems and they use a number of sensors attached to a computer through an interface. The sensors take regular readings of measurements such as temperature or sound and input them to the controlling computer. The computer analyses the readings and decides whether any action is necessary. If action is needed, the computer sends out a signal to operate a device such as a heater or an alarm.

Environmental control

In a heating system, there is a sensor that takes regular readings of the temperature of a house. Temperature is an analogue measurement so it must be converted into a digital measurement to enable the computer to process it. This conversion is done by an analogue-to-digital converter (ADC).

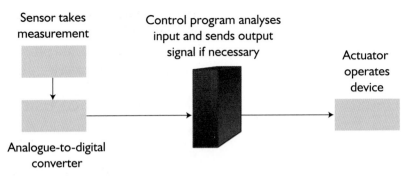

Figure 5.4 A simple heating control system

> Actuator: A motor that can operate a device when it receives a signal.

> Example
>
> A fan heater will come on if the temperature reaches a certain level.
>
> 0 = "Switch Off"
>
> 1 = "Switch On"
>
> The input bits are:
>
> Temperature in the room is too cold: 0
>
> Temperature in the room is too hot: 1
>
> The output bits are:
>
> Turn the fan off: 0
>
> Turn the fan on: 1
>
> Turn the heater off: 0
>
> Turn the heater on: 1
>
> If the input is 0 (because the room is too cold), the output is 11 (turn fan and heater on)
>
> If the input is 1 (because the room is too hot), the output is 10 (turn fan on, heater off)

> A passive infrared (PIR) sensor: is a device for detecting movement.

When the computer receives the data, the control program analyses the reading. If the reading is too low, the computer sends a control signal to an **actuator** that can turn a heater on. If the reading is too high, the computer sends a signal to switch the heater off.

A similar system could be used to control the temperature and humidity in a greenhouse. Sensors measuring the temperature and humidity are connected to a computer that can turn sprinklers on if the air is too dry, or open and close ventilators if the temperature is not within an acceptable range. The measurements from sensors can be taken at regular intervals and input to the controlling computer, which then analyses the data to decide if any actions need to be taken.

For many measurements, there will be a range of values within which the reading from the sensor should always lie. If the measured value lies outside that range then the controlling program will decide that some action needs to be taken. If action is needed, the computer will output a control signal to devices that operate the system. An actuator is a device that controls a motor, a switch or a tap. It receives a signal from the controlling computer either through a cable or by means of a wireless signal and activates a device.

An output signal may be in the form of a **bit pattern**, that is, a number of binary digits (0s or 1s). Each bit may control a separate device.

Alarm systems

A number of different sensors could be used in an alarm system in the home. **Passive infrared (PIR)** sensors measure the infrared radiation of a room and can detect any changes caused by movement. Proximity sensors have two parts that activate a signal when they are separated. They can be used on windows or doors to detect when they have been opened. Pressure sensors can be placed under mats to sense when a person stands on them. All of these sensors, if activated, send a signal to the controlling computer, which outputs a control signal to an alarm device.

There is usually a short delay between receiving a signal and an alarm being activated, which allows the owner of the house

time to switch the system off by entering a security code. If the security code is not entered, then the alarm sounds. When an intruder is detected, the system may activate a siren that makes a loud sound or switches on the lights. Some alarm systems connect to an automatic telephone dialler, which sends a recorded message to the police.

Microprocessor control

There are many electrical appliances in the home that have microprocessors or microcontrollers in them. We are sometimes unaware of them or take them for granted. A microprocessor is just an integrated circuit (a "chip") which can perform a lot of processing activities on very small circuitry.

An example of a device that has a microprocessor is a washing machine. There is a control program stored in it, which can run the different wash sequences set by the user. Once started, the washing machine does not need to be supervised because the program is run automatically; it sets the water temperature and goes through the appropriate wash, rinse and spin cycles without any need for intervention.

Devices that are controlled by a microprocessor are often called embedded systems. They have become possible because of the small size of the microprocessors and the fact that programs (sequences of instructions) can be stored in them.

Some devices in the home that are controlled by microprocessors include:

Microprocessors and microcontrollers are integrated circuits (chips) and they can be found controlling many household appliances.

● Dishwasher: A selection of different sequences and temperatures can be selected and a delay timer can be set. Some models have sensors that detect the amount of dirt in the water and adjust the cycle accordingly.

● DVD/Blu-ray recorder: The time at which recording starts and ends can be set and the channels to be recorded are selected.

● Microwave oven: Different programs can be run for different foods.

● Refrigerator: A microprocessor controls the temperature inside.

● Mobile phones: Phone numbers can be stored and text-messaging programs run.

● Personal digital assistants(PDAs): A microprocessor stores all kinds of information as well as phone numbers and addresses. It can remind you of tasks to do and birthdays to remember, record pictures and movies, and much more.

● Games consoles: These are small computers dedicated to playing games.

… and many more, such as televisions, MP3 or MP4 players, digital cameras, remote-control toys, etc.

Activity A

Internet investigation

A glimpse of the future? Find out what a **domotic system** is.

Weather forecasting

Some of the world's most powerful computers are used to forecast the weather. Accuracy of forecasts is improving all the time and many people rely on these forecasts: TV companies, shipping, farmers, the military, etc.

Computer systems are also used for hurricane and tornado tracking (not really needed in the UK!). If weather disasters can be predicted then people can be warned before they happen and take precautions. Whole areas may be evacuated before a hurricane strikes, saving many lives. Large computers are also used to monitor global warming: the increase in the average temperature of the Earth's surface. They also monitor the ocean temperatures and currents. El Niño is a warming of the eastern Pacific Ocean that affects global weather patterns every few years.

Many millions of items of data are collected daily from all round the world. The data may consist of readings of temperature, humidity, atmospheric pressure, rainfall, visibility, even radar data or infrared levels. Sensors commonly used for measuring the weather are listed below.

- A thermometer measures the air or sea temperature.
- A barometer measures the atmospheric pressure. Changing pressures are the main influence on weather.
- A rain gauge measures the amount of precipitation (rain, hail, sleet or snow).
- A hygrometer measures the amount of water vapour in the air.
- A psychometer consists of two thermometers (a wet one and a dry one) and measures relative humidity.
- A anemometer measures wind speed.

Many weather sensors are connected to a computer and readings are taken automatically at regular intervals. Some weather stations in remote places have to be manned and so meteorologists take the readings visually and record them.

Figure 5.5 Extreme weather – a satellite image of a hurricane over the southern states of the USA

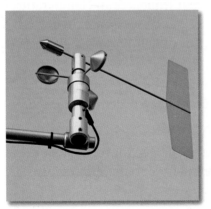

Figure 5.6 An anemometer is used to measure wind speed

Weather centres collect data from all over the world and even outer space.

The sources of this data are:

- weather stations sited all round the world, even in some of the remotest regions

- satellites constantly transmitting weather readings to weather centres on Earth (visual and infrared images of weather systems can be built up from the received data)

- weather balloons, in the atmosphere taking weather readings

- aircraft flying through the upper atmosphere

- radar stations

- weather ships out at sea

- weather buoys permanently anchored out at sea.

Figure 5.7 Satellites orbiting the Earth transmit visual and infrared data so that pictures of weather patterns can be viewed from space

In the UK, the computer system at the Meteorological Office in Exeter collects the weather data from all these sources, validates the data and uses it as input for its weather program. Millions of items of data have to be processed (often called number-crunching), so high-powered computers (supercomputers) are needed with fast processors, large memories and large disk storage capacities to process the data quickly enough to give a weather forecast in time to be useful.

Producing weather forecasts is a very complex process that involves solving large numbers of mathematical equations. Only the most powerful computers can do this effectively.

The data is processed to produce the following forms of output:

- charts, such as maps of atmospheric pressure, wind maps, rainfall charts: a succession of charts show how the weather is changing
- forecasts: previous weather patterns are used to predict future weather
- warnings of predicted weather problems, such as flooding or difficult driving conditions.

All the data is stored in archives. The more information that is known about previous weather behaviour, the better the predictions of future weather will be.

There is a network of weather stations around the country and around the world. Many airfields have weather stations and can transmit their readings automatically across the network. All these weather stations share data with each other so that a pattern of world weather can be built up. The internet has made weather data and forecasts more widely accessible and websites, such as www.metoffice.gov.uk, provide up-to-date and reliable weather information.

Summary

S

- Computer-aided learning (CAL) is a way to learn a skill using a computer and interactive software.
- An interactive white board enables a teacher to produce more interesting lessons.
- Distance learning allows someone to study at home using a computer without being in the presence of a teacher.
- Schools can use ICT for registration with OMR, swipe cards or portable computing devices.
- Using a computer to create the school timetable means it will be done more quickly and there will be fewer mistakes.
- A number of other school administration tasks could be helped by ICT:
  - Spreadsheets can be used to plan the school budget.
  - A word-processing program can be used to prepare circulars or letters to parents.
  - Orders and invoices can be tracked by recording them on a computer database.
  - Pupil exam entries can be stored in a database.
  - Library books and other equipment owned by the school can be tracked.
- Data logging is a term used to describe the automatic collection of data from a number of sensors.
- Weather forecasting relies on ICT systems:
  - Millions of data readings are collected from sensors all over the world.
  - Sensors measure temperature, air pressure, humidity, wind speed and rainfall.
  - A large mainframe computer is needed to process the data.
  - Complex modelling calculations are performed to output weather forecasts and charts.
  - Weather warnings can be given in plenty of time.

Practice questions 5

1 A pupil is preparing some coursework and needs to find out information about the topic she is studying. Give **three** different ways in which the pupil can use a computer to research the topic. [3]

2 Computer use in the home has increased rapidly in recent years. Give an example of how a home computer user might use each of the following:

   (a) a spreadsheet [1]

   (b) control software [1]

   (c) desktop publishing [1]

   (d) a database. [1]

3 Computer games are often played by pupils at home.

   (a) Give **one** reason why playing a computer game may be a good thing. [1]

   (b) Give **one** reason why playing a computer game may be a bad thing. [1]

4 People often use computers to learn at home.

   (a) Give **two** advantages of home learning. [1]

   (b) Give **one** reason why it might be difficult to learn at home. [1]

5 (a) What does CAL stand for? [1]

   (b) Name **two** sensors that may be used in a computer-controlled alarm system in a home. [2]

   (c) A control system may include an ADC. What is an ADC? [1]

   (d) Why might an ADC be needed in a control system? [3]

6 Computer systems are used to process many millions of weather data readings to produce weather forecasts.

   (a) State **three** different types of sensor used to take weather readings. [3]

   (b) Give **two** situations where accurate weather forecasts are needed. [2]

7 Life-support systems are used to monitor patients in hospitals. [3]

   (a) State **three** sensors used in a life-support system.

   (b) Give **three** advantages of using a computer-controlled, life-support system. [3]

Chapter

6

ICT and learning

In this chapter, you will learn about the graphical user interface (GUI). You will look at a number of ways of using a computer interface and special ways that people with disabilities can use a computer. You will also learn about using the computer to learn at a distance, rather than having to be in a classroom to learn something.

○ Understanding the desktop environment

When you switch on your computer, you will probably have a view something like the screen shown in Figure 6.1. This is known as a desktop environment. On it, you have access to all the useful tools you need to get on with the work you are doing using a computer. Microsoft Windows is an example of a graphical user interface (GUI). A GUI is a desktop environment that contains icons, windows, toolbars and folders. A GUI that uses **W**indows, **I**cons, **M**enus and a **P**ointer is sometimes called a **WIMP environment**.

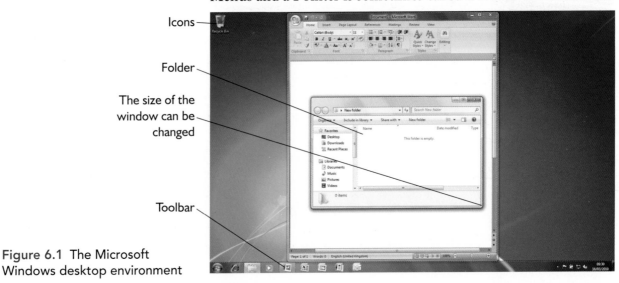

Icons

Folder

The size of the window can be changed

Toolbar

Figure 6.1 The Microsoft Windows desktop environment

To move a pointer around the screen, we can use a number of devices such as joystick, touch pad, tracker ball or, most commonly, a mouse.

Mouse

Mouse: A common input device. Movement of the mouse controls the movement of a screen pointer. Clicking the mouse buttons allows the user to interact with the computer according to the selection made by the screen pointer.

A mouse is an input device that should be very familiar. Moving the mouse across a flat surface controls the screen pointer because there is a ball in the mouse and small sensors measure the amount of the rotation. In an optical mouse, there is no ball and the movement is measured using light sensors; a laser mouse uses a laser beam. Cordless mice use wireless technology to transmit their signals to the computer.

Two (sometimes three) buttons on the mouse are used to send a signal to the computer to perform an action such as opening an application, selecting a menu option or printing a document. Some mice have a wheel for scrolling through a list or a long document and this wheel may act as a third button if it is clicked. A few have extra buttons that act as shortcuts when navigating web pages.

Figure 6.2 A cordless mouse with a scroll wheel

Touchpad

Drag a finger across the surface of a touchpad and it acts like a mouse. A pointer moves across the screen in the same way as the motion of the finger. Touchpads are built into laptop computers as they are much easier to use in confined spaces than a mouse. When the pad is tapped, it acts like the click of a mouse but there may also be buttons to click.

Touchpads are useful on laptops if they are being used where there is no flat surface to use a mouse.

Tracker ball

A tracker ball is a bit like an upside-down mouse. The ball is on the top and is rotated by hand. The movement of the ball controls the movement of a screen pointer. Tracker balls may be found built into some laptop computers.

Other input devices

A joystick is used mainly for playing games or for simulation programs, such as flight simulators; they may also be used to control the movement of robotic devices. Movement of the stick can be in any direction and there are some buttons on the joystick base. Other methods of interacting with simulation software are through steering wheels, foot pedals, pressure pads (as in simulated ski runs) and, of course, devices such as the Wii which allow the movement of your body to be transmitted to the action on the monitor.

Surgeons can operate on patients in hospitals thousands of miles away by wearing special gloves fitted with sensors that control remote robot surgical devices.

Figure 6.3 A touchpad is a common input device on a laptop computer

Figure 6.4 Controlling simulation programs

○ Desktop environment customisations

A desktop environment (DTE) can be altered or **customised** to suit the user. Many aspects of the DTE can be changed and some of these are explained below.

Mouse settings

Because individuals are different and people have different reaction speeds, it is possible to change the setting for the input devices described above. For a mouse, it is possible to change:

● double-click speed

● whether it is for a left-handed or right-handed person

● pointer speed

● pointer trails

● the size and shape of the pointer.

Figure 6.5 Mouse properties

Figure 6.6 Large icons

Mouse settings

There are other changes which can be made to mouse settings. On your computer go to the control panel, click on Mouse and explore the settings available.

Icon size

Figure 6.6 shows large icons. To suit your taste, you can choose large, medium or small (classic).

Desktop settings

1 Right-click your mouse somewhere on the screen and you always get a menu. The menu is different depending on where you click.

2 Try changing your desktop background and icon sizes.

(You may need to ask your teacher to give you permission to do this as your school may have locked some of these properties. If you have a computer at home, try it there.)

Other personalisation options for the display

The following examples use Windows 7, but other operating systems use similar methods to personalise the way your screen displays objects and data.

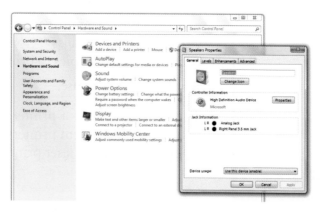

Figure 6.7 Personalisation in Windows 7

You can change many aspects of your desktop environment. For example, you can make changes to:

● screen resolution, which changes the number of pixels on the screen – the more pixels the more detailed the images

● desktop font size (number of dots per inch, DPI) to make the text more readable

● colours (of almost anything)

● the position of icons and windows

● login graphic

● screen contrast

● volume.

Figure 6.8 shows that the properties of almost every factor of the computer can be changed by the user.

Figure 6.8 Windows 7 control panel

Print settings

Whenever something is printed, options are offered that allow you to do a number of different things. The options offered in a printer dialog usually include:

● which pages to print:
  – all the pages
  – only the current page
  – a selection of pages

● the number of copies to print

● which printer to use.

The ability to select a printer is useful if you are working on a network with different printers attached, such as a colour printer, a photocopier and a laser printer.

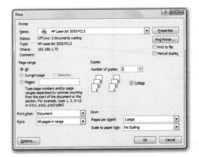

Figure 6.9 Print dialog

Password protection

If you are leaving your computer logged in for any reason, it is important to make sure that your work is secure and that no one other than you can access your work area. Pressing Control + Alt + Delete brings up a menu which can be used to lock the computer. A password is needed to unlock it again.

Shortcuts

There are many ways to make working in a desktop environment more efficient and quicker. **Shortcuts** allow a sometimes complex series of actions to be carried out using a mouse click or pressing a key. Some of the shortcuts in Microsoft Windows are shown in the table below. The actual shortcuts depend on which operating system or software you are using, but they all have shortcuts.

Shortcut	Action
Click an icon on the desktop	The application loads or the folder opens.
Press function key 3 (F3)	A search box opens.
Control + escape	The start menu is displayed.
Right-click on an object	A menu associated with the object appears.
Control + B	Highlighted text becomes bold.

To see a full list of shortcuts, type "shortcuts" into the online help box.

On-screen help

Almost all commercially available software comes with on-screen help built in to the package. With many products, this is accessed by pressing a shortcut key, such as F1, or clicking on the question mark on the menu bar. Some applications have a search box always displayed and a request for help can be typed into the box. If the computer is connected to the internet, the search for help may also produce answers from other users of the package. Hovering a mouse pointer over an icon or button on the screen may produce a short summary (a "tooltip") of what will happen when the icon or button is clicked.

Figure 6.10 Pop-up tooltip

Learning devices to support disabilities

There are pupils in school with physical problems or learning difficulties. ICT can help these pupils with their learning. There are many programs to help pupils with learning difficulties improve their reading or writing skills or help them with basic mathematics so that they can be better included in classes for other subjects. These programs use colourful, exciting and interactive methods to help motivate the pupil and make learning an interesting experience.

> Concept keyboards have special overlays that help a physically disabled pupil to input data.

Voice-recognition software

Pupils who have difficulty typing can use a microphone to speak to a computer, either to issue commands or to use the applications available. The software converts the sound waves from the pupil's voice into words on the computer. There are word banks and prediction software, which offer choices of words or phrases that can be selected to speed up the production of text. The system has to be trained to understand a particular voice as everyone has a slightly different accent or way of pronouncing words.

Text-to-voice software

For those that have difficulty seeing the screen, text-to-voice software synthesises speech and reads out whatever is on the screen, outputting the sound through speakers. Users can choose a synthesised male or female voice.

Braille keyboards

There are specialist input devices such as Braille keyboards for people who cannot see, though most people can be trained to be touch typists. A Braille keyboard has the Braille dots for the character that the key represents embossed on the key. A more common type of Braille keyboard is an electronic form of the Brailler which is used to emboss Braille dots on paper.

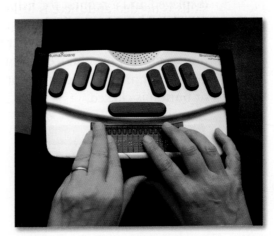

Figure 6.11 One of the many types of Braille keyboard

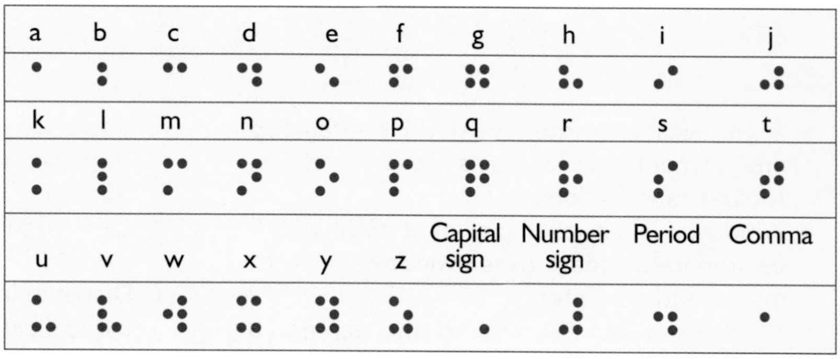

a	b	c	d	e	f	g	h	i	j
•	:	••	•:	•.	:•	::	:.	.•	.:

k	l	m	n	o	p	q	r	s	t
•	:	••	•:	•.	:•	::	:.	.•	.:
•	•	•	•	•	•	•	•	•	•

u	v	w	x	y	z	Capital sign	Number sign	Period	Comma
•.	:.	.:	••	:•	:.	.	.:	•:	•
••	••	••	••	••	••				

Figure 6.12 The English Braille alphabet

Touch-sensitive data entry devices

Some devices work by a user touching them. The position at which the device is touched is sensed and used as data. A touch screen might have a menu displayed on it. The user selects an option by touching the screen at one of a number of predefined positions.

Touch screens are often used in places where devices such as a mouse or a keyboard may get stolen or damaged. There are no loose or detachable parts.

Touch screens are often situated in places where members of the public can use them. For example, they may be found in museums, banks or doctors' surgeries. The screen may offer information about the museum or explain to a customer the services the bank can offer. Touch screens are used in some doctors' surgeries to allow a patient to register their attendance without needing to see the receptionist. Touch screens can often be seen in restaurants or bars. Each item a customer buys is touched on the screen by the member of staff and the total bill is automatically calculated and displayed.

Touch screens are also used in factories where dirt and grease could damage keyboards. Touch screens can be wiped clean easily. They can also be used where there are liquids present or a damp atmosphere, such as inside a greenhouse.

The advantages of touch screens are that a low level of ICT skills is needed and there is little possibility of damage or theft. A disadvantage is that a touch screen that is used a lot may become scratched and difficult to read.

A touch screen is a user-friendly method of selecting options by touching the screen. The user does not need to be an expert in ICT.

Summary

- A graphical user interface (GUI) is a desktop environment that contains icons, windows, toolbars and folders.
- Windows is an example of a GUI WIMP environment that uses windows, icons, menus and a pointer.
- To move a pointer around the screen, a number of devices (such as a joystick, touch pad, tracker ball or mouse) can be used.
- The desktop environment can be altered or customised to suit the user.
- A control panel allows the properties of almost every factor of the computer desktop environment to be changed by the user.
- Password protection of your computer can make sure that your work is secure and that no one other than you can access your work area.

- Shortcuts help to make working within a desktop environment more efficient and quicker.
- On-screen help is often built in to a software package.
- Distance learning is a means of studying for a qualification at home, in your own time and at your own speed.
- ICT can help pupils with learning difficulties or physical disabilities:
  - concept keyboards
  - voice-recognition software
  - text-to-voice software
  - Braille keyboards
  - touch screens.

Practice questions 6

1 Fill in the blanks in the sentences below.

   (a) A WIMP environment is made up of:

   W_____, I_____, M_____ and P_____ [4]

   (b) A GUI is a:

   G_____ U_____ I_____ [3]

2 (a) Describe **two** differences between a tracker ball and a mouse. [2]

   (b) Describe **two** differences between a joystick and a touchpad. [2]

3 Explain why it is a good idea to password protect your computer if you have to leave it for a short time. [2]

4 Describe **three** ways in which computers can be adapted to help students with:

   (a) learning difficulties [3]

   (b) physical disabilities. [3]

5 Explain what is meant by a "customised desktop environment" and give an example of one. [2]

Chapter

7

Applications software

In this chapter, you will learn about how to use software to carry out different tasks. You will look at software for creating graphs, presentations, letters and databases and how different audiences require information to be presented to them in different ways.

○ Sources of information

People frequently need information, for example to write a business report, complete a homework assignment, solve a problem or create a presentation for a children's party. There are many sources of information these days and, when information is needed, the first step is to decide where to look.

Here are some places where information can be found. Not all of them may be suitable for a particular search.

> Finding relevant and up-to-date information can take some time and you need to know where to look.

Databases

A business may have a large database with useful information that is needed by its employees. Your school may have a database that allows staff to quickly find information such as the home address of a pupil.

Searching a database is done by creating a **query**, which specifies the data you are searching for and the fields that you would like displayed in the result. The items of data that you are searching for make up the **search criteria**. If the search involves only one criterion, then it is called a simple search. If the search involves more than one criterion, it is called a complex search.

> A **criterion** is the general term given for one thing that is being searched for, such as a search for all the boys in Year 11. Two or more criterion are called **criteria**.

Internet

The internet is a valuable source of information but you must be careful! It is better to find more than one source of information and go to reputable websites. To find information on the internet,

> Don't be led astray by old websites that are not up to date and may provide incorrect information.

use one of the many search engines. You need to be precise with searches or you may get overwhelmed with the number of responses! (See Chapter 4 for information on searching.)

CD-ROMs and DVDs

There are CD-ROMs and DVDs available which have searchable databases on them. Some have whole encyclopaedias including text, sound and video clips and some are available for specialist topics.

Files on disk

Information is often found in files on disk, such as an address book or sets of holiday photographs stored on a memory stick.

Files such as documents may be saved on a disk and used again or edited later, but it is sometimes difficult to remember where you saved them. It is important to do some proper "house-keeping" of your files:

> Keep your saved files organised and you will not waste time trying to find them.

- Make sure each file is given a **meaningful name** when it is saved.
- Create a **proper directory (folder) structure** with sensible names. This should be arranged in a hierarchical structure, that is, a main folder with subfolders. Each of these subfolders may themselves have subfolders, and so on.
- If you use disks, memory sticks or flash cards, they should be **clearly labelled**.

Computers have search facilities to find files saved on disk. You can search for a file with a particular name, or use wildcards for partial names. You can also search for text files that have particular words or phrases contained in them, or files that were saved at given times.

Figure 7.1 Windows allows you to search for files which have the word "Homework" in them

Information-handling software

Files of data rarely remain the same for very long and often need to be changed. Businesses change all the time. They may expand, taking on new staff or moving to new premises, they may grow smaller, or the goods they sell may vary. Schools appoint new staff, change the timetable, pupils come and go, change their addresses or even their names. There is no point in having data that is incorrect or out of date, so data files need to be constantly updated.

The order in which the data is stored may need to be changed. Imagine a telephone directory where the names are stored in numerical order of the phone numbers. It would be easy to find the person whose phone number is 639247 but very difficult to find the telephone number of a particular person! The data needs to be sorted in alphabetical order of the person's name before it becomes easy to find the phone number for Thompson P.J., for example.

Data can be sorted into ascending or descending order. In a classroom register, it would be appropriate to have the names in ascending alphabetical order, whereas for the results of an examination or competition it would be better to have the results displayed in descending order with the highest mark shown first.

The data itself may need to be edited. The following table gives the four main reasons for updating files and uses a library application to illustrate each one.

> Data files need constant updating as the businesses and organisations that use them change.

File update	Reason
Sorting the data	**To speed up searching the data** When data is sorted, it makes it much easier to search. Imagine trying to find a person's telephone number, if the names in the telephone directory were not sorted into alphabetical order.
Editing the data	**To change or correct the data** A member of the library may move house and their address would need to be changed on the members file.
Adding new data	**To add a new record to the file** A book is added to the library's stock, so the data needs to be added to the stock file.
Deleting old data	**To remove a record from the file** A book may be permanently lost or too damaged to lend, so it would be removed from the library's stock file.

○ Developing information

When you have found the information you need, what next? Well, that depends on what type of work you are doing. If it is research, a homework task or a piece of coursework, you need to get all the text, statistics or graphics together in one place. The easiest way of doing this is to open a new file, in word-processing, DTP or spreadsheet software, and then copy the information you have found and paste it into the new file – then make sure you save it.

Files can be imported into your project from wherever they are stored. Text files can be imported into a document or publication, data files can be imported into a database or into a spreadsheet. Graphic images can be imported into almost any application.

Once the data is in your project, you can start to develop the information.

Type of application	Development
Document or publication	The layout of text and images can be manipulated in a word processor or DTP software to make sure the finished project looks good: ● The text may need to be adjusted to fit into the space allocated. ● The size of the font can be changed for headings. ● Final formatting of the text will make words or phrases catch the eye. ● The size of images may need to be adjusted to fit better, but bitmap images lose their quality if enlarged too much.
Presentation	The contents of each slide of a presentation can be animated to change the way they appear or disappear. For example, they can be set to fly in from any direction or just appear suddenly, or fade slowly away. Slide transitions – the way one slide changes to another – can be defined in various ways, such as dissolve, wedge, wipe down, fade smoothly and many others. **Sounds** or **music** may be added to enhance the presentation and make it more interesting to view. Some of the slides may have **hyperlinks** to other slides within the presentation, other presentations, other programs, music files or the internet. There are many possibilities.
Website	**Hyperlinks** need to be defined on each page so that the viewer can navigate between the pages of the site. Some of the links may be to other websites and some may be defined to send an email or download a file.
Spreadsheet	Spreadsheets can be used to perform calculations. Provided the formula is correct, the calculations will always be accurate. When the data has been entered correctly and the formulae defined correctly in the cells of a spreadsheet, it can then be used to carry out investigations. Many spreadsheets simulate events in the real world, and the definitions of the **formulae** are designed to imitate behaviour in the real situation. Models of situations that are difficult or dangerous to reproduce can be simulated using spreadsheets – you could not conduct an experiment on nuclear fusion in the classroom, but you could use a spreadsheet to simulate it. **Simulations** can be explored by examining the effects of changing the information in a spreadsheet, and predictions can be tested. **Charts** and **graphs** can be drawn from the data to illustrate the results of an investigation.

Database	There may be a number of files (tables) in a database and **relationships** between some of the data fields can be defined. This is normally done by having common fields in each of the related files, but these should only be key fields. The data may be **sorted** into alphabetical or numerical order to make it easier and faster to find information. **Searches** can be defined by creating queries, organising the data to be displayed and the search criteria to be used. Preparing **reports** to be printed will involve deciding which fields are to be included, how they are to be searched and how the results are to be sorted and grouped. Calculations such as totals or averages may also be included.

○ Presenting information

> The way of presenting information must take into account the needs of the audience and it must suit the specified purpose.

In practice, a project probably consists of a combination of the methods described in the previous section and the results need to be presented in a variety of different ways. An example may be a researcher using a database to carry out searches of data, entering the results in a spreadsheet, drawing graphs of the results and presenting the final conclusions on a website.

There are a number of different ways of presenting information, and it is important that the most appropriate method is chosen. The method selected and the style must take into account the target audience (i.e. it must meet the needs of those who are going to view it) and it must suit the specified purpose of the project.

The style of writing is also important. It is no good using difficult words if your audience is a group of children and don't write slang if the viewer is your boss!

Presentation medium	Style
Printed document or publication	These may be formal documents such as legal letters or offers of job interviews, or they may be informal, such as party invitations. The choice of style must be appropriate. The style is defined by the layout, fonts used and graphics selected. For example, a letter of resignation to your boss would need a different style to an invitation to a children's birthday party. The first would need a formal document with professional layout and font, but the second can be more informal and use plenty of colour, graphics and weird fonts. Some publications, such as advertisements or magazines, need to be eye-catching to attract viewers, so plenty of bold and colourful lettering and graphics may be needed. Large publications also need consistency of layout and style. It is a good idea to use a template for each page of a large publication. Reports created by databases are usually printed results of a query. Other reports can be created using a word processor or desktop publisher. A report generally uses outlined numbering to make sections clear and incorporates graphs and images to support points made.

Screen display	Output may be displayed on a screen. Layouts should be simple but interesting with only necessary information displayed. It is difficult to look at a cluttered, disorganised screen of information. The advantage of screen displays is that sounds and video clips can be included – you cannot do this on a printed document.
Multimedia presentation	Multimedia presentations are more appropriate for situations where a speaker will give information to an audience. Slides are displayed on a screen and may include text, graphics, sound or video clips. There may be a few bullet points displayed on a slide and a speaker explains each of them. Animation effects can be used to capture the attention of the audience. They can also be used for single-user presentations where the slides are presented on a monitor and a user interactively works through the display, with a soundtrack recorded to explain the information.
Website	Pages of text can be displayed on websites with hyperlinks between them. This method of presentation attracts a worldwide audience and must be made to look attractive if it is an advertisement designed to attract customers to a business. Websites are interactive and allow the viewer to select the pages they wish to see.
Sound	Information can be presented as a recorded soundtrack – it may even be a piece of music.
Video	A video clip can combine moving pictures and a soundtrack. Videos can be included in web pages or multimedia presentations.

However the information is to be presented, it must be accurate and it must be clear. Spellcheckers can be used on documents to make sure text is correctly spelled and data used in a project should be validated to ensure that all the data used is sensible data.

Information can then be stored for future use but make sure it is saved with recognisable names in an appropriate folder, so that it can easily be found when it is needed again.

Summary

- Data files frequently need updating:
  - sorting records into order
  - editing data in records
  - adding new data
  - deleting old data.
- Data may come from documents, databases, the internet, CD-ROMs, DVDs or other files saved on disk.
- Files saved on disk must be given meaningful names and placed in an organised collection of folders.
- Information can be brought together using copy and paste or by importing.
- Information can be arranged on documents and publications to give an appropriate layout and style.
- Information must be checked carefully for accuracy.
- Presentations can be animated and used to give out information.
- Websites reach a worldwide audience.
- Spreadsheets can be used to model real-life situations.
- The effects of changing information shown on spreadsheets can be studied.
- Charts and graphs of spreadsheet results can be created.
- Printed reports can be created using data from databases.
- Information must be presented in a way that is appropriate to the needs of the audience and must suit the specified purpose.
- Information may be presented as:
  - a printed document or publication
  - a screen display
  - a multimedia presentation
  - a website
  - sound or video.

Practice questions 7

1 Data files often need updating. These updates could be amendments, deletions or insertions. Choose whether each of the following updates to a school database is **amend**, **delete** or **insert**.

 (a) Adding a new pupil to the school. [4]

 (b) Changing the address of a pupil.

 (c) Removing a pupil from the database when they leave.

 (d) Recording the GCSE examination results.

2 (a) Give **one** source of data for a sports club members' database. [1]

 (b) Give **one** source of data for a GCSE history project. [1]

3 A business wants to create an advertisement for a new product.

 Describe **three** different ways that this advertisement could be presented by its sales department and give an advantage of each. [6]

4 Explain why the internet might be a better way of advertising products than using a paper-based catalogue. [3]

Chapter 8

Information-handling software

In this chapter, you will learn about databases and the special words associated with the use of databases, such as files, records and fields. You will learn a number of ways in which data and information can be found (known as information sources) and the importance of checking the data you find for accuracy.

All businesses need to store data of some kind. It may be the details of all their customers and the orders that have been placed to buy goods. It may be the details of their staff so that their pay can be calculated at the end of the pay period.

A computer uses a database to store information. Once the data has been entered, it can be edited, searched or sorted easily, or deleted if it is no longer needed. A database provides facilities for organising the data in different ways, such as sorting alphabetically, and there will be ways of finding information quickly. The main benefit of a large database is the fast speed at which information can be found.

The data stored in a database can be used in a number of different ways. It can be used to produce reports or exported to other applications such as spreadsheets or word-processing programs. In an office environment, the database is usually stored on a network's file server so that every other user on the network can access the information and be able to update it.

The benefits of using a database include:

- Fast access: Finding data on the database is much faster than in a system where the data is stored on paper in filing cabinets.

- Easy to edit: Whenever data needs to be updated, a database makes it easy to find that data and change it.

- Validation: There are ways of setting checks on the data as it is being entered to make sure that no inappropriate data gets into the database.

- Reports: Results of searches can be used to produce printed reports that may help the management of a business in their

> A database is an organised collection of related data. It is possible to add, edit, manage and retrieve data from a database. The structure of a database allows data to be found and used quickly.

decision-making. Reports can appear in a wide variety of formats.

- Sharing: The database can be shared with any number of users on a network and any user can access and edit the data.
- Security: Passwords may be set so that no unauthorised user can access the database, which may contain personal and sensitive data.

There are many different programs that help you create and manage a database. Microsoft Access is one of them.

What you can do with a database:

- add new data, change or delete data
- search the data
- sort the data into a given order
- print reports about some aspect of the data
- use the data in other applications.

A database may have a number of different files (these are called tables in Microsoft Access) and they are related in some way. A database for your school may have a table with pupils' details, and another table containing data about their classes, and yet another table about the examinations they are taking. The relationship is that they all contain data about your school. A table will have a number of records in it. Each record will have a number of fields.

Figure 8.1 shows four records in a table:

- Each row displays the data of one record: the data about one pupil.
- Each record has five fields.
- Each column displays a different field.
- Each field is a category of information about the pupil.

PupilID	Surname	FirstName	Form	DateOfBirth
901	Johnson	Sam	10Y	19/04/1998
902	Smith	Alison	10G	02/01/1998
903	Bland	Louis	10Y	10/11/1997
904	Thomas	Glyn	10S	29/07/1998
905				

Figure 8.1 Part of a table showing four records

○ Creating a database

As with most things in ICT, it is really important to design the database properly, as this will save time and create fewer problems later on. You need to decide what information is stored in the database and, for each table, what fields of data are going to be stored.

The type of each field needs to be defined, for example whether it is a text field, a number, a date or currency, etc. One of the fields of each table must be designated as a **key field**. This is the item of data that uniquely identifies each record ensuring that each record is different so they can't be confused.

An important part of creating a database table is to set **validation rules** for some of the fields. As the data is entered it is checked to see that it obeys the rules; any data that does not obey the rules is not accepted. In Microsoft Access, you can set the **validation text** (the message that is displayed if the data is not acceptable).

> A key field uniquely identifies each record. No two records will have the same data in their key field.

General	Lookup
Field Size	Integer
Format	
Decimal Places	Auto
Input Mask	
Caption	
Default Value	
Validation Rule	>1999
Validation Text	The ID number must be 2000 or more
Required	No
Indexed	Yes (No Duplicates)
Smart Tags	
Text Align	General

Figure 8.2 A range check is set as a validation rule for a field in a table

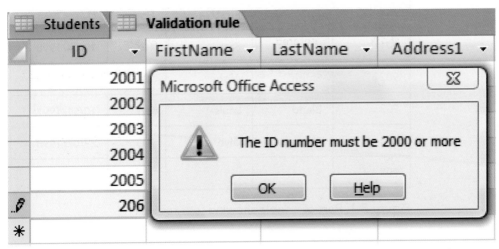

Figure 8.3 The error message that is displayed when invalid data is entered

There are a number of ways of validating data. Remember that validating input data is to make sure that the data is sensible and obeys the rules for that input field.

Validation method	Description	Example
Range check	The data entered must be in a sensible range.	If a test is out of 100 marks then only marks in the range 0 to 100 are acceptable.
Type check	This check ensures that the data is of the correct data type.	If the number of rooms in a house is being recorded, only an integer (a whole number) is accepted by the database.
Length check	The length of the input is checked for the number of characters used.	If a name is being entered into the computer, it is reasonable to assume that it will be between 2 and 18 characters long.
Lookup list	If the data entered consists of a limited number of possible entries then the computer can compare the entry with a list of allowed answers.	If the predicted grade for an examination can be A, B, C, D, E, or U, only these inputs are allowed.
Picture or format check	If the data being entered has a particular pattern, such as a postcode or a car registration number, an **input mask** can be used to force the data to conform to the rule.	The computer checks to see that the entry conforms to that pattern. The input mask for a postcode would be LLN NLL where L is a letter and N a number.
Presence check	Some data has to be entered.	If you were ordering goods from the internet you would have to give your address and the item you were ordering. An error would occur if this data was not filled in and the computer would not allow the processing to take place.

Remember that these validation methods can only ensure reasonable or sensible data is input to a system. There is no certainty that the data is accurate or true.

○ Searching for data

Searching a database is often referred to as "querying a database". **Field names** must always be given in a query, as well as the value being searched for. This value is known as the **search criterion**.

One of the main uses of a database is to allow you to find information quickly. To search for data you need to use a **query**. A query specifies what records you are looking for and what fields from the records you would like to display. A **simple search** looks for data in one field only and a **complex search** looks for data with more than one criterion.

There are a number of **operators** which can be used in searches and these are shown in the table below.

Operator	Description	Example	Resulting records
=	Equals	Form = 10Y	901, 903
<	Less than	DateOfBirth < 02/01/1998	903
>	Greater than	Surname > Smith	902
<>	Not equal to	Form <> 10Y	902, 904

A simple search

Let's query the data in Figure 8.1 (page 65) to find all the pupils in 10Y.

The search criterion is **10Y**.

The search could be written: **Form = 10Y**

This search would find two records: 901 Sam Johnson and 903 Louis Bland.

Complex searches use multiple criteria and the logical operators **AND, OR**.

Complex searches

1 Let's query the data in Figure 8.1 (page 65) to find all the pupils in 10Y who were born on 10/11/1997. This would be written as:

   Form = 10Y
   AND
   DateOfBirth = 10/11/1997

   This search would find record 903 Louis Bland.
2 Let's query the data in Figure 8.1 to find all the pupils in 10Y or 10G. This would be written as:

   Form = 10Y
   OR
   Form = 10G

   This search would find records 901, 902 and 903.

Wildcard characters

It is possible to use wildcard characters in searches for data that you only know part of. For example, you might want a list of all the pupils born in March or all the pupils whose surname starts with the letter "S" or within a given range of letters.

The table on page 69 shows the wildcards that you can use in query selection criteria and their meaning.

Wildcard	Meaning	Example	
*	Any number of characters	Like "S*"	Finds Smith, Smithers and Scott
?	Any character	Like "Ca?"	Finds Cat and Cab but not Cart
[ ]	Any character in the brackets	Like "10[YG]"	Finds 10Y or 10G
[-]	Any character within a range of characters	Like "10[A-M]"	Finds 10B and 10G but not 10T
!	Any character not in the brackets	Like "10[!YG]"	Finds 10B and 10T but not 10Y or 10G

Sorting data

One powerful feature of a database is that the results of queries can be presented in sorted order, either in alphabetical or in numerical order. Sorts may be made in ascending or descending order and can be performed on numerical or text fields. The field that is being sorted needs to be specified. For example, the pupils in form 10Y could be listed in ascending alphabetical order of surname.

PupilID	Surname	FirstName	Form	DateOfBirth
903	Bland	Louis	10Y	10/11/1997
901	Johnson	Sam	10Y	19/04/1998

Figure 8.4 Sorted data from a database

Forms

A form can be produced to make data entry more attractive and secure, rather than just putting the information into the raw tables. It is more secure for looking through and displaying the data because the person putting in the data need not see all the other data or even all the fields. It also allows instructions to be entered. The form's navigation buttons allow movement between records.

> Forms are often used for inputting data. They can be made to look more attractive than showing the raw data.

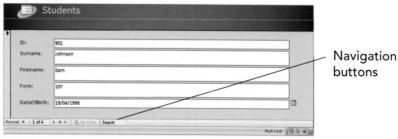

Navigation buttons

Figure 8.5 A form for entering a pupil's record

○ Reports

A report is a printed document that contains data from the database that is organised and analysed in a specific way. An example of a report that lists the pupils in each class in alphabetical order may look like that shown in Figure 8.6.

Students

ID	Surname	Firstname	Form
903	Bland	Louis	10Y
901	Johnson	Sam	10Y
902	Smith	Alison	10G
904	Thomas	Glyn	10S

Page 1 of 1

Figure 8.6 A printed report of pupils

Activity

Download the Microsoft Access database **trip.mdb** and use it for the following exercises. The database has data about pupils and teachers travelling by bus on a school trip. There are two buses.

1 Use the database to find out:

   (a) How many tables are there in the database and what are they called?

   (b) What is the key field of the pupils table?

   (c) How many records are there in the pupils table?

   (d) How many fields are there in each record?

2 One pupil has been left out. Sarah Smith of 7B has been assigned to Bus 2 for the trip. Add her to the database.

3 Search and print out all the pupils in 7N.

4 Search and print out all the pupils in 7N who are assigned to travel on Bus 1.

5 When the buses returned to school, one of the teachers found a coat left on Bus 2. There was a name label in the coat but it was very faded and all that could be seen was that the surname started with the letters "Je". Use a query with a wildcard search to find the telephone number to ring to let the owner of the coat know.

○ Files, records and fields

Data types

Computers can process a wide variety of different types of data. The table below lists the main types of data.

Data type	Example	Description
Number (integer)	43	A whole number (positive or negative but no fractions)
Number (real)	432.51	Any number, including whole numbers and fractions
Text or string	John Smith	Letters, numbers or other characters such as punctuation marks
Date/Time	04/10/06 12:23:09	Any time or date; the way the time or date is displayed depends on how it is formatted
Currency	£12.50	Money (including foreign currencies, such as $ or €)
Boolean	Yes	Two opposing states, such as yes or no, true or false, male or female
Lists	Red Green Blue Yellow	A list of values, sometimes called a "drop-down" list; only data from the list can be selected
Picture		Image data, from a digital camera, mobile phone, the internet, a clip-art library or a scanned drawing
Sound	A sound or music clip	A beep from a barcode reader or a popular song
Video	A moving picture	A video introduction to a computer game or a downloaded film/TV programme

Field: An individual data item within a record

Record: A collection of related fields

File: A collection of related records

The last two data types (sound and video) demonstrate the disadvantage of paper as these two types of data cannot be shown on the printed page, whereas computers can produce sounds and display video clips or animated graphics.

Fields

A field is a single data item. When data is stored in a field, the type of data has to be specified and no data of other types can be stored in it. Examples of fields and their types:

● surname: text
● date of birth: date/time
● selling price: currency.

71

Records

A record consists of a collection of related fields. For example, a pupil's record in a school database only has fields related to that pupil (surname, forename, date of birth, form, etc.) and not any of another pupil's data.

Files

A file is a collection of related records. An example of a file is the file of records of all pupils in the school.

For example, a school would like to create a simple file of pupil names and their dates of birth. The file of pupils' data has the following data structure table:

Field name	Field type
Pupil ID	Integer
Surname	Text
Forename	Text
Date of Birth	Date/time

The file itself is displayed in the next table:

PupilID	Surname	Forename	DateOfBirth
4001	Jenkins	Jennifer	16/05/1998
4002	Smith	Sally	04/09/1997
4003	Thomas	David	12/05/1998
4004	Williams	John	16/04/1998
4005	Williams	Walter	03/06/1997

This file consists of five records (each row in the table is one record). Each record in this file has four fields (each column in the table represents a field).

Key fields

A key field uniquely identifies each record. No two records will have the same data in their key field.

One of the fields is used to uniquely identify each record. This is called the key field. The key field in the example above is the Pupil ID field. No two pupils would have the same Pupil ID number (but, for example, they may have the same name or date of birth). A file may be sorted in order of its key field.

Sometimes more than one field is used as a key and they are then referred to as the primary key field, the secondary key field, and so on.

Calculated fields

Some information needed in a report produced by a database may not be stored in the database because it can change over time. For example, a teacher may wish to produce a list of pupils with their ages. However a pupil's age changes day by day. Today they may be 14, tomorrow 15. The solution is for the database to use the recorded date of birth to **calculate** the age by subtracting the date of birth from the date of the report.

Another example is the total number of marks scored in an examination. The database might hold a record of the scores in individual papers and calculate the final score.

A calculated field only exists when it is needed, such as at the time of running a query or printing a report. The field can be given a field name but no data is held permanently in the database.

A business wants to produce a report to show the total gained from the sale of each item they have sold in a week.

The database contains the two fields **NumberSold** and **Price**.

To print the report a Total field will have to be calculated using a query, and the query will be used to produce the report.

The formula used would be:

Total: [NumberSold]*[Price]

Total Cost of Items

NumberSold	Price (£)	Total (£)
23	1.30	29.90
12	2.50	30.00
12	5.60	67.20
435	6.75	2936.25
6	23.00	138.00
67	12.00	804.00

Figure 8.7 Using a calculated field

Security issues with databases

Security is a major issue with most businesses and organisations. The problems that arise with the loss of important data could have serious consequences for a business and may result in:

● loss of customers – unhappy customers will go elsewhere

● payments for goods not being received

● bad publicity – a business relies on its good reputation

● cash flow problems

● management unable to make decisions due to lack of information.

> A biometric system is a security system that uses physical characteristics, such as fingerprints, voice, facial features and eye scans, to identify people.

> Authentication means identifying a person and verifying that they are who they claim to be.

Data is often stored on the hard drives of computers, so it is important that the computers themselves are safe. There are a number of physical methods of making sure that data on computers is secure, and there are also some software methods.

Physical methods include locks on doors, alarms, ID cards, fingerprint recognition and other biometric systems, such as voice recognition or iris scanning.

If data is secure then:

- It cannot be destroyed.
- It cannot be accidentally or maliciously altered.
- It cannot fall into the hands of unauthorised people.

Software methods for keeping data secure

Password system

One way of identifying a user is a password system. Every authorised user of a computer system is given a username, which is recognised by the system. Each user also has a password that must be entered every time they log in. The computer will only allows access to a username that it recognises when the correct password is also entered.

Single files can be protected by a password. The user has to enter a password before being allowed to use the file.

Back-ups

Important data should be backed up regularly. This means making a second copy of the data. If a problem arises with the data file, then the back-up copy can be used instead.

Back-up copies of data files can be made locally (the back-up is saved on the same computer hard drive as the original) but there is no point keeping the back-up on the same computer if that computer is stolen or gets destroyed in a fire. Back-up copies can be made on removable media such as CD, DVD or tape cartridge. The back-up copy of the data should be kept in a secure place such as a locked room or a fireproof safe and preferably in a different location to the original.

Many organisations back up their data every working day. Computers can be scheduled to make back-ups at regular time intervals (possibly every night, when the computers are less busy).

> Back-up: A duplicate copy of a file kept in case the original is lost or corrupted.

File attributes

There are some characteristics of a file, called the **file attributes**, which the user can set. One of them is a "read-only" attribute.

If this is set, then the file can be viewed but cannot be changed. Many data problems are caused by users accidentally changing or deleting files and the setting of the read-only attribute prevents this happening.

Summary ⓢ

- A database is an organised collection of related data.
- A database allows you to find information easily and quickly.
- Benefits of using a database:
  - fast access to the data
  - easy editing of data
  - validation of data
  - easy production of reports
  - sharing data, so that more than one person can enter and edit it
  - security – the data can be password protected.
- With a database you can:
  - add new data
  - change or delete data
  - search the data
  - sort the data into a given order.
- A key field uniquely identifies each record.
- Data can be validated using
  - range check
  - type check
  - length check
  - lookup list
  - picture or format check
  - input mask
  - presence check.
- Validation ensures reasonable or sensible data is input to a system.
- A query (or search) specifies which records you are looking for and which fields of the records you would like to display.
- A complex query looks for data with more than one criterion.
- The search criteria of a query consists of the field names and the values being searched for.
- A form can be produced to make data entry more attractive and secure than just putting the information into the raw tables.
- A report is a printed document that contains data from the database organised and analysed in a specific way.

- Data types allow the computer to process a wide variety of different sorts of data:
  - number (integer)
  - number (real)
  - text or string
  - date/time
  - currency
  - Boolean
  - lists
  - picture
  - sound
  - video.
- A field is an individual data item within a record.
- A record is a collection of related fields.
- A file is a collection of related records.
- A key field uniquely identifies each record.
- A calculated field is a field produced by the database.
- Data is often stored on the hard drives of computers, so it is important that the computers and the data are kept safe.
- Physical methods of security include:
  - locks on doors
  - alarms
  - ID cards
  - biometric systems, such as fingerprint recognition, voice recognition or iris scanning.
- A biometric system is a security system that uses physical characteristics such as fingerprints, voice, facial features and eye scans to identify people.
- Authentication means identifying a person and verifying that they are who they claim to be.
- A back-up is a duplicate copy of a file kept in case the original is lost or corrupted.
- File attributes can be set to increase security of data.

Practice questions 8

P

The following questions are all about the school swimming club database, part of which is shown in the table below. The best time is measured in seconds for one length of the school pool.

1 (a) From the database, name **one** field. [1]

(b) How many fields are in **one** record in this database? [1]

(c) Which field would be the best field to use as a key field? [1]

2 Copy and complete the table below.

Field name	Data type
FirstName	
LastName	
Event	
BestTime	
Gender	
DateOfBirth	
TeamNumber	

[7]

3 Design searches to find:

(a) female swimmers [1]

(b) male breaststroke swimmers [3]

(c) female crawl swimmers whose best time is faster than 40. [4]

4 Using the database, find the results of the searches designed in part 3. [3]

FirstName	LastName	Event	BestTime	Gender	DateOfBirth	TeamNumber
James	Smith	Crawl	39	M	01/01/1996	101
Sonia	Edwards	Crawl	40	F	13/05/1997	209
Rebecca	Shaw	Crawl	36	F	11/07/1996	33
Rose	Hawes	Breaststroke	42	F	05/07/1995	344
Jack	Ford	Crawl	39	M	30/09/1998	195
Bryn	Evans	Breaststroke	41	M	11/11/1997	66
Tilly	Chang	Backstroke	32	F	12/12/1996	457
David	Cribbin	Butterfly	33	M	14/08/1995	568
Fenna	Vander	Crawl	34	F	12/10/1995	239
Alex	Slabbert	Butterfly	36	M	05/05/1996	110
Sam	Hopley	Backstroke	37	M	17/12/1999	131
Emma	Edwards	Backstroke	35	F	23/12/1998	412

Chapter

9

Email

In this chapter, you will learn about emails, what is possible with an email application and what to watch out for when receiving emails from other people.

Electronic mail (email) is a system of sending messages from one computer user to another either on a local network or over the internet. To use email, both users must be subscribers to the internet and have email software installed or they need to be working on a local area network, such as within a school or business. It is then possible to send and receive internal emails without using the internet.

Every email user must have an email address. This is usually provided by an internet service provider (ISP) and looks something like this:

`john.smith@myprovider.co.uk`

"john.smith" is the name of the user and "myprovider.co.uk" is the name of the domain used by the ISP to which the user is subscribed. Every email address is unique, which means that no two users have the same email address and other people cannot read your emails. There is no problem with having more than one email address and sometimes people use different email addresses for different purposes. For example, a person may use one email address at home and a different one in their workplace.

> Email is a system that allows a network user to send a message to another network user.

> Every email user has a unique email address.

Sending an email

If you send an email to another person on the internet, you need to specify the address of the person you are sending it to, and give the email a subject (a heading to indicate what the email is about). The subject you enter is what appears on the list of emails of the person receiving your email. You type the actual message in a larger box underneath.

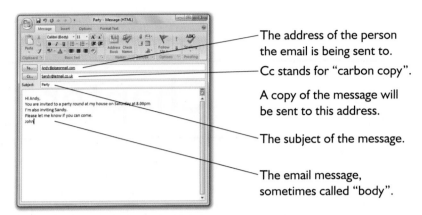

The address of the person the email is being sent to.

Cc stands for "carbon copy".

A copy of the message will be sent to this address.

The subject of the message.

The email message, sometimes called "body".

Figure 9.1 A typical email screen

Once you have typed your message, you need to send it. If you are not connected to the internet, it is placed in your "outbox", where it stays until you connect. This is one of the most important advantages of emails: you can collect and send your messages at a time that suits you.

You can also choose when you receive messages. This has the advantage over telephone calls, which interrupt what you are doing and demand immediate attention, no matter how inconvenient that is.

When you log in to your computer and open the email program, a connection is made and any emails waiting for you are downloaded. Any emails in your outbox are uploaded to your ISP's computer, which then transmits them to the computer of the recipient's ISP, where they are stored until they log in and download them.

Received emails are stored in the **inbox**. Emails waiting to be sent are stored in the **outbox**.

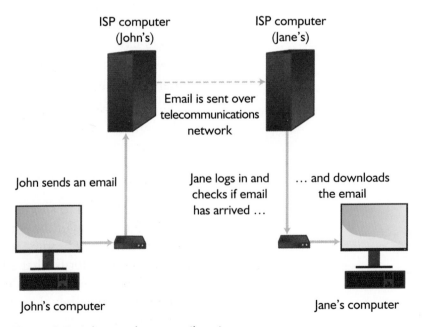

Figure 9.2 John sends an email to Jane

Email programs generally have the following facilities:

- Address book: This allows you to store the email addresses of people to whom you may wish to send emails, and sort them into alphabetical order. Email addresses can often be long and difficult to remember and the address book offers a convenient way of storing them and searching through the list for a particular address. Once in your address book, email addresses can be referred to by the name of the person rather than the address. When you create a new email, you can select one of the addresses stored in the address book without having to type the whole address. You can also create **groups** of addresses in the address book such as a group of people in your class or a group that belong to the same club, so a message can be sent to a group without having to type in all the individual email addresses.

- Inbox folder: The emails you receive are stored in the inbox folder, but you can create your own folders, and rules can be set for the program to know which folder to store emails in when they are received. For example, you can set a rule for the program to store all emails from a friend's address in a separate folder. When you see an email in the inbox, you can open it and read it or print it out, but you can also **reply** to it and write a message back to the sender, or you can **forward** it on to another email user's address.

- Outbox folder: This contains all the emails that are waiting to be sent. When a connection is made, this folder is emptied as all the emails are uploaded to the ISP's computer.

- Sent items folder: A record is kept of all the emails that you have sent.

- Deleted items folder: All the emails that you delete are stored in this folder until you choose to empty it, when they are permanently removed.

- Multiple copies: You can send the same email to a number of different addresses.
  - The addresses can all be placed in the address space separated by commas or semi-colons.
  - The **carbon copy** (Cc) box can be used to send a copy to someone else.
  - If you don't want the main recipient to know you have sent a copy to someone else, use the **blind carbon copy** (Bcc) box.
  - Create a **group** and put the group name in the address space.

- Attachments: Any file that can be stored on a computer, whether it is a document, a picture, a sound file or a video clip, can be attached to an email and sent to another user. However, you have to be careful that the file is not too large. Most email systems have restrictions on how big a file can be and also how much can be stored in someone's mail folder.

● Signature: A standard message can be set up to be attached to all your emails automatically. This might just be your name or, if you are in business, it might be your business address and mobile phone number.

Activity

Signature

Find out how to create a standard message or "signature" for your email.

The sending of emails is now commonplace and is rapidly replacing the conventional methods of communication. The first task done when a person turns on a computer is often to "check the mail".

Advantages of email

● Emails arrive within seconds. The postal service takes a day or two and is sometimes referred to as "snail mail".

● It is a cheap method of communication as there are no extra charges for sending emails, beyond the normal monthly payments to your ISP.

● It does not matter if the recipient is online when the email is sent. It can be received at a time that is convenient for them.

● An email can be sent to a number of different users at the same time.

● Files may be attached to an email and sent with it.

● Emails can be forwarded to other people, such as to a different department in a business, and you can write a note to go with it if you wish, e.g. "Here is the price list I received from the suppliers this morning".

Disadvantages of email

● Objects cannot be sent, for example, you cannot send a parcel by email.

● A large amount of unwanted emails are received. These are called "spam" and ISPs sometimes place spam filters on their computers to try to remove them.

● A paper document must be scanned before it can be sent by email.

- Some legal processes require original documents and do not accept scanned copies so they have to be sent by conventional post.

- There is sometimes a limit to the size of an attached file, so very large files may not be sent.

Webmail

> Webmail is a means of sending and receiving emails using a website.

Webmail allows users to send and receive emails by visiting a website. The computer hosting the website stores all the emails and they are not sent to your computer. The main advantages of this is that emails can be checked from anywhere in the world with an internet connection. For example, you can check your emails even if you are on holiday. You automatically have your address book to hand when you log on to the email website. Finally, if you change your ISP, you do not have to change your email address.

Figure 9.3 Google Mail is an example of a webmail site

Security

There are problems associated with emails. Care must be taken to use an email system wisely. Here are some of the problems:

- A **computer virus** might be attached to the message. You can help prevent this problem by using an up-to-date anti-virus program and never open emails that look suspicious or come from people you have never heard of.

- **Spam** (consisting of unwanted advertising) can quickly clutter up your system. Your ISP usually filters most of this and so does a good anti-virus program.

- **Phishing** emails pretend to come from a bank or eBay or tell you that you have won a prize in a draw you never entered. Never reply to them as they are trying to get personal details from you and, in the worst case, steal money from your bank account.

● Emails are sometimes used to send offensive and hurtful comments to someone (known as **cyber bullying**). This is a foolish thing to do as the sender is always shown on the email and copies can be printed off and shown to an adult. It is also a cowardly way of amusing yourself at someone else's expense. Always report an abusive email if you receive one.

Activity

Google Mail

Before you start, you need to ask your teacher if you are allowed to access Google Mail. If you cannot use Google Mail then ask your teacher how you can do this activity using the email system you have.

1 If you do not already have a Google Mail account, go to www.google.co.uk and create one.

2 Find out the Google Mail addresses of other members of your class and put at least three of them in your address book.

3 Create a group of email addresses called **myclass** and send the whole group the message "Group emails saves remembering the addresses of everyone in the group".

4 There are already some folders for you to store your emails, such as All Mail, Sent Mail and Bin (for deleted mail). Create a new folder called **Homework**.

5 Ask a friend to send you a message about homework you need to do. Move the message into the Homework folder.

Summary

- Email is a system that allows a network user to send a message to another network user.
- Every email user must have an email address. This is a unique address.
- Email programs generally have the following facilities:
  - an address book
  - the ability to create groups of addresses
  - an inbox for the emails you receive
  - an outbox for emails waiting to be sent
  - a sent items folder containing all the emails that you have sent
  - a deleted items folder containing the emails that you have deleted.
- You can send the same email to different addresses:
  - The addresses can all be placed in the To address space, separated by commas or semi-colons or you can use the carbon copy (Cc) box.
  - If you don't want the main recipient to know you have sent a copy to someone else, use the blind carbon copy (Bcc) box.
- Attachments are files that are attached to an email.
- A signature is a standard message automatically attached to all your emails.
- Webmail is a means of sending and receiving emails using a website.
- There are some security problems associated with emails. These include:
  - computer viruses
  - spam
  - phishing
  - cyber bullying.

Practice questions 9

1 Sarah regularly sends emails to her friends.

   (a) What is email? [1]

   (b) Give **two** advantages of using emails rather than the normal postal service. [2]

   (c) Give **two** disadvantages of using email. [2]

2 (a) Explain the use of Cc in an email. [2]

   (b) Explain the use of Bcc, making sure that you show why it is different to Cc. [2]

3 Explain **three** problems that can arise when using email and how these problems can be avoided. [6]

Chapter

10

Spreadsheets

In this chapter, you will learn about spreadsheets and how they can be used for processing numbers, solving problems, exploring possibilities and producing graphs. You will look at different data types and learn the language associated with spreadsheets, such as cell, row, formula, variable and so on.

Spreadsheets are widely used in offices for any application that needs some calculations performed or some graphs drawn. For example, a spreadsheet could be used to plan the annual budget of a department in a business, so that the management know how much money they can spend on items such as advertising or whether they can afford to employ a new secretary.

The spreadsheet can then be used to investigate the best allocation of money by changing the numbers. Various spending plans can be looked at to see if the total amount to be spent is less than the full amount planned within the budget.

Text, numbers and calculations are placed in a grid of rectangular cells called a **worksheet**. A spreadsheet may consist of a number of worksheets that are related to each other and interact.

◯ Benefits of using a spreadsheet

- Automatic recalculation: Every time the content of a cell is changed, calculations are performed and other cells are updated if necessary.
- Graphs and charts can be drawn using the data in selected cells. These have greater visual impact and are easier to understand than complex sheets of data. Trends and patterns are easier to see on graphs.
- Replication: Once the first formula is correctly entered, it is possible to drag across the adjacent cells in a row or column so the computer copies the pattern of the calculation.

● **What-if calculations** allow you to use the spreadsheet to see what would happen if you changed certain figures in the spreadsheet. Spreadsheets have a "knock-on" ability. If you change one figure, all the figures in the spreadsheet associated with it change too.

● Formulae can be stored and reused.

● Calculations involving large numbers are possible.

● You can use the **fill** feature to copy formulae after the formula is input.

> A spreadsheet is a means of performing calculations and of modelling real-life situations.

If there are calculations involved in your data, then a spreadsheet is needed. Spreadsheets organise data and perform calculations. Microsoft Excel is an example of a program that is used to create spreadsheets.

Activity

Budget spreadsheet

1 Download the file **budget.xls** from the website mentioned at the start of this book. This is a simple budgeting spreadsheet for a newsagent. There are two worksheets to this spreadsheet:

● Budget calculates the overall net profit for the month. The net profit is how much is left of the income after all expenses have been paid.
● Monthly Wages calculates the monthly wages bill.

You can flip from one worksheet to the other by clicking on the tab at the bottom of the page.

2 Use this spreadsheet to answer the following questions:

(a) How much could the shop spend on marketing this month and keep its net profit at least £2000?

(b) Could the shop hire another shop assistant and still keep the net profit over £2000?

(c) If newspaper sales fell to £12,000 and they made one of their three sales assistants redundant, would the shop still show a net profit?

	A	B	C	D	E	F	G	H	I
	A5		ƒₓ New Zedline						
1	Monthly Budget								
2									
3	Maggie's Magz								
4	15, Rappit Road,								
5	New Zedline								
6									
7			Amount						
8	INCOME								
9	SALES								
10		Newspapers	£16,200						
11		Magazines	£8,452						
12		Confectionery	£15,966						
13		Stationery	£6,875						
14		Others	£4,200						
15		Total	£51,693						
16	EXPENSES								
17		Admin	£1,200						
18		IT Support	£800						
19		Wages	£9,400						
20		Supplies	£20,000						
21		Marketing	£14,000						
22		Premises	£2,550						
23			£47,950						
24									
25		Net Profit	£3,743						
26									
27									
28									
29									

Budget and Monthly Wages tabs

Figure 10.1 The budget spreadsheet

Cells

A spreadsheet consists of rows and columns of boxes called cells. The rows are labelled with numbers and the columns with letters. Each cell is referenced by a combination of the column letter and row number. For example, the cell B5 is highlighted in Figure 10.3.

I am sure that you can see that you could have cell references going up to column Z (e.g. Z999) but what happens after that? Well, new columns are labelled AA, AB, AC, …, BA, BB, BC, BD, …, all the way up to ZZ. If you are a mathematician, you could try to work out how many possible columns that makes!

Sometimes you might want to refer to a range of cells. As shown in Figure 10.2, (B5:B9) means all the cells in the column from B5 down to B9. A block of cells can be referenced in a similar way, for example (B5:D9).

> A cell reference always starts with a letter and ends with a number (e.g. C5).

> Wherever you are in a spreadsheet you can always get back to cell A1 by holding down the **CTRL** key and tapping the **Home** key on the keyboard.

Figure 10.2 Ranges of cells in a spreadsheet

The width of the columns may be changed by dragging the line of the column boundary on the column heading to the size required. Row height may be changed in a similar way. If several columns or rows are to be adjusted, it might be best to use the format button on the toolbar.

Data can be entered into any cell. This data can be of different types (text, number, currency, date, etc.) and can be formatted in the usual ways (font, size, colour, alignment). There are also ways of formatting the cells with background colours, single or double grid lines, and borders.

Each cell can contain:

- a **label** – text used largely for description purposes; labels are not used in calculation

- a **data** – numbers to be used in a calculation; the results of one calculation may be used in another

- a **formula** – a mathematical calculation automatically carried out once you have entered it correctly.

Figure 10.4 shows labels, data and a formula. The formula appears in the **formula bar** but the cell which contains the formula normally displays the result of the calculation.

Drag here to change width of column B

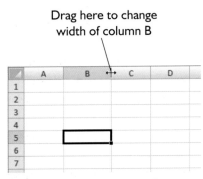

Figure 10.3 The width of a column can be changed

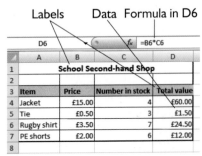

Figure 10.4 Labels, data and a formula

Formulae

Formulae are automatically recalculated every time the data on the spreadsheet is changed.

Formula example

In Figure 10.4, the data in cell B6 is to be multiplied by the data in cell C6 and entered in cell D6.

The formula entered in cell D6 is = **B6*C6**

Spreadsheets do more than just display data in a neat way. Some of the cells will contain a mathematical formula. The calculation will be performed every time any of the data on the spreadsheet is edited. It is these formulas that make a spreadsheet useful.

In Excel, a formula is differentiated from other data by placing an equals sign ("=") at the beginning. Cell references (such as **D3** or **C5**) are used in the formulae. The symbols for the four main mathematical operations are:

+ Add

– Subtract

* Multiply

/ Divide

If you want to use the spreadsheet to add up the total costs of the jacket, tie, rugby shorts and PE shorts shown in column D in Figure 10.4, you can enter the formula:

=D4+D5+D6+D7

There are some abbreviations to make formulae simpler to enter. The formula above is the same as the following abbreviated formula:

=SUM(D4:D7)

In this case there is not much difference, but imagine if there were lots of items to add up. **=SUM(D4:D99)** is much easier to write than **=D4+D5+D6+D7+D8+…** all the way to D99.

SUM is an example of a **function**. There are many other functions that can be used in a spreadsheet program for instance AVERAGE, COUNT, MAX and IF. The current time and date can be entered into a cell with the formula **=NOW()**.

There are lots of functions. You can find out about them by using the "Help" on your spreadsheet. There are also lots of shortcuts from the keyboard. For instance, **Ctrl+;** makes the current date appear. For the current time, press **Ctrl+:**.

A spreadsheet normally displays the result of a calculation rather than the formula itself. The formulae are kept hidden so that they do not confuse the user, but you can set the spreadsheet to display the formula in Excel by holding down the Control key (Ctrl) and pressing the key to the left of 1.

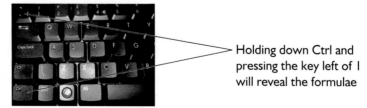

Holding down Ctrl and pressing the key left of I will reveal the formulae

Figure 10.5 Using the keyboard to display formulae

Formatting

In a spreadsheet, you can format the way that items are aligned in a cell (left, right or centre alignment).

Cells can be merged together and any cell or group of cells can be coloured or have borders (see Figure 10.6).

Within a cell, the characters can be formatted for font style, size and colour. Cells are also formatted to reflect the data that is to be held in them. Computers store different data types in different ways and the software needs to know the data type in order to display it properly and to manipulate it properly in calculations. Data types you may use when formatting cells are:

- currency
- number (real and integer, or whole number)
- date
- text.

School Second-hand Shop			
Item	**Price**	**Number in stock**	**Total value**
Jacket	£15.00	4	£60.00
Tie	£0.50	3	£1.50
Rugby shirt	£3.50	7	£24.50
PE shorts	£2.00	6	£12.00

— Cells merged and text centred
— Cell background colour filled
— Cells formatted as currency
— Border around cells
Text left aligned
Numbers right aligned

Figure 10.6 Formatting features

Copying cells in a spreadsheet

Cells can be treated in three ways apart from the normal one of just filling them with data values or formulae. You can:

- drag a cell and its contents to another part of the spreadsheet
- highlight a cell or group of cells
- replicate the cell (a kind of intelligent copying which we look at in this section).

You get a clue as to what will happen to the cell by the shape of the cursor on the screen. It all depends where you place your pointer in the cell as to what effect it has. The pointer changes shape as shown in Figure 10.7.

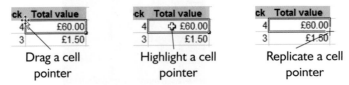

Drag a cell pointer

Highlight a cell pointer

Replicate a cell pointer

Figure 10.7 Pointers on cells in a spreadsheet

○ Replicating cells

When you position the mouse pointer in the bottom right-hand corner of the cell and drag down or across, the spreadsheet tries to respond intelligently. If there is a formula in the cell, the spreadsheet tries to adjust it as it goes down the page to fit in with the new position and the cells being referred to.

Activity

Cell replication

You can have a bit of fun learning about cell replication.

1 Open a blank spreadsheet.

2 In cell A1, type "Monday".

3 In cell A2, type "Tuesday".

4 Highlight those two cells and then position the pointer in the bottom right of the combined cells to get the replication symbol. Drag the replication pointer down column A. The result might surprise you!

5 Try using different data, such as "January" and "February" or numbers such as 2 and 4 or 10 and 20.

Relative cell references

If a formula is copied by filling down, the cell references are adjusted as you drag the replication pointer down the page. This is because it uses the **relative addresses** of cells, based on their position in the sheet.

In Figure 10.8, the highlighted cell (D4) contains a total calculated by multiplying a price (stored in cell B4) by the number in stock (stored in cell C4). Cell D4 is copied (or filled down) into the cells D5, D6 and D7 and the cell references are automatically adjusted for each row.

	A	B	C	D	E	F
1		**School Second-hand Shop**				
2						
3	**Item**	**Price**	**Number in stock**	**Total value**		
4	Jacket	£15.00	4	£60.00		=B4*C4
5	Tie	£0.50	3	£1.50		=B5*C5
6	Rugby shirt	£3.50	7	£24.50		=B6*C6
7	PE shorts	£2.00	6	£12.00		=B7*C7
8						

Figure 10.8 Relative addressing

Absolute addresses have a $ character in front of the column letter and row number that are required to stay the same.

When copying cells containing formulae, relative addresses change but absolute addresses do not.

Absolute cell references

In Figure 10.9, cell C4 contains a formula that calculates a new price based on a percentage increase on a price stored in cell B4. The amount of the percentage increase is stored in cell F2.

Cell C4 has a relative address (B4) in its formula as well as an **absolute address ($F$2)**. When the formula is copied into the cells below, the relative address changes but the absolute address does not. (A good way to remember this is to think of the dollar sign as glue! It glues this cell into every formula.)

	A	B	C	D	E	F
1			School Second-hand Shop			% Increase
2						15
3	Item	Price	New Price	Number in stock	Total value	
4	Jacket	£15.00	£17.25	4	£60.00	
5	Tie	£0.50	£0.58	3	£1.50	
6	Rugby shirt	£3.50	£4.03	7	£24.50	
7	PE shorts	£2.00	£2.30	6	£12.00	
8						

	A	B	C	D	E	F
1			School Second-hand Shop			% Increase
2						15
3	Item	Price	New Price	Number in stock	Total value	
4	Jacket	£15.00	=B4+(B4*$F$2/100)	4	£60.00	
5	Tie	£0.50	=B5+(B5*$F$2/100)	3	£1.50	
6	Rugby shirt	£3.50	=B6+(B6*$F$2/100)	7	£24.50	
7	PE shorts	£2.00	=B7+(B7*$F$2/100)	6	£12.00	
8						

Figure 10.9 Absolute addressing

The IF function

It is possible to make the data in one cell conditional on the content of another cell using the IF function.

For example, the delivery charge of an item depends on its total price. The delivery charge is 10% of the value but delivery is free if the item costs over £50.

Assume the total cost is in cell E6. The formula to calculate the delivery charge, written in English, is: if the price in E6 is more than £50 then delivery is free, if it is £50 or less then delivery is 10% of the price in E6. The way this formula is written for the spreadsheet is:

= IF(E6>50, 0, E6*0.1)

There are three parts to the IF function and they are written in this order inside the brackets:

- the condition that is being looked for (in this case, **E6>50**)
- the value to use if the condition is true (in this case, **0**)
- the value to use if the condition is false (in this case, **E6*0.1**)

The data in some cells can be set depending on the data in other cells using the IF function.

Activity

Create your own "expert" system

In Figure 10.10, the spreadsheet adds up the number of times you answer "yes" and makes a judgement based on your answers.

	A	B	C	D	E	F
1						
2	The Amazing "Are you well enough to come to school?" Calculator					
3						
4	Please answer the following questions.					
5						
6	Do you feel rotten?	no	0			
7	Have you done your homework?	no	0			
8	Will you have your favourite lesson today?	no	1			
9	Have you called a doctor?	no	0			
10	Will be at home alone today?	yes	0			
11	What time did you go to bed last night?	11	0			
12	Have you got a pet?	yes	0			
13	Is there a good programme on TV today?	no	1			
14	Is your favourite video due for return tomorrow?	no	1			
15	Will you have your worst lesson today?	no	1			
16			4	For staying in		
17			6	For going out		
18	The calculator says	Go to school!				

Figure 10.10 The amazing "Are you well enough to come to school?" calculator

The formulae are shown in Figure 10.11. The long formula in cell B18 is known as a "nested IF". It is an IF inside an IF. You can try to unravel it if you want or just use it for a bit of fun.

	A	B	C	D	E
1					
2	The Amazing "Are you well enough to come to school?" Calculator				
3					
4	Please answer the following questions.				
5					
6	Do you feel rotten?	no	=IF(B6="yes",1,0)		
7	Have you done your homework?	no	=IF(B7="yes",1,0)		
8	Will you have your favourite lesson today?	no	=IF(B8="yes",0,1)		
9	Have you called a doctor?	no	=IF(B9="yes",1,0)		
10	Will be at home alone today?	yes	=IF(B10="yes",0,1)		
11	What time did you go to bed last night?	11	=IF(B11>10,0,1)		
12	Have you got a pet?	yes	=IF(B12="yes",0,1)		
13	Is there a good programme on TV today?	no	=IF(B13="yes",0,1)		
14	Is your favourite video due for return tomorrow?	no	=IF(B14="yes",0,1)		
15	Will you have your worst lesson today?	no	=IF(B15="yes",0,1)		
16			=SUM(C6:C15)	For staying in	
17			=COUNT(C6:C15)-C16	For going out	
18	The calculator says	=IF(C1			

=IF(C16=C17,"Make up your own mind!",
IF(C16>C17,"Stay at home!", "Go to school!"))

Figure 10.11 The amazing "Are you well enough to come to school?" formulae

1 Copy the calculator and try it out.

2 Now make up a similar spreadsheet to decide whether you should go to the cinema at the weekend or not.

3 Make up another expert system of your choice (e.g. to decide if someone should be included in a team).

○ Charts and graphs

Spreadsheet data can be selected and a chart or graph of this data can be created. There are many different types of chart and it is important to select the one that is most appropriate. In other words, you need to choose the type of chart that best illustrates the information.

Figure 10.12 Excel offers a wide variety of graphical representations

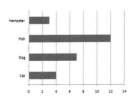

Figure 10.13 Bar chart – the longest bar shows the favourite type of pet

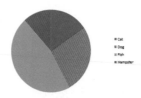

Figure 10.14 Pie chart – the slices show the proportion of each type of pet

Charts make information easier to read and understand. Patterns and trends are easier to see.

Bar and column charts may best be used to compare different values (i.e. numbers and headings from several columns). The biggest bar or column shows the greatest value.

Pie charts show how a total is subdivided among a number of different categories.

Line graphs display a trend of sequences of values by using plotted points.

The purpose of graphs and charts is to display data visually to make it instantly clear to the reader what they are seeing. There are many other types of graph, such as doughnut, bubble and radar, but many of them do not show the data as clearly as bar, column, pie and line charts. It may be better to stick with these types for most purposes.

Figure 10.15 shows the Class 10H pet data represented as bar, pie, column and line charts. Which of these four charts has no sensible meaning?

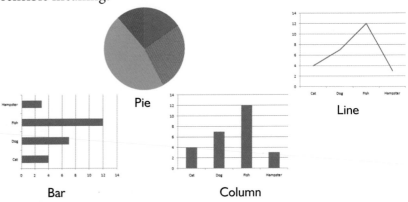

Figure 10.15 Various charts showing the same data

All graphs and charts should have a purpose. They should illustrate a fact or a trend, or prove a theory about the data in the spreadsheet. It must therefore be clear to the person looking at the chart what is being shown, so you need to make sure all the axes are clearly labelled.

Summary

- Spreadsheets display data in a neat way but also perform calculations automatically.
- Each cell is referenced by a column letter and a row number (e.g. D10).
- Data in a cell may be text, numbers, dates, times, currency, logical values, errors or even graphics.
- A formula can be placed in a cell to perform a calculation.
- Each time data is changed, the formulae recalculate automatically.
- Several sheets can be used in a workbook and these sheets can interact with each other.
- Rows of data can be sorted into alphabetical or numerical order.
- In a formula, cell references can use relative addresses (e.g. B3) or absolute addresses (e.g. $B$3).
- When a formula is copied or filled into adjoining cells, relative addresses change but absolute addresses do not.
- Data can be represented as charts, such as bar, column, pie and line charts.

Practice questions 10

A school drama club uses a spreadsheet (see below) to budget the cost of putting on a show.

1 (a) Which of these formulae could be used to give the difference between the estimated cost and the actual cost of publicity (D4)?

    (i)   =B4+C4

    (ii) =B4-C4

    (iii) =D2-D3 [1]

  (b) Which of these formulae could be used to give the total estimated cost (B8)?

    (i)   =B8-C8

    (ii) =SUM(B2:B7)

    (iii) =D8-C8

    (iv) =B2+B3+B4+B5+B6+B7 [1]

  (c) If the actual cost of costumes (C2) was changed to £290, what **three** other cells would change? [3]

2 (a) Write down a formula that could be used for the total in C8. [1]

  (b) Write down a formula that could be used for the total in D8. [1]

3 The formula in B8 could have been copied to C8 and D8. Would this use absolute or relative replication? [1]

4 Which would be the best type of chart to illustrate the actual costs of the **six** different expenditures in an article for the school magazine? [1]

	A	B	C	D
1	Expenditure	Estimate	Actual Cost	Difference
2	Costumes	£350.00	£300.00	£50.00
3	Printing	£250.00	£250.00	£0.00
4	Publicity	£200.00	£180.00	£20.00
5	Props	£100.00	£110.00	−£10.00
6	Lighting	£300.00	£250.00	£50.00
7	Sound	£300.00	£300.00	£0.00
8	TOTAL	£1500.00	£1390.00	£110.00

Chapter 11

Desktop publishing

In this chapter, you will learn the meaning of WYSIWYG and how to use desktop publishing software to produce posters, leaflets, newsletters and other documents. You will learn about images and how to resize, flip, crop and rotate them.

Desktop publishing (DTP) software is used to create complex documents that a word-processing program may not be able to produce. Publications such as newspapers or magazines, brochures and advertisements are created using DTP software.

Pages are created using frames, which may be positioned anywhere on the page. These frames contain text or graphics, and can be used to create a number of columns on the page.

The text that is to be used in the publication is usually prepared using a word processor and then imported into the appropriate frame on the page. Similarly, any graphics are prepared using a graphics package before being imported. The DTP program should only really be used to arrange the items on the page and for special effects.

Benefits of DTP:

- High-quality, professional-looking publications which have impact can be created.

- Ready-made templates are available for many types of document, such as letters or business cards.

- It is easy to edit the layout of a publication.

- The display shows what will be printed.

- Publications can be made with a consistency of style. A company may have its own style for publications.

- Ready-made colour schemes are available.

- It is possible to create more complex layouts than with a word-processing program.

Word-processing software

A word-processing program is used to create a document that can be printed or emailed as an attachment to another computer user. Many word-processing programs use a **what-you-see-is-what-you-get (WYSIWIG)** approach to creating documents. There are many different programs available but one of the most widely used is Microsoft Word.

You will probably notice that your word-processing program contains many of the functions previously only available in DTP programs. As software has developed, the distinction between the two has tended to blur.

> WYSIWYG (what you see is what you get): The display on the screen is how the document will look when printed out.

Planning a document

There are a number of things to decide when planning your document. These include:

● the layout of the page

● the fonts you wish to use

● justification (alignment)

● tabulation

● headers and footers.

You may wish to include **tables,** which will need planning separately. There are often **style sheets** and **templates** available. All these are explained below.

Page layout

It is most important that care is paid to the layout of the page before even a word of text has been typed. When you create a new document, you will need to plan for the following features:

● the page size – the size of paper on which you want the finished document to be printed; most printers use A4 paper and so pages should be set to A4 size (29.7 cm by 21.0 cm)

● the orientation of the page (portrait or landscape)

● the size of the margins (top, bottom, left and right)

● the spacing between the lines (single-line spacing is normal; double-line spacing can be used to give more space between lines).

Portrait   Landscape

Figure 11.1 Portrait and landscape orientation

Fonts

Once the page size and margins have been set, you are ready to start typing the text. Before you do, select the font that you are going to use and the size of the text. There are many different fonts, each of which displays the text in a different style, and the choice of font often depends on the document you are typing and the target audience. Is it a serious piece of coursework or is it a fun message for your friends?

Some fonts, such as Arial, are plain looking and some have little lines attached, known as **serifs**. The fonts without the lines are known as **sans serif** fonts. (If you know French, you will know that this means "without serif".) The serif is useful as it helps to distinguish letters which look similar.

> Do not use too many different fonts in the same document. A document that has a lot of different fonts looks untidy and is difficult to read.

> Consider the word "ill" at the start of a sentence.
>
> Using Arial (Sans serif), it would be Ill.
>
> Using Times New Roman (serif), it would be Ill.
>
> The font using serifs is a bit clearer to understand.

Figure 11.2 Font size, type and style can be easily set

Justification

Text can be aligned to the left, right or centre or fully justified. This is known as text justification or alignment. Once justification has been set, the text that follows remains with that justification until the justification is changed.

This text is left justified. It is written with every line
starting neatly on the left.

                    This text is right justified. It is written with every line
                                          starting neatly on the right.

            This text is centre justified. It is written with the
            centre of every line in the middle of the page.

If   text   is   fully   justified,   it   is   spaced   out   so   that   each   line   of   text   is
exactly   the   same   length.   This   is   often   done   in   books   and   newspapers.

Figure 11.3 Justification of text

Tabulation

To make lists of data items more readable, they are often placed in columns. A tab is the jump made by the text cursor when the tab key is pressed on the keyboard, and the lengths of these jumps can be set by dragging the tab stops along the ruler bar at the top of the page to the positions you want the columns to be. If you need more precision, the distances of the tabs can be entered using the Tabs dialog box.

The TAB key is on the left of the keyboard and is usually shown with double arrows on it. Pressing TAB moves the pointer left to right. Holding SHIFT with TAB moves the other way (right to left).

Figure 11.4 The TAB key

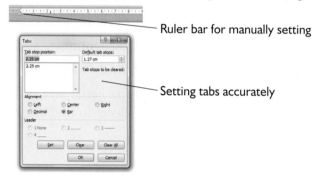

Ruler bar for manually setting

Setting tabs accurately

Figure 11.5 Tabs can be set accurately or by dragging using the ruler

Once the tab stop positions have been set, it is easy to line up columns of data on the page using the tab key.

Mark	Thompson	1	0	C
Thomas	Smith	1	0	Y
Jane	Jones	1	0	Y
Alice	Jenkins	1	0	B

Figure 11.6 A tabbed list

Tables

If lists of data are to be displayed in a grid, then a table should be used. The number of rows and columns can be set, and dragging the vertical lines on the table can change the widths of the columns.

First name	Surname	Form
Mark	Thompson	10C
Thomas	Smith	10Y
Jane	Jones	10Y
Alice	Jenkins	10B

Figure 11.7 A table

Headers and footers

A **header** is a section of a page that, once you have set it up, appears at the top of every page of a document when it is printed. A **footer** appears at the bottom of the page. They are useful for displaying information about the document. Information appearing in headers and footers may include:

- the title of the document
- the name and author of the document
- page numbers
- the date and time of printing
- the name and path of the file on the disk drive (this makes it easier to find again on the computer).

> Headers and footers can be used for automatic page numbering.

Styles

When creating large documents, such as your coursework documentation, it is a good idea to define some text styles. These make sure there is consistency in the way the document looks and makes it appear more professional. When setting a style (e.g. Headline), you can specify the font, size and colour to be used and any formatting of the text, including line spacing. A description of a style is known as a **style sheet**.

Figure 11.8 Setting a new style using a style sheet

Templates

Setting up a template for a frequently used type of document can save a lot of time. Styles and layouts can be pre-set on the template and used every time a new document is created.

Businesses use letterheads printed on the top of all their stationery, showing details about the business, such as the name, address, email, telephone numbers and possibly a small logo. These can all be placed in position on a template, which means that they do not have to be typed every time a letter is written. In order to give a more professional look to letters, the same font and text size is used for every letter that is written and these can be defined in the template.

Spellchecker and thesaurus

A spellchecker checks spelling, but it does more than that. Every word that is typed is checked to see if it exists in a dictionary; if it does not, then that word is highlighted as a possible spelling

mistake. Alternative spellings are suggested and the correct one can be selected. If the word is not in the dictionary (it may be a person or place name), then it is possible to add it so that it is not shown as a spelling error next time it is typed.

There are some problems with spellcheckers:

- A word used incorrectly may be a perfectly valid word. For example, if you mean to type the word "which" but spell it wrongly as "witch", no error is detected.

- Words can be spelled differently in US English and in UK English. For example, "colour" in the UK is spelled "color" in the USA.

- A word may be correct but not in the dictionary, such as your surname or the name of the town you live in.

A grammar-checker suggests problems with the way sentences are structured and can find repeated words or incorrect punctuation.

A thesaurus can give alternatives for words. For example, a thesaurus may suggest "pleasant", "kind", "lovely" and other words with a similar meaning as alternatives for the word "nice".

Careful! Spellcheckers do not always get it right!

Figure 11.9 A thesaurus can give alternative words with a similar meaning

○ Mail merge

Much of the junk mail we receive has personalised information on it, such as our name, address or town that we live in. Many other people receive the same letter, but with different details. The way this is done is by using mail merge. There are three main stages to this process:

1 A form letter (see Figure 11.10) is created which has the main text of the letter as well as place markers to show where the data fields, such as name and address, are to be inserted.

2 A database of the data that is to be used in the letters (see Figure 11.11) is created.

3 The mail merge operation places the data from the database into each individual letter and prints them, one for each record in the database (see Figure 11.12).

Figure 11.10 A form letter with the field placeholders

Title	Surname	MemberNum	StartDate
Mr	Jones	325	12/06/10
Mrs	Hunter	326	23/06/10
Ms	Flash	327	25/06/10

Figure 11.11 Data to be used in the form letter

  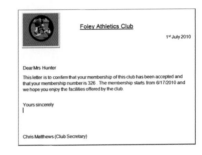

Figure 11.12 Output from the mail merge operation

A large proportion of junk mail uses mail merge.

There are many different types of document that use mail merge. Businesses send circulars to their clients, companies send bills or payment reminders to their customers, and school pupils receive their exam results on mail-merged letters.

Borders

Borders can be placed around text, graphics, or even pages. Borders help to make a document more attractive and can cause sections to be separated from each other or make other sections stand out from the rest. Borders can be different colours, styles and thicknesses.

Figure 11.13 Choosing a border style for a text box

Graphics

A graphic is a picture (sometimes called an image). It might be a picture you have taken with a digital camera or downloaded from the internet, or a piece of clipart.

Graphics software is used to create or edit an image, whether it is a picture for a school newsletter, a company logo to be placed on a letterhead, or even a family photo you are sending by email.

Graphics can be manipulated in a number of ways. These include resizing, cropping, rotating and flipping (producing the mirror image). Figure 11.14 shows some of these manipulations.

> **Clipart** is ready-made graphics, often in cartoon form, which can be used to illustrate a document.

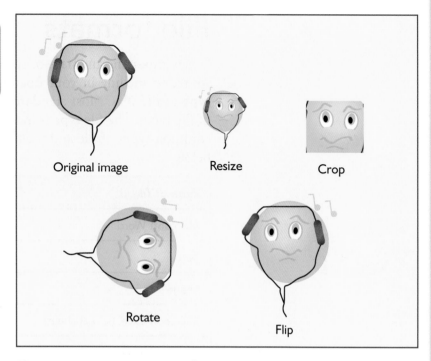

Figure 11.14 Ways to manipulate graphics

There are shapes included in many word-processing packages. These are known as "auto shapes" in Microsoft Word.

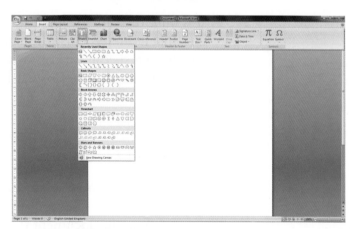

Figure 11.15 Auto shapes in Microsoft Word

Activity **A**

Clipart

1 Select a piece of clipart.

2 Using appropriate software, try to:

- enlarge it
- rotate it
- crop a portion from it
- flip it to create a mirror image.

File formats

When importing an image or some other sort of file from another source to include in your document, you must take care which **type of file** it is. Most standard software can recognise a variety of file types. The file type is indicated by the **file extension**. Some common types of file and their extensions are shown in the table below.

Type of file	File extension
Microsoft Word	.doc or .docx
Text	.txt
Image	.jpg or .png
Microsoft Excel (spreadsheet)	.xls or .xlsx
Comma-separated variable	.csv
Rich text format	.rtf
Database	.mdb

It is important for an application to recognise what type of file it is so that it can recognise the data held in it. Each piece of software has its own special way of saving data and the application must interpret what data is a formatting command, a number, a colour in an image, and so on.

Watermarks

A graphic or text can be placed on a **master page** where it becomes a **watermark** for the rest of the document. Everything else appearing on the document is written over the watermark, which shows through faintly from the background.

> The word DRAFT is a watermark on this page and will be removed when the text is finalised.
>
> This text is draft text and should only been seen as such.

Figure 11.16 A master page with the word "DRAFT" as a watermark

Summary

- Desktop publishing (DTP) software is used to create documents containing mixtures of text and graphics.
- WYSIWYG (what you see is what you get) software displays on the screen how the document will look when printed out.
- Changes can be made to the style of a document:
  - font size, style and type
  - line spacing
  - page size and orientation
  - page justification – left, right, centre, full
  - watermarks.
- Documents can be checked using a spellchecker or words can be looked up using an online thesaurus.
- Mail merge allows a standard letter to be linked to a database for personalised mail shots to be created.
- Files have different file types.
- Lists can be set out using tabulation or placed in tables.
- Borders can be placed around words, objects or pages.
- Graphics can be manipulated using:
  - resizing
  - cropping
  - rotating
  - flipping (reflecting).
- Auto shapes are pre-drawn shapes available in the software.

Practice questions 11

1 Explain **three** things you should take into account when planning a document. [3]

2 Some fonts are "serif" fonts and some are "sans serif".

  (a) Explain the difference between serif and sans serif fonts. [2]

  (b) Give the name of an example of each type of font. [2]

3 When a personalised letter is sent to a number of people, the process of mail merge is used.

  (a) Define "mail merge". [2]

  (b) Put the following steps in the mail-merge process into the correct order:

    1 Print the merged letters.

    2 Prepare a data source.

    3 Prepare the letter.

    4 Insert the <<fields>>.

    5 Merge the fields with the data.

    6 Save the mail merge. [6]

Chapter

12

Web and presentation software

In this chapter, you will learn about web pages and the different features and effects that can be used with them. You will learn about multimedia presentations and what is possible within individual slides. You will learn about slide animation, transitions and the different effects that can be achieved.

○ Multimedia presentations

A multimedia presentation usually involves a sequence of slides projected onto a screen or interactive whiteboard. It is used to communicate information in a way that is interesting for the viewers so they can more easily understand the topic being presented. Animations, video clips or sound may further illustrate the topic. Examples may include a teacher explaining a topic to a class in a lesson or a salesperson explaining to a panel of business personnel about their latest products.

Usually, the person who is explaining the topic also controls the slide show and the slide only moves on when the speaker is ready. However, sometimes the slides are set to move on after a given time interval.

Microsoft PowerPoint is an example of presentation software. A single slide consists of a number of frames and each frame may have some text or a graphic in it. Sound or video clips may also be placed on a slide.

> Multimedia presentations are an effective way of communicating information. They are more interesting than just listening to somebody talking.

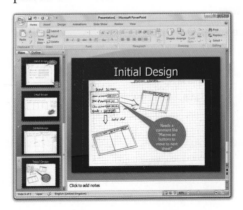

Figure 12.1 Each slide of the Microsoft PowerPoint presentation is individually designed

Animation and transitions

The objects on a single slide need not all be displayed at once. Each object can be programmed to appear after a set time or at the click of a mouse or the press of a button on a remote control. The way each object appears can be selected from a number of **animation effects**.

Figure 12.2 Each word can fly in from the top, accompanied by the sound of breaking glass, for example

Slide transitions and animations can be really irritating to viewers so do not use too many different types in the same presentation.

The way one slide changes into another is called the **slide transition**. This can be programmed as well and there are many different options to choose from.

Action buttons and hyperlinks

Action buttons can be placed on a slide to perform such tasks as:

- moving on to the next slide
- moving to the home slide
- opening a document
- running a movie clip
- linking to the internet or another slide via a **hyperlink**.

A section of text or a graphic may be set up as a hyperlink to another slide. When the mouse button is clicked with the pointer on the hyperlink, the next slide is displayed.

Creation of a slide show

It is most important to design the content of each slide carefully. The order in which the slides are displayed, what animation and effects are to be included and the methods of slide transition must be planned. This design is often called a storyboard.

The next step is to prepare the different elements that are going to be contained on the slides. Graphics need to be drawn or collected, text prepared and sounds and video clips recorded. Then all these elements can be assembled on the slides. It is also possible

to record a spoken narration for the slide show to allow people to watch it and understand it without the need for a presenter.

Templates for slides can be used to create consistency of formatting and layout. When the data has been placed on the slides it is possible to further edit it. Many of the features of a word processor are available, such as text formatting and spellchecking.

Test the slide show for timing and make sure the transitions work. Then you are ready to present your slide show.

> Always test your slide show. It can be embarrassing if it does not work in front of an audience!

Activity **A**

Multimedia presentation

1 Download the presentation **animate.ppt** from the website for this book.

2 Run the presentation, which illustrates animation effects available in Microsoft PowerPoint.

○ Web pages

Many millions of websites now exist on the World Wide Web, and creating your own is not difficult. There are two ways of creating web pages:

- Use a special language called **Hypertext Mark-up Language (HTML)** to inform an internet browser (such as Microsoft Internet Explorer or Google Chrome) how to display the page.

- Use a special web page creation program.

You can open any page on the internet and view its "source". This displays the text and the HTML code (or "tags") that tell the browser how to display the page. The code looks complicated but is easily understood by an HTML programmer. With a web page creation program, you do not need to know so much about HTML.

Web page creation programs are very similar to word-processing programs. Text can be added to the page and formatted. Bullets, colours and text alignment can all be used and graphics included. The layout of a page is usually managed by putting text and graphics into the cells of a table. These cells can be resized or merged together to give different spacing.

Web

A **web** is a folder on your computer that contains all your web pages. When it is complete, a web can be uploaded to an intranet or to a website on the internet.

Some web pages have counters on them that monitor how many people have visited the web page.

> Web page 'hit' counters show how popular a website is.

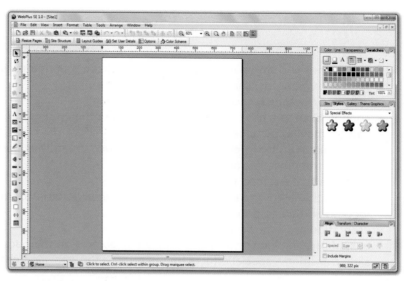

Figure 12.3 A web page creation program

Hyperlinks

The design of web pages is important. There must not be too much information on any one page, and colours need to be used carefully.

Any section of text or even a graphic can be set up as a hyperlink to another page. When a hyperlink is clicked, the new page is displayed in the browser. This is how you navigate between pages within a website or to other websites. A **navigation bar** should be placed on every page of a website so that you can return to the home page or move quickly between different sections.

○ Considering the audience

Careful design saves time. The design of a presentation or web page must take into account the purpose and the needs of the audience.

When a web page or presentation is designed it is important to take into account the target audience who are to watch it. A presentation to a primary school would use simple graphics, straightforward language and probably contain sounds to enliven the slides. A presentation to a group of scientists would probably have tables, graphs, mathematical equations and so on and possibly no sound at all. Similarly, you must remember that not all people can see or hear as well as others.

Some considerations that can be given to audiences are:

● Text should be large enough for most people to see from the back of a room.

● Font styles should not be fancy or bizarre, unless in a title.

● Do not to cram too much information together on a page.

● Make good use of contrasting colour to ensure information is clear.

● On a web page, hovering a mouse over an image can produce pop-up text that describes the image, for people using a speech synthesizer.

Summary **S**

- Presentations and web pages have a number of common features:
  - text, such as words, characters or numbers
  - images or graphics, such as photos or cartoons
  - sounds, such as a clip of music, voice or some other sound
  - videos, moving pictures
  - hyperlinks that, when clicked, move the viewer to another part of the presentation or outside the presentation
  - hotspots that respond to a mouse click
  - buttons that allow the user to move to another slide or introduce a special effect
  - looping and timed pages.
- Presentation slide shows also have:
  - animation – movement of the text or other objects on the page
  - slide transition – special effects that happen when one slide changes for another.

Practice questions 12 **P**

1 A school is having an open day. In the entrance hall, they would like to show a slide show of sporting achievements by pupils in the past year.

   (a) Choose whether the school should use automatic or manual transition of slides. [1]

   (b) Explain why they would use the method you have chosen. [2]

2 (a) Describe **two** different types of animation that could be included in a slide transition. [2]

   (b) Describe what could be added to a slide of a student scoring a goal to make it more interesting for the audience. Say why it would make it more interesting. [2]

3 Web page designers use HTML.

   (a) What is HTML? [1]

   (b) Explain the difference between writing HTML and using a special web page program to write your web pages. [2]

4 Name **three** features that are specific to multimedia software. [3]

Chapter 13

Health, safety and other issues

In this chapter, you will learn about some of the laws that govern our use of ICT. You will look at ways in which computers could affect your health and how you can prevent that happening. You will look at how to stay safe in a computer environment and how to keep your data safe too.

As ICT users you have many responsibilities. You need to be aware of:

● laws relating to the use of ICT

● ways in which you can keep data safe

● ways in which you can keep yourself safe when online

● health problems that might affect you when using ICT systems.

○ Copyright law

Anything that has been produced by someone and is based on their own ideas can be subject to the **copyright** laws of this country. Literally, if you have the copyright of something then you are the only one allowed to copy it. This covers books, music, images, films, software and so on.

It you want to copy someone else's work, for instance a song they have written, then you can apply for permission to copy it and usually this is allowed on payment of a fee. When you are copying information, pictures or software from the internet, you might be infringing the copyright laws. For example, if a logo belonging to a company or business is used in this book, the publishers of the book have to ask permission to use it.

The most common form of breaking copyright laws is in the illegal copying of CDs, DVDs and computer games. It may be easy to do in some cases but it is illegal. It is also wrong, because someone has worked hard to produce whatever you have just stolen and they rely on the money it makes to feed and clothe themselves and their families.

Software piracy is the stealing or copying of software without the permission of the copyright holder.

Computer software companies have a big problem. People obtain illegal copies of their software without paying for it, either by making a copy of somebody else's disk or by downloading it from the internet. Developing and testing of software is an expensive business, and software piracy is costing companies a lot of money.

The Copyright, Designs and Patents Act 1989 makes software piracy illegal. It is a criminal offence to steal or copy software without the permission of the copyright holder or the owner of the software. It also states that it is an offence to run pirated software on your computer. The problem for software companies is that this law is very difficult to enforce. Software piracy is very common, but it is difficult to detect and even harder to prove.

Some software requires the user to enter a special licence number when installing the program. This licence number is given to the purchaser of the software, or included in the documentation and is an attempt to prevent software piracy.

Some companies buy site licences for software. This means they are legally allowed to run the programs on a given number of computers on their site, which may be an office, a school, or a college campus.

Accidental damage to files

Once data is stored on a computer system it is still not safe. It is all too easy for a user to accidentally destroy data.

Back-up copies of important data need to be made frequently and stored in a different place from the original data.

It is important for an organisation to have a proper back-up strategy. A back-up of the data is an extra copy of the data stored somewhere different from the original. If a disaster happens to the data then the back-up copy can be used instead. If it is required that a back-up is taken at the end of every day, then the computer may be set to automatically store the data on tape overnight. The tapes for each day could be stored in a fire-proof safe in a different building and only re-used after a week has passed.

When you do your coursework, it is vital that you have more than one copy of your work. Make frequent back-ups and store them in different places if you can. Make sure you name the back-up copies carefully so you know which is the most recent. If you lose your work for some reason, then it will be possible to get most of it back without having to do it all again.

Another way of protecting data from accidental deletion is to change the attribute of the file to "read-only". This is a setting that can be made on the computer, which means the file cannot be accidentally changed or deleted.

Viruses

Stored data files may need to be protected from some types of malicious damage that are deliberately caused. The most common source of such damage are programs called viruses. A **virus** is a computer program which can:

● copy itself from one computer file to another

● attach itself to an email so that it has the ability to spread from one computer system to another

● cause damage to files stored on a computer's hard disk.

Each virus has a different name and can spread itself so fast that computers all over the world can be infected within just a few days. Some viruses are called Trojans or worms.

Computer users need to protect their files from possible damage by a virus. The best way of doing this is to install special **anti-virus software** on the computer. This software not only detects if a virus has been received but also tries to remove it. The program checks all the hard disks and removable drives, such as a pen drive when it is inserted into your computer.

Virus-protection software needs to be kept up to date as new viruses appear all the time.

Here are some precautions to take to prevent infections by a virus:

● Try not to use a disk or memory stick on one computer and then transfer it to another computer unless you are sure that virus-protection software is running on both computers.

● Do not open an email from a sender who you do not know. In particular, never open an attachment file that comes with it.

● Do not download data or software from the internet unless it is from a well-known and trusted site. This is one of the main ways in which viruses spread.

● Run a virus check on a regular basis. Virus-protection software is usually loaded every time you start up your computer.

● Virus-protection software uses **virus definitions** to identify viruses. These definitions and software updates are usually downloaded automatically from the internet every time you start up your computer.

● Don't forget to take back-ups regularly in case files get damaged!

Figure 13.1 The best defence against viruses is to install virus-protection software

A

Activity

Internet search

On Wednesday, 22 January 2003, a judge passed a prison sentence on the writer of the Gokar virus, which is said to have infected 27,000 computers in 42 different countries. Use the internet (suggested search: +Gokar +2003) to find answers to the following questions:

1 Where did the writer of this virus come from?

2 What does this virus place in the Microsoft Windows folder of the infected computer?

3 What sort of virus is this and how does it spread?

4 What are the names of the two other viruses that he wrote?

5 How long was the prison sentence?

○ Hacking

A hacker is a person who gains unauthorised access to data stored on a computer.

Hacking has become a problem since networks have been developed. In particular, the internet has allowed hacking to become a global problem. A hacker is someone who deliberately accesses data stored on a computer without authorisation.

Hackers may change the data to their advantage, or they may delete or damage the data. There have been a number of stories of people who have been sacked from their jobs hacking into their ex-employer's computer and destroying the files out of malicious revenge. Others may hack computers to gain data for criminal purposes, such as blackmail.

Banks are frequently the targets of attack from hackers. Attempts are made to break into a bank's files or hackers may try to monitor files which are being sent to the bank in the hope of obtaining customer bank details and security information. Once they have that information they can pretend to be that person and withdraw money from their account or use their credit card to buy goods. It may be difficult to know how much hacking is happening, as banks are unwilling to admit to any failures in their security systems.

Not all hackers are bad! Hackers are now being employed by some organisations to "hack the hackers". They call themselves "ethical hackers" or "intelligence consultants". Their job is to track down the criminal hackers and bring them to justice.

Organisations have to try to keep one step ahead of the hackers and devise ever more sophisticated methods of preventing them accessing their files. This is often seen as a challenge by hackers who communicate with each other over the internet and offer help with ideas of how to get past new security measures.

Figure 13.2 Passwords – the best defence against hackers

Hacking may be prevented by using a password system, logging off properly, disconnecting computers from networks, using a call-back system or installing firewall software. Data may be encrypted to prevent intercepted data from being wrongly used.

To protect a network from hackers:

- A system of passwords should be used. Each user enters a username and password when logging on to a system. Passwords need to be changed regularly and obvious passwords, such as dates of birth or pet names, should be avoided. A user should never tell their password to anyone else.

- Users must log off properly every time they have finished using a computer.

- Computers should be shut down properly when not in use.

- To prevent important data being intercepted and used for wrongful purposes when it is transmitted down a network, the data may be encrypted. This means the data is changed so that a hacker cannot understand or use the data.

- A special type of software, called a **firewall**, can be used to prevent hackers from accessing a network. A firewall is usually included when you buy virus-protection software.

Staying safe online

The following SMART rules for being online and using social networking sites have been developed by Kidsmart.

Safe   Keep safe by being careful not to give out personal information – such as your name, email, phone number, home address or school name – to people who you have only met online.

Meeting   Meeting someone you have only been in touch with online can be dangerous. Only do so with your parents' or carers' permission and even then only when they can be present.

Accepting   Accepting emails and messages or opening files, pictures or texts from people you don't know or trust can lead to problems – they may contain viruses or nasty messages!

Reliable   Someone online may be lying about who they are, and information you find on the internet may not be reliable.

Tell   Tell your parent, carer or a trusted adult if someone or something makes you feel uncomfortable or worried. You can report online abuse to the police at **www.thinkuknow.co.uk**.

Health and computers

There are a number of health issues when using computers for long periods of time, such as in an office, or playing computer games for hours on end. Many of these concern ergonomics (the study of a worker and the environment). Careful consideration must be given to the design of the chair, desk, computer, telephone and other equipment to increase efficiency and avoid discomfort, fatigue or health problems.

Common health problems include:

- Back or neck strain: Using a badly positioned desk, chair and computer for long periods can lead to aches in the back or neck.
  - Chairs should be adjustable and set at the correct height (forearms should be horizontal).
  - Take frequent short breaks and walk around.
  - Use a footrest.
- Eye strain: Poor quality monitors, poor lighting and long hours staring at computer screens may lead to eye problems.
  - Computer screens should be set at the correct distance – an arm's length away.
  - Monitors should not flicker or be turned up too bright. They should be able to swivel and be positioned at a comfortable angle.
  - Blinds should be placed over windows to minimise glare from the sun and reflection on the screen.
  - Take regular breaks.
- Repetitive strain injury (RSI): Constant use of the joints in fingers, hands or wrists can lead to long-term pain or stiffness in the tendons. This is a common problem for office workers or serious computer games players, who spend long hours using a keyboard or mouse, and surgery is often undertaken to help alleviate the symptoms.
  - Use rests for wrists or arms.
  - Take frequent short breaks from typing or using a mouse.
  - Perform hand and wrist exercises regularly.
  - Relax. Grip the mouse lightly (tension can cause RSI).
  - Position the keyboard and mouse at a proper distance and height and make sure you are sitting comfortably.

> Neck strain, eye strain and RSI are all preventable problems. Office managers must make sure that their staff are seated comfortably and properly so that these problems can be avoided.

Safety and computers

Computers and peripherals are often heavy and computer rooms by their very nature are full of electrical sockets and wires, all of which could be safety hazards.

- Trailing wires could be tripped over or caught and may pull heavy equipment off shelves or benches. Keep all wires cleared away or placed in "cable tidies".

- There is a risk of fire and electrocution from bare or worn wires or badly wired plugs. Plugs and wires should be regularly inspected and wiring should be carried out by a qualified person.

- Unsecured equipment, such as monitors or large speakers balanced on shelves, may fall. Make sure shelves are firmly fixed and the equipment is secure on them.

- Food and drink are bad news near a computer. Crumbs of food can enter the keyboard and cause sticking keys and disease. Any liquid and electrical equipment is a recipe for disaster. Never have food or drink near a computer.

- Water and electricity can cause electrocution and damage equipment. Never have a source of water in a room with a computer. Fire extinguishers must be of the powder or carbon dioxide type.

Activity **A**

Health and safety

Read the following paragraph and identify all the things that are against health and safety common sense. In each case, decide whether it is a matter of health or safety.

Mr Careless entered the room carrying a large box containing a computer.

"Take the computer out of the box and put it on the draining board next to the sink," he called to me. "Plug it in on the far wall and run the extension cable over the floor and behind the taps."

Mr Careless then went out and came back with the monitor and keyboard. He put them down on the floor and went over to the sink.

"Plug these in and then switch on." He said, "I'm going to make a cuppa. I'll try not to splash my nice new machine. I can always wash it afterwards though I suppose if it gets dirty."

We got the computer set up and working and Mr Careless sat at the keyboard typing with one hand while he held his lunch – a large sticky bun – in the other.

"Computers might be a fire risk," he said. "We had better install sprinklers in here. And while you are at it you might as well bring in my favourite armchair so I can be comfortable while writing my memoirs. When I get going, I can type for hours on end without any breaks at all."

After I had helped drag in the old sagging armchair and positioned it near the computer, it was time for me to go. Mr Careless called "goodbye" cheerily.

"Thanks for your help. Leave the blinds up so that the sun can shine in here and cheer the place up."

And with that he turned his back to me, hunched over the computer and began to type.

Summary

S

- Software piracy is the stealing or copying of software without the permission of the copyright holder.
- Stay safe online by using the SMART rules.
- It is essential to make frequent back-ups of important data.
- Viruses are small programs that can spread from one computer to another. They can be detected and prevented by installing special virus-protection software.
- A hacker is a person who gains unauthorised access to a computer system.
- Prevention is usually possible by using a system of usernames and passwords.
- Data is often encrypted so that hackers cannot use it. But the downside of this is that the person to whom you are sending the encrypted data needs to be able to decrypt it at the other end.
- Health problems can be caused by over-use of a computer if proper precautions are not taken.
- Safety in the computer room is important to avoid injury or electrocution.

Practice questions 13

P

1 Explain what a computer virus is and how you can protect a computer against virus attack. [3]

2 Explain what hacking is and how you can protect a computer against it. [3]

3 Describe **three** health problems that can occur when using a computer for a long period of time and describe ways of preventing those problems. [6]

4 Describe **three** safety problems that can occur in a computer room and ways of preventing the problems. [6]

5 Explain what is meant by the copyright laws and why it is necessary to have these laws. [4]

Chapter 14

Data, information and knowledge

In this chapter, you will learn more about data, information and knowledge. You first studied this in Chapter 1 but now we look at data in much more detail. You will learn about the binary number system and ways for encoding data as well as ways of keeping data secure.

As with most technologies, there are good things about ICT and there are some not so good things. We will look at both the advantages and disadvantages of using ICT.

○ Advantages of using ICT

- When data is stored using ICT, it needs less storage space. The old methods of storing data on sheets of paper or record cards and filing them away in filing cabinets are now being replaced by methods of storing data on computer systems.

- Data stored using ICT can be kept more securely. The data can be encrypted so that unauthorised people will not be able to understand or use it.

- If data is stored on a computer system, then it can be accessed quickly. This means that finding data is much faster.

- Back-up copies of data stored on computer systems can easily be made and these can be kept for security reasons. If data is accidentally destroyed then it can be replaced by the back-up copy.

- Data stored in a computer system can be changed easily. It is more difficult to alter text that has been printed on paper.

- Processing data is much faster on a computer.

- Fewer staff are needed but they must have the necessary ICT skills.

- Data can be presented in many different ways:
  - Information may be displayed as printed text or in tables of data.
  - Charts may be drawn to illustrate some information.

Figure 14.1 Old methods of storing and distributing data have been replaced by ICT methods

Remember **encryption** means that data is changed into a form that no one without a **decryption key** can understand. If it is intercepted in transmission it is useless without the key.

– Pictures or moving videos may be shown or presentations consisting of a number of slides may be used.
– Computers can also output sounds or music.
● Data stored on a computer network can be accessed by any user on the network.
● Computers can send data from one computer user to another in just a few seconds, even if the users are in different parts of the world. This speed of communication is an essential element in many business systems.

Disadvantages of using ICT

The disadvantages are much harder to find, but there are some …

● The cost of equipment can be high. Many businesses or people may not be able to afford to buy the most up-to-date computers and all the associated equipment.

● Difficulties may arise because people do not know how to use a computer system. A business may have to spend time and money on training its staff so they can use a computer system effectively.

● Viruses or hackers may damage data on computer network systems.

There are clearly more advantages than disadvantages for businesses using ICT to give the best possible service to their customers.

Advances in ICT have caused many changes in the way businesses and organisations operate. We now see computers helping with management decision-making or planning financial budgets. There are fewer staff employed but they are better trained in the use of ICT. Marketing in many cases has become global and businesses can advertise their goods all over the world using the internet.

Businesses have been able to expand their operations worldwide.

Data

Data is only useful if it is valid and sensible. Data **validation** is used to make sure that the data being entered into the system is reasonable. It would not be reasonable to enter a person's height as 21.0m or the cost of a loaf of bread as £45. There are many ways to try to ensure that data is valid, which are explained below. Data **verification** tries to ensure that the data being entered has been entered correctly. This is why you are often asked to enter your password twice when setting it up, to **verify** that you typed it correctly.

Verification and validation checks **cannot** ensure that the data is correct. If someone wants to lie about their age, the date of birth they enter into a computer is both valid and verified but still wrong.

○ Validation

It is often very important to make sure that no "freak" readings are entered into a data processing system. Data validation is the process of making sure the data meets these requirements. In other words, validation makes sure that the data is sensible data.

It is important for businesses to check data carefully. Incorrect data can cause customer dissatisfaction if incorrect bills are sent out, or if incorrect amounts of money are deducted from people's bank accounts. Businesses spend a great deal of time and money in making sure that there are no mistakes in their input data.

> Data validation is used to check that data is sensible before it is processed. Typical validation checks are range checks, presence checks, format checks and the use of check digits.

Range check

A range check makes sure that an item of data lies within a specified range of numbers. A "smallest" allowable value is set as well as a "largest", and every time a numerical item of data is entered a check is made to see whether it falls within this range of values. If it does not, the data is not accepted for processing. The following list gives examples of range checks:

- The month part of a date must lie between 1 and 12.
- A pupil's percentage exam mark must lie between 0 and 100.
- Appointment times for a doctor: the hour part must lie between 0 and 24.

Ranges are usually set for numerical data, but ranges may be defined for other types of data. For example, an exam grade may be restricted to a set of characters "A" to "G".

> Data is rejected if it is outside the specified limits of a **range check**. This is a check for data that has been recorded or transcribed incorrectly.

Check digits

Another type of validation check involves an extra digit that has been added onto the end of numerical data. This check digit is calculated from the other digits using a predefined formula.

When the data is entered, the calculation is performed by the computer to make sure the check digit is correct. If it is not, then it means the data has not been read correctly and it is not accepted for processing.

Check digits are used on data that is input using devices such as barcode readers or card readers. The following list gives examples of the use of check digits:

- **Barcode:** In 13-digit barcodes, the 13th digit is a check digit calculated from the first 12 digits. When a barcode is read by a barcode reader, the computer calculates the check digit to make sure it is correct. If it is not, the barcode is rejected.
- **ISBN:** Most books have an international standard book number (ISBN). The final digit of this is a check digit.
- **Credit and debit cards:** Some credit and debit card numbers are quite long (16 digits) and the last digit is a check digit.

> A digit is a single character taken from the set 0, 1, 2, 3, 4, 5, 6, 7, 8, 9.

> Using a check digit makes sure that data automatically input has been read correctly.

Activity　A

Check digit calculator

1 Find an item with a 13-digit barcode on it (e.g. 5016442001876).

2 Make a note of the first 12 digits.

3 Create a barcode calculator that will check the 13th digit:

　(a) Put the first 12 digits into the first column of a spreadsheet starting from cell B3, as shown in Figure 14.2.

　(b) Enter calculations into column C as follows (make sure you enter a formula in each cell from C3 to C14):

● The digits in cells B4, B6, … (every other digit) are multiplied by 3.
● The digits in cells B3, B5, … remain as they are.
● The results are added up in cell C15.
● Cell C16 calculates the check digit as the number that needs to be added to the total in cell C15 to make the result an exact multiple of 10, that is **=10 – MOD(C15,10)**.

4 Now try it out on other 13-digit bar codes you can find on items from your kitchen.

	A	B	C	D
1				
2		Bar code	Calculations	
3		5	5	
4		0	0	
5		1	1	
6		6	18	
7		4	4	
8		4	12	
9		2	2	
10		0	0	
11		0	0	
12		1	3	
13		8	8	
14		7	21	
15			74	
16		Check digit is:	6	
17				

Figure 14.2 Check digit calculator

Presence check

The computer makes sure that a field is not null. A null field is one where data has not been entered when it should have been. A presence check is a check for missing data: data that may have been missed when transcribing or maybe somebody forgot to enter it.

For example: When supplying details on an on-screen form, users have to enter items such as their name, address, postcode, telephone number, etc. This form may be part of a database system, or it may be a web page application such as a member registration form. Some of the fields may be marked as essential and the data will not be accepted if any of these fields are left blank.

A **presence check** is a validation that makes sure that all important data has been entered and there is no missing data.

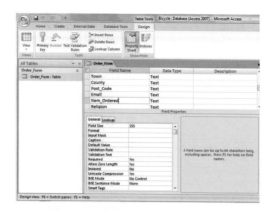

Figure 14.3 In Microsoft Access, users can designate fields as essential by setting the **required property field** to "Yes"

Batch total

> A **batch total** is a validation that checks whether numerical data is missing or has been entered incorrectly.

If a number of records of data are collected together and entered at the same time, a batch total may be included. The batch total is calculated using the data from all the records. When the data is entered, the batch total is also entered and the computer checks that the batch total is correct. If it is not, then it usually means that some item of data has been missed out or one of the numbers has been incorrectly entered.

When keying in numbers it is easy to transpose some of the digits. For example, the number 12345 may be entered as 12435. The batch total will not then agree and the computer will indicate that an error has occurred.

For example, a list of 20 items and their prices are entered into a database. The prices are added to provide a batch total. When the data is keyed in, the batch total is also entered. The computer checks whether the total is correct and does not accept the data if it is not.

Hash total

> A **hash total** is a batch total that is "meaningless".

A hash total is really the same as a batch total but the resulting number has no meaning. For example, it may be the sum of people's telephone numbers or the sum of account numbers.

Verification

If data is copied from one medium to another, for example when data on paper is keyed into a computer and saved on the hard disk, it is called transcribing the data.

Data may also have been sent (transmitted) from one computer medium to another, and verification checks are needed to make sure the data received is the same as the data that was sent.

Verification checks whether data has been transcribed correctly. The problem with people is that they get tired and make mistakes, and mistakes in data could cause serious problems for some businesses. These copying mistakes are known as **transcription errors.**

Transcription errors may be:

- omissions: leaving data out
- transpositions: for example, typing 1324 instead of 1234
- spelling mistakes: for example, typing Davies instead of Davis.

Visual check

One of the simplest ways to verify data that has been typed into a computer is to compare visually the source data and the transcribed data.

If the data that has been typed is a document, this is called proofreading. There are many errors that are not found by a spellchecker, such as words that are perfectly valid but used incorrectly, and these can only be noticed using a visual check. Visually checking large amounts of data can become very tiring and it is easy to miss errors, so this method of verification is not guaranteed to find all the transcription errors.

> Proofreading documents is a **visual check** of the copied data against the original data. It will find some transcription errors but it can be very tiring for large amounts of data.

Double keying

A more reliable method of verification is double keying. The data is entered twice, usually by two different data entry personnel and the two versions of the data are compared by the computer. If they are identical, the computer accepts them for processing, but if there are any differences, this means that one or other of the clerks has made a mistake, and the data is checked or entered again.

It is extremely unlikely that two different people will make the same typing mistake, and although double keying of data takes much longer and is double the amount of work, it is a very effective way of making sure no errors are made when transcribing data.

> **Double keying** of data is an effective method of verification even though it takes much longer than normal data entry.

Parity check

Parity is a method of verifying that transmitted data has not been corrupted. If data is transmitted through telephone lines or over a network there are many possible sources of "noise" where the data may be accidentally changed.

Parity methods are not able to correct the error, they can only detect whether an error has occurred. If there is an error, the data must be transmitted again.

All data in computer systems, whether it is text, graphics, sounds or video clips, is represented as numbers. These numbers are usually thought of as binary numbers that only involve 0s and 1s, so an item of data may look like:

> A **parity check** is a means of checking for data transmission errors. An extra bit is added to the end of each binary number.

01001011

ASCII: The American Standard Code for Information Interchange is a system of binary digits representing letters, numbers and other characters that are found on the keyboard. It is the most widely used system of allocating a numerical code to each character.

Parity checks involve adding an extra bit (a binary digit) onto the end of a binary item of data. An even parity system makes sure that the total number of 1s in each number is even; an odd parity system uses an odd number of 1s.

For example, assume an even parity system is being used to send a data item. Characters are represented by seven-bit ASCII codes. An eighth bit is added onto each number before it is transmitted. 0110100 has a total of three 1s, so a parity bit of 1 must be added to make an even number of 1s. The number is now 01101001. 0101110 has a total of four 1s, so a parity bit of 0 must be added making it 01011100. When the transmitted data is received, each number is checked to make sure that the total of all binary digits in each number is even.

Activity A

Parity

A computer using even parity receives the following data. Each 8-bit number consists of a seven-bit ASCII code and a parity bit.

10010000
10001011
10011000
10100000
01000001
10011010
10001011

1 Which number has been corrupted?

2 Find a table of ASCII codes on the internet and use it to translate this message into text.

○ Encoding data

When data is stored it is often encoded. This means that a simple representation replaces a more complicated one. For instance, if you were selling three different colours of laptop bag, you might encode the data as in the following table:

Colour	Code	Size	Code
Red	R	Large	L
Black	B	Medium	M
Grey	G	Small	S

So a large red laptop case would be encoded as LR.

The advantages of encoding data are that:

- Less computer memory is used.
- It is faster to enter or write down the data once you know the codes.
- There are usually fewer errors made in the accuracy of the data recorded.

○ Speed of access to data

Once data has been recorded onto a computer device, it can be retrieved very quickly. Computers are able to search through vast quantities of data at very high speed and produce an answer almost instantly. Most businesses have a database containing details of their customers, including their names, addresses, what they have purchased and so on. A computer can search for a particular customer's telephone number and find the answer almost at once. Using manual methods, such as looking through a phone book, would take much longer.

> Businesses can usually improve their services to customers by using ICT methods.

Summary

S

- ICT has had some impact on people. Fewer staff may be needed in some businesses. Staff may need to be trained to improve their ICT skills.
- Data can be presented in many different ways, for example, text, tables, charts, graphs, pictures, videos, sounds or music.
- Data can be sent between computers on a network.
- ICT costs may be high initially.
- Validation is a method of checking whether data is sensible.
- Range checks make sure that data lies within predetermined limits.
- Check digits are extra digits added onto numerical data. Computers check that the check digits are correct when data is input.
- Presence checks make sure that no essential data is missing.
- Batch totals are totals of similar numerical data items. The batch total is also input so the computer can check it is correct.
- Verification checks for transcription errors or transmission errors.
- Proofreading a document is an example of a visual check.
- Double keying involves entering data twice. The computer only accepts the data if the two copies are identical.
- Parity bits are extra bits added to data to check for transmission errors.

Practice questions 14 (P)

1 Describe a suitable validation check for each of the following types of input data:

(a) The month part of a date given in numerical format (e.g. 12/04/05). [3]

(b) A set of exam marks. [1]

(c) The number of a credit card account. [1]

2 John Smith was born on 12/09/85. When his data was entered into a computer database, the data appeared as John Ssmith and 12/99/85. Which of these two errors would be most likely to have been picked up by a validation check and which one by a verification check? [2]

3 (a) Why is parity used? [1]

(b) What does it mean if a system uses even parity? [2]

4 A solicitor's office has recently changed from a paper-based system of storing documents to an ICT system using computers and hard disks.

(a) Describe **one** advantage to the workers at the office. [1]

(b) Give **one** advantage to the firm of solicitors. [1]

(c) Give **one** disadvantage to the firm of solicitors. [1]

Chapter 15

Multimedia components

In this chapter, you will learn about digital cameras, digital images and units used with pictorial data. You will look at the various techniques that can be used with computer applications that are designed to deal with images and you will learn a number of ways to change the appearance of an image.

○ Hardware

If you have ever tried to play a computer game on an inadequate computer, you will probably have experienced slow play, jerky movements, poor sound and coarse graphics. This is because the requirements of a multimedia system are generally more demanding than using a computer for email, social networking, homework and so on. For a good multimedia system, you need:

● a good-sized, high-resolution screen

● a mouse, game pad or tracker ball

● good-quality speakers

● a fast processor

● a high-specification graphics card

● a large hard drive

● a DVD or Blu-ray drive.

Screen size is measured by an imaginary line drawn diagonally across from corner to corner.

You might also need other hardware devices such as a touch-sensitive input device (for example, a touch pad) or a microphone if you wish to input voice, music and other sounds.

Figure 15.1 Drawing with a graphics tablet is easier than drawing with a mouse

A graphics tablet is sometimes called a graphics pad or a graphics digitiser.

Digitising means converting into digits (in other words, numbers). A computer can then process the data.

A **pixel** or picture element is one dot of a graphic which is a particular colour.

Graphics tablet

A graphics tablet is a board covered by a touch-sensitive membrane that can detect the position of a pointing device on its surface. It can be used to hold a drawing while the user traces it, or to hold a sheet of menus, icons and shapes, which the user can select.

A **stylus** is a pointing device for a graphics tablet. If you have a personal organiser (PDA), it probably comes with a stylus for writing on the touch-sensitive surface.

Scanner

A scanner can be used to digitise graphics that are printed or drawn on paper. With a flat-bed scanner, the paper (or photo) is placed face down on a glass screen under a closed lid. Light is systematically beamed onto the image from a moving scan bar and the reflection patterns analysed and converted into numbers before being input to the computer.

Different scanners have different resolutions. This is measured in dots per inch (dpi) and high-resolution scans result in better quality images.

Digital cameras

The images on a digital camera are stored on a memory card. These cards are removable and blank cards can be inserted to store more images. Thousands of images can be stored on one card. Cameras usually have editing software built in so images can be deleted or changed without moving them from the camera.

It is possible to take the memory card to a camera shop or supermarket, insert the card, choose the images you want and print them off. Alternatively there are many online services where you can load the camera images into your computer and then upload them to the site. After a short time, your pictures are sent to you in the post. You can also of course print them for yourself.

Many people do not bother to print digital images since they can be stored in electronic photo frames or displayed on social networking sites such as Facebook.

Many mobile phones have a digital camera. This has the advantage of taking a picture and sending it to someone or a website quickly and easily directly from the phone.

Images have different quality depending on the **resolution**. More expensive cameras have higher resolutions. You can set the resolution of the images using the camera software. If you choose a low resolution you can store more images, but the quality is not as good as with a high-resolution setting.

The resolution of a picture is measured in **pixels**. A pixel is a dot of colour or **picture element**. When you see an image described as a 640 × 480 image it is 640 pixels wide and 480 pixels high. If the vertical and horizontal resolutions are multiplied together and

divided by 1 million you end up with the number of **megapixels** of the image.

If you have a "9-megapixel" camera it should be capable of taking images approximately 3000 × 3000 pixels. Of course, such huge images would rapidly fill your camera memory and most computer screens do not have the resolution to be able to display all the pixels.

Digital camera memories are measured in **gigabytes**. One gigabyte is 1024 × 1024 × 1024 bytes of memory or over 1000 million bytes.

When an image is displayed, the **resolution** is described by how many pixels per inch (ppi) are capable of being shown on the monitor. So if you have a high-density screen, the picture is clearer than on a low-density one. If you right click your desktop and go to Properties, you will find a display similar to the one shown in Figure 15.2. This dialog not only shows you the resolution of your screen but also allows you to experiment with different screen resolutions.

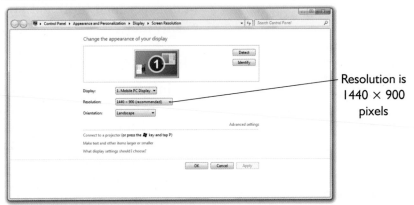

Resolution is 1440 × 900 pixels

Figure 15.2 Screen resolution

Activity A

Calculate pixels per inch (ppi)

1 Read the resolution of your screen (as shown in Figure 15.2).

2 Measure the width of the screen in inches and call it **w**. (For example, the screen I am looking at is 17 inches wide, so w=17.)

3 Measure the height of your screen and call it **h**. (For example, the screen I am looking at is 9 inches high, so h=9.)

4 Divide the first number in the resolution by **w** and call it **a**. (For me, a =1600/17 = 94.)

5 Divide the second number on the resolution by **h** and call it **b**. (For me, b=900/9 = 100.)

6 Work out the average of **a** and **b** and round down to the nearest whole number. (For me, (94+100)/2 = 97 ppi.)

The resolution of a printer is often called **dots per inch** (dpi) rather than ppi.

○ Tools and techniques for creating and manipulating still images

Whether you wish to create an image from scratch or edit an existing image, such as a digital photograph, you need an applications package to help you do this task. Each application offers a number of tools. Some of the standard tools are described below.

Zoom

Zooming allows you to view the image on the screen larger or smaller than it is. This is really useful if you want to do some delicate close-up work such as getting rid of a spot on a photo.

Figure 15.3 Zoom into an image to edit it

Selection

The selection tool is really useful for choosing part of an image to work on. The selection tool lets you form a barrier from the rest of the image so that what you do inside the selected area does not affect the rest of the image.

Transforming

Images can be transformed from one state to another with a graphics package. We have seen some of these, such as **rotation** and **reflection**, in earlier chapters.

Scaling and sizing

Images can be scaled which means that they can be resized or distorted in some way. Resizing just means that the image is made smaller or larger but the proportions stay the same. With scaling, the image can be changed as a percentage of the original.

Magazines are sometimes accused of scaling their cover models so that they look taller and thinner than they do in real life.

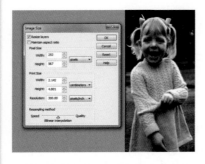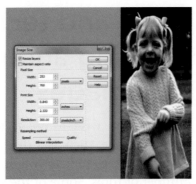

Figure 15.4 By **not** maintaining the aspect ratio it is possible to make the little girl look taller and thinner

Summary **S**

- For a good multimedia system you need:
  - a good-sized, high-resolution screen
  - a mouse, game pad or tracker ball
  - good-quality speakers
  - a fast processor
  - a high-specification graphics card
  - a large hard drive
  - a DVD or Blu-ray drive.
- Other hardware devices needed might be:
  - a touch-sensitive input device, such as a touch pad
  - a microphone, if you wish to input voice, music and other sounds.
- Screen size is measured by an imaginary line drawn diagonally across from corner to corner.
- A graphics tablet is sometimes called a graphics pad or a graphics digitiser.
- A stylus is a pointing device for a graphics tablet.
- Digitising means converting into digits for a computer to process.
- A scanner can be used to digitise graphics that are printed or drawn on paper.
- A picture element (pixel) is one dot of a graphic which is a particular colour.
- When an image is displayed, the resolution is described by how many pixels per inch are capable of being shown on the monitor.
- Digital camera memories are measured in gigabytes. One gigabyte is 1024 x 1024 x 1024 bytes of memory or over 1000 million bytes.
- The resolution of printers is often called dots per inch (dpi) rather than ppi.
- Zoom allows you to view the image on the screen larger or smaller than it is.
- The selection tool is really useful for choosing part of an image to work on.
- Images can be scaled, which means that they can be resized or distorted in some way.

Practice questions 15 **P**

1 Describe the hardware requirements of a good multimedia system. [6]

2 (a) Describe a **pixel**. [2]

  (b) Explain what is meant by a **megapixel**. [2]

  (c) Explain what is meant by the resolution of an image. [2]

3 Using examples, describe **three** different types of transformation that can be performed on digital images. [6]

Chapter 16

Art in ICT

In this chapter, you will learn more about the manipulation of images and also the role played by sound in computers. You will look at cloning, layering and transparency and study the difference between bitmap and vector graphics. You will also learn about the hardware and software necessary for creating and storing graphics files, including video files, and about the units we use to describe the size of a file.

○ Graphics software

Brush settings

Most graphics packages offer a large variety of brush tips and colours. Many are straight forward shapes as shown in Figure 16.1, but there are also odder ones such as Sci-Fi and Sparkle.

Figure 16.1 Brush tip settings

Distortion

Distortion can add movement and interest to an image. It is possible for you to produce the effect of movement or action or just artistic interpretation using these tools. Different packages have different types of distortion which might be called "twirl", "ripple", "wave", etc. Some examples are shown in Figure 16.2.

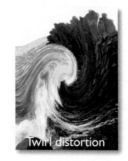

Normal image Twirl distortion Ripple distortion

Figure 16.2 Distortions

Cloning

If you wish to remove a part of an image it can be changed to look like another part of that image by **cloning**. This involves using a "magic brush" or clone tool that traces over part of the image and produces a copy of it on another part of the image. The size of the brush can be altered to carry out fine cloning or coarse cloning.

If you take a really good picture of a friend on holiday but there is another tourist in the image, you can remove them by cloning the background over their image. It could also make you appear alone on a crowded beach!

Layering

When you draw an image, for example, a logo, it can be built up from a number of layers. The order in which the layers overlap can be changed, so that something at the back can appear at the front and so on. The transparency of a layer can be changed too so that it is possible to see through the layer to what is behind it.

Figure 16.3 The logo can be moved about as it is on a different layer from the picture

You can move or **toggle** between layers by using "send to back", "bring to front" and so on or use the layering tools of the package to choose the layer you are working on or viewing.

Colour effects, colour palettes and colour gradients

These have already been discussed elsewhere. The important thing for you to do is to explore whatever image editing package you are using and find out what effects can be achieved and how. Don't be afraid to experiment, there is usually an undo button. If in doubt, save first!

When something is **transparent** it means that it is possible to see through it. The degree of transparency of an object can be changed so that it is either 100 per cent transparent (you can see right through it to the background) or 0 per cent transparent (you cannot see through it at all).

The opposite of **transparent** is **opaque**. You may sometimes see "opacity" referred to rather than transparency.

Figure 16.4 Different degrees of transparency applied to a rectangle

Vector and bitmap graphics

Bitmap graphics are made up of pixels. Each pixel has a position and a colour and is usually square. Many thousands of these dots are grouped together and to the human eye they appear to be connected. However, the larger the image the more dots are needed to maintain quality, and the larger the size of the image in terms of computer memory. If small graphics are enlarged, the image becomes "pixellated", that is, as the individual pixels get bigger, the image becomes distorted.

Vector graphics are made of points which are described by their relative distance from the point of origin in the form of equations. Components are described by length, thickness and colour. Because the points are generated mathematically, the images can be scaled up without loss of quality.

If you were designing a poster that might eventually end up very large and displayed on a hoarding, you might use vector graphics.

○ Digital video camera

A digital video camera is similar to a digital camera. A digital video camera stores video clips as digital files in the camera, which can be downloaded directly to a computer. Many video cameras also take still photos (and many digital cameras take movie clips).

○ Webcam

A webcam is a digital camera directly connected to a computer. Many laptops have a webcam in the lid. This is very convenient if you wish to send someone a picture of yourself working hard on your computer!

A webcam is a digital video camera connected directly to a computer and set up in a fixed position. The webcam can be used to feed a stream of video or still pictures at regular intervals to a website. There are now many thousands of web pages with webcam images on them and it is possible to view real-time images of places all over the world.

Webcams are often set up to monitor conditions such as the weather, skiing conditions on mountains or traffic on congested roads.

A webcam can be used to feed pictures to a website. There are many webcams viewing sites around the world. You can log in to the sites and see live pictures of radio studios, Parisian streets or the Antarctic.

Webcams are also used in teleconferencing to allow computer users in different places to communicate through video and audio links.

Activity

Webcam network

Go to the website www.earthcam.com and look at some of the many public webcam services around the world.

Microphone

Microphones are used to input sound into a device. Most digital cameras have the ability to record sound as well as pictures when taking moving pictures. A microphone can be used as an input device but the sound needs to be sampled by a sound card inside the computer or camera to convert it into a digital file before the computer can process it.

Microphones are used for teleconferencing or in speech-recognition systems where the user can speak commands to the computer. This is useful for people whose hands are occupied (surgeons, people driving vehicles or flying aircraft).

Microphones can also be used in offices for dictation systems: for inputting spoken words into a word processor.

Sound and music

Musical instruments can communicate with a computer using a defined standard called "Musical Instrument Digital Interface" (**MIDI**). MIDI instruments are musical instruments that can be connected to a computer. As you play the instrument, digital signals are input and these can then be stored as a data file and later processed, edited or played back through the instrument.

For example, on a MIDI keyboard, you can play a piece of music that is directly input to the computer and stored digitally. The piece can easily be edited with special software by changing the notes, tempo, dynamics and even the sound of the instrument before playing it back through the keyboard.

Other common MIDI instruments are guitars, drums and synthesizers which generate artificially produced sounds.

Any device with a MIDI-OUT port can control any device with a MIDI-IN port. This is because MIDI is a defined standard.

Sound storage devices

Sound can be stored in a number of ways. It can be stored in an analogue fashion such as on old fashioned records where the

grooves on the record represented the sound or in a more modern way where the sound waves are **digitised**. The digitised files might be in the form of **.wav**, **.mp3** or some other form. These files can then be saved on CD or DVD, on hard drives or flash cards. Most of you probably have the devices to play these files such as CD, DVD or MP3 players.

Sound cards

Computers have sound cards that process the sounds produced by the computer and send them to the speakers. You can look at the case of your computer to see where the sound card has an interface that allows you to plug in a microphone and speakers or lets you transfer sound to another device. Different speakers have the capacity to play different frequencies of sounds. Generally, the bigger the speaker, the lower the sound frequency that can be played using it. Big heavy speakers are sometimes called **woofers** and high-frequency speakers are called **tweeters**.

Sounds are produced as waves, which are analogue, but computers and their devices deal in digital quantities. There needs to be conversion from analogue to digital and digital to analogue in order for sounds to be recorded on a computer or played back from it.

Computers are capable of generating music by using software and hardware. **Synthesizers**, usually in the form of musical keyboards with the capability of producing or **sequencing** many different musical sounds, can be connected to the computer using a MIDI interface. The computer can be used to record a musical track, playing one instrument on the synthesizer. Another **track** can then be played and recorded alongside the first. In this way, it is possible to build up a whole orchestra of musical sounds. Voice can be added if required. **Sequencers**, or multi-track recording studios, are software designed to help produce music using a computer. Musical scores can be written using a **notator**.

Figure 16.5 A representation of a sound wave

Sound-wave editors

Sounds are analogue signals and are heard when a sequence of sound waves hits our ear-drums. It is possible to sample and edit these waves to change the sound we hear. There are many **sound-wave editors** and some may be downloaded free from the internet.

○ Internal memory and backing store

All computers and devices such as cameras and printers have some memory. It is a place where data and programs can be temporarily stored while the central processor needs to use them.

Data can be read from or saved to memory very quickly, much faster than from a backing storage medium, such as a hard disk, so data that is currently being used by the central processor is stored in the memory to speed up the operation of the computer. Generally a computer with more memory runs programs faster than one with less memory. Memory size is limited, so data that is not being used is stored in backing storage. Think of memory as the workspace of the computer.

The complexity of computer systems and networks, combined with the ever-increasing demands of users, has led to modern software needing more and more memory.

RAM and ROM

The main types of memory are:

- Random Access Memory (RAM): Data can be read from it and saved to it. In other words, data stored on RAM can be changed. Modern computers may have more than three gigabytes of RAM.

- Read-Only Memory (ROM): Data can be read but no data can be saved. The data stored on ROM cannot be changed.

Data stored in RAM is volatile. This means that the data is lost when the power is turned off. Data stored in ROM is permanent.

Disk cache

Accessing data from a disk is much slower than accessing data from memory.

Sometimes a program frequently requires reading large amounts of data from a disk. This can dramatically slow a program down so, to speed up processing, part of the memory is set aside to be used as a disk cache and any data recently read from the disk is stored in it. When the central processor needs an item of data, it first checks the disk cache to see if it is there, and only accesses the disk if it is not.

Moving data in memory is about 1000 times faster than moving data in backing storage.

Units used in ICT

In the system of counting you use every day, you use something called the **decimal** (or **base 10**) system. When you were little, you probably called this system "tens and units".

We think that base 10 was first used by humans because before they learned a complicated language and had different words for one, two, three and so on, it was easy to hold up a number of fingers to indicate how many of anything you were describing.

As life became more complicated, it was necessary to talk about larger numbers of things so humans developed a way of

---

Memory is also known as immediate access store (IAS).

Data stored on RAM is temporary. Data stored in ROM is permanent.

Access time is the average time it takes a storage medium to respond to a request for data. In other words, it is the average time it takes your hard drive to find a file after you have clicked on the icon to load it up.

> We call the numbers 1, 2, 3, …, 9 **digits,** which is also the name we give to our fingers and toes.

saying "one lot of ten and five units". As people learned to write, this would become 15 which we call "fifteen". The story of how numbers developed is very interesting but unfortunately there is no space in this book to write any more about it.

In ICT, we use the **binary system.** This is sometimes called the **base 2** number system because there are only two digits in it. These are 0 and 1 and all data held in the memory of a computer is made up of combinations of 0 and 1. The following table shows the units we use to measure storage in a computer or any device related to a computer:

Unit	Equivalence	Description
bit		A bit can hold 0 or 1. It can be used to represent two-state values such as TRUE or FALSE, MALE or FEMALE, YES or NO. Sometimes you see a light switch or an electric socket marked with "0" meaning "off" and "1" meaning "on".
byte	8 bits	A byte can hold a character such as the letter "A", the digit "7" or the symbol "?".
kilobyte (KB)	1024 bytes	A kilobyte can hold 1024 characters or about one page of this book.
megabyte (MB)	1024 KB	A megabyte is about the size of a digital photo.
gigabyte (GB)	1024 MB	A gigabyte can hold approximately one billion characters.
terabyte (TB)	1024 GB (approx one trillion bytes)	External hard drives are often able to hold a terabyte of data or more.

> The reason for the strange number of 1024 being used instead of the more familiar 1000 is that a base 2 number cannot produce 1000 exactly. In base 10, we can write 10 x 10 x 10 and get 1000 (1000 grams = 1 kilogram, 1000 metres = 1 kilometre). The nearest we can get to a "kilo" in base 2 is 2 x 2 x 2 x 2 x 2 x 2 x 2 x 2 x 2 x 2 = 1024.

Activity

Memory size

1 Find out the size of the memory in your computer. In Microsoft Windows, you can do this by right-clicking on the My Computer icon and then selecting Properties.

2 Use the internet to find websites of computer retail companies and study the specifications of the computers they sell. What is the size of memory in them? How do the memory sizes of laptop computers compare with desktop PCs?

Backing storage

The disadvantages of storing data in RAM are that:

- The storage capacity is relatively small.
- It is volatile – the data is lost when the power is turned off.

Backing storage is used to store data and programs that are not currently being used. It is non-volatile storage, so data is permanently saved. The disadvantage of backing store is that loading and saving files is slower than from main memory (RAM and ROM) but this is outweighed by the fact that you can store all your pictures, music, games, work and so on in one place and retrieve them whenever you want.

There are many devices that can be used for backing storage:

- **Hard drives** are the most common type of backing store; all computers are sold with a hard drive in them. Storage capacities are high and increasing every year. A hard disk is a magnetic medium. Circular plates of metal or glass are coated with a magnetic material. Data is saved by magnetising particles on the disk surface. The drive is a sealed unit containing the disk, which rotates at high speed. A moving arm has the read/write head at the end of it.

- **CDs, DVDs** and **Blu-ray discs** are used by many multimedia applications because of their large storage capacity and the fact that they are easily portable:

  - CDs can store around 650 MB of data, enough for an album of songs.
  - Digital versatile disks (DVDs) can store up to 8 GB of data and so they can be used for full-length feature films.
  - Blu-ray discs can hold around 50 GB of data and later developments may mean as much as a TB. This will mean several full-length films on one disc.

- **USB memory sticks** allow you to work on your coursework in school and at home. They are very small and easily lost but can be an extremely convenient way of keeping and transferring data.

- **External hard drives** sit on your desk and are connected to your computer through the USB port. They can hold huge quantities of data and are portable.

Multimedia software

The advantages of using multimedia software are that:

- It is easy to standardise the slides.
- A presentation can be saved to disk or memory stick.
- It is easy to edit and change the order of slides.
- Special effects, such as sound, video and animation, are possible.
- There are supplied template designs to choose from.

The disadvantages of using multimedia software are that:

● It relies on a computer.

● Someone must be trained to use the computer.

● Computers can sometimes be unreliable and crash or not connect to the projector.

● Expensive equipment, which could be stolen, might need to be carried around.

● It is difficult to annotate slides during a presentation.

Apart from giving demonstrations, lectures or presentations, it is possible to use interactive multimedia for other activities, such as quizzes, questionnaires or games.

By placing links on the pages, answers can be given to quizzes, new questions can be asked in questionnaires and so on. For instance, if a questionnaire asks if the user is male or female, pressing the Female button could give access to one lot of questions and pressing the Male button would give a different set of questions.

Similarly, in a quiz when a button is pressed, it could say whether the user is correct and give the right answer if the user is wrong.

Activity A

Multiple choice quiz

Use presentation software to make a simple multiple choice quiz containing five questions. Set up the questions in a similar way to those shown in Figure 16.6.

Figure 16.6 A multiple choice quiz question

Figure 16.7 Answer to a multiple choice quiz question

Each option is a button that has a hyperlink to another slide. Remember to put a button on every slide to allow the user to return to an appropriate place. For instance, if the user presses "A Jupiter", they should see the slide in Figure 16.7, which contains a button to go to the next question.

Summary

- Bitmap graphics are made up of pixels. Each pixel has a position and a colour and is usually square.
- Vector graphics are made of points which are described by their relative distance from the point of origin in the form of equations.
- A webcam is a digital camera directly connected to a computer.
- MIDI stands for Musical Instrument Digital Interface.
- Any device with a MIDI-OUT port can control any device with a MIDI-IN port.
- Random Access Memory (RAM) can have data saved to it and read from it.
- Read Only Memory (ROM) can have data read from it but not saved to it.
- Internal memory (RAM) of a computer is also known as immediate access store (IAS).
- Data stored in RAM is volatile (temporary) and is lost when the power is turned off.
- Data stored in ROM is non-volatile (permanent).
- Access time is the average time it takes a storage medium to respond to a request for data.
- A music notator is a computer program for editing and producing musical scores using a computer.
- A synthesizer can be used to create musical sounds electronically.
- Sound-wave editors allow sounds to be sampled, saved and edited on screen.
- The binary (base 2) number system is made up of combinations of 0 and 1.
- Units of storage are:
  - a bit (0 or 1)
  - a byte (8 bits)
  - a kilobyte (KB, 1024 bytes)
  - a megabyte (MB, 1024 KB)
  - a gigabyte (GB, 1024 MB)
  - a terabyte (TB, 1024 GB).
- Animation means making something move.

Practice questions 16

1 Look at the advert below and then answer the questions.

   (a) What does RAM stand for? [1]

   (b) The processor has a 4 MB cache. How many bytes in 4 MB? [1]

   (c) How many megabytes does the 1 TB hard drive hold? [1]

   (d) Explain how the Blu-ray read/write device can be regarded as an input, output and storage device. [3]

2 Explain the difference between bitmap and vector graphics. [4]

3 Describe the components needed for an interactive multimedia system. [4]

The GameExtreme machine comes with the following spec:

23-inch monitor

6 GB RAM with a 2.5 GHz processor containing 4 MB cache

I TB hard drive for storing all your games, films and photos

I GB GeeWizz GT9999 graphics card for brilliant smooth gaming and seamless movements

DVD and Blu-ray read/write

Chapter 17

Presentation software

In this chapter, you will learn more about presentation software. You have already learned about slide shows and now some more advanced features are introduced such as hotspots and hyperlinks. You will also find out the meaning of house style and corporate image and how these can be preserved or promoted in a presentation.

Creating a presentation has already been discussed briefly in the short-course material and you should refresh your knowledge by re-reading Chapter 12. Some further ideas for presentations are explained below.

Presentation software, such as Microsoft PowerPoint, is often used to help with teaching, to show an automatic display of slides at an exhibition or as a display in a shop window or entrance foyer to an office. A set of slides is created, each one containing text, images, sound and video. Various effects can be included to vary the way that the information appears on the screen. This is known as slide animation.

○ Animation effects

Any element of a presentation can be animated. This includes text, graphics, video and charts. Animation is carried out to emphasise important points and to control the flow of information within the presentation.

Amongst animation effects available are:

- Bulleted lists can appear on a slide, one bullet at a time when the presenter clicks the mouse.

- Bullets can fly in from the left or right.

- Text can appear by the letter, word or paragraph.

- Text or objects can be dimmed or change colour.

- Animations can occur automatically without human intervention.

Slide transitions are animations with effects that happen when one slide changes to another. There are many effects, such as fade, wipe, explode or fly-in. The timing of the animations can be preset or operated by a click of the mouse.

⭕ Objects

This table summarises the objects that can appear in presentations:

Feature	Description
Text	Words, characters or numbers should be carefully used to reflect the abilities and age of the audience watching the presentation. The amount of text on each slide should be restricted so as not to overwhelm the audience.
Image	A picture or cartoon can be used to draw attention to a point or make something easier to understand. ("A picture is worth a thousand words.")
Sound	A clip of music, voice or some other sound, such as applause, animal noises or a car starting up, can draw attention to a point or make it clearer.
Video	A clip of moving pictures is especially useful to illustrate how an action is carried out, for example, showing an operating procedure to doctors.
Hyperlink	When the link is clicked, the screen shows another part of the presentation or something outside the presentation (such as a web page). Hyperlinks are usually shown as a different colour to the rest of the text and underlined.
Hotspot	A hyperlink may be defined on an area of text or graphics so that it responds to a click of the mouse button.
Button	Like a hotspot, a button responds to a mouse click. A button may be labelled.
Navigation bookmark	A bookmark is a link that is recorded so that you can jump back to it at any time. If the presentation is linked to the internet, a bookmark can be a URL to an external slide or page.

⭕ Design templates

A **corporate style** is used to present an image of a company which is instantly recognisable. This is achieved by the use of particular logos, font styles and colours. Corporate style is also called **house style**.

Using the master slide facility on a presentation package, it is possible to set backgrounds, fonts, colours and another aspects of the layout of a slide without entering specific content. This information can be saved as a template which can be used in different presentations and by different people.

Templates ensure that the slides in a presentation are uniform and less confusing to the audience. They can also project a **corporate style**.

Many packages already have templates set up for such things as quizzes, photo albums and calendars. There are thousands of templates available on the internet which have been designed by other people. You can take an existing template and adapt it for your own use or create one from scratch.

Figure 17.1 Design a template

Transitions and timings

Slides can be set to change automatically or manually (when the presenter clicks a button).

Automatic transition of slides is when the presentation is set to run continuously without human intervention. You sometimes hear people referring to a **loop** when describing automatic transition of slides because, when the slides get to the end, they loop round and start again from the beginning. This is useful in situations such as a museum where the presentation describes a particular exhibit or at a school speech day where a presentation continuously runs about the achievements made by the school during the previous year.

Automatic presentation does have its disadvantages. For instance, it might move too slowly (or too quickly) to satisfy the audience. It might break down and nobody notices. It is not possible for the viewer to ask questions or to receive further information about a particular slide.

Manual transition is when the presenter moves the slides on by clicking a mouse or pressing a button on a remote handheld device. This method is useful when the presenter is engaging with the audience, answering questions and expanding on a point. The main disadvantage of manual transition is that a speaker has to be present.

Narration and speaker notes

If the presenter of a slide presentation wishes to talk while the slides are being shown, it is often useful to make notes on each slide which can be seen by the presenter and not by the audience.

This is helpful as it keeps the notes with the slides, rather than having separate documents. The notes act as an *aide memoire* for the presenter.

Printing formats

Figure 17.2 Print options in PowerPoint

It is possible to print out copies of the slides in a presentation using the facilities of the presentation software. Options may include:

- individual slides
- several slides to a page
- printout with notes
- outline view
- delegate's copy with area for notes.

Advantages and disadvantages of presentation software

The advantages of using presentation software are that:

- It is easy to standardise the slides using templates.
- A presentation can be saved to disk or memory stick.
- It is easy to edit and change the order of slides.
- The slides cannot be dropped and become out of order.
- Special effects, such as sound, video and animation, are possible.
- A presentation can run automatically.

The Pack & Go facility saves the presentation and the Viewer file to an external device so that the computer at the venue doesn't need the presentation software in order to run the presentation.

The disadvantages of using presentation software are that:

- It relies on a computer.
- Someone must be trained to use the computer.
- Computers can sometimes be unreliable and crash or not connect to the projector.
- If there is no computer or projector at the venue, expensive and heavy equipment needs to be carried around.
- It is difficult to annotate slides during a presentation.

Summary

- Text, graphics, movie and charts in a presentation can be animated.
- Corporate style is used to present an image of a company which is instantly recognised.
- House style is another phrase for corporate style.
- Design templates ensure the slides in a presentation are uniform and less confusing to the audience.
- Slides can be set to change automatically or manually at the click of a button.
- It is possible to move from one slide to another using hotspots, hyperlinks and buttons.

Practice questions 17   P

1 A school is going to set up a slide show to run on speech day showing the sporting triumphs of the year.

  (a) Choose whether an automatic or manual presentation would be best to use. [1]

  (b) Explain why your choice of method would be best. [2]

2 Examine the slide below and then copy and complete the table. You can use the letters more than once if necessary.

Feature	Letter
Hyperlink	
Graphic	
Button	
Hotspot	
Text	

[5]

3 Describe **three** slide transition effects. [3]

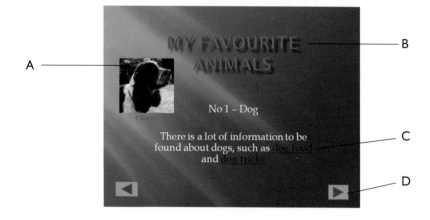

Chapter 18

Multimedia industries

In this chapter, you will learn much more about web pages and the way in which websites are set up. You will learn how files can be compressed, so they take up less memory and are faster to transmit, and how different files can be saved in different formats depending on their contents. You will also learn about the relationship between binary and hexadecimal numbers and what they are used for.

○ File storage

Files may have a structure other than a collection of related data records. For example, graphics files and sound files have different structures.

When a file is saved onto backing storage, it is given a name and an extension. For example, a word-processed document may be saved as **project.doc** on the hard disk of a computer. The file name can be any text that enables the user to easily identify the file but the extension, which is added by the software, indicates which software was used to create the file. Some common file extensions are shown below:

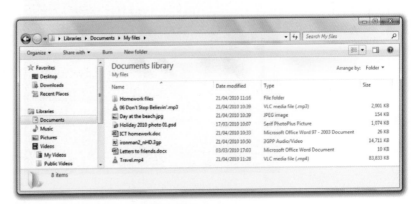

Figure 18.1 Common file extensions

File extension	File type
.doc or .docx	Microsoft Word document
.mdb	Microsoft Access database
.xls or .xlsx	Microsoft Excel spreadsheet
.ppt	Microsoft PowerPoint presentation
.txt	Text file
.bmp	Bitmap graphic
.jpg	Compressed bitmap graphic
.htm or .html	Web page
.exe	Application (executable file)

It is possible to change the extension of a file but it is not advisable as the standard conventions enable the computer operating system to identify the type of data a file contains and automatically load the appropriate software to process it.

All backing storage devices have limited capacity. Large files fill up the available storage space quickly, so a general rule when creating files is to keep them as small as possible. Large files also load up slower than small ones and may take longer to find and access the data. If data is transmitted across a network, smaller files are sent faster than large ones.

Data compression

Data compression is a way of making file sizes smaller. A variety of techniques can be used to "pack" the data of a file so it takes up less storage space when it is saved or transmitted over a network. Before the data file can be processed, it needs to be de-compressed.

Advantages of data compression are:

● smaller file sizes when saved on a hard disk or other storage media

● faster transmission when sent over a network or downloaded from the internet.

Text files

Text files can be compressed by replacing a common combination of characters with a single character. For example, the following sentence has 88 characters (including spaces):

● There are several methods of compressing files so they are smaller when they are stored.

● If the character combination "re" is replaced by the character "@", the paragraph only has 82 characters, as follows: The@ a@ several methods of comp@ssing files so they a@ smaller when they a@ sto@d.

● By replacing more of the common character combinations by a single character, the file size can be made much smaller.

Graphics files

Graphics files have different methods of compression. Bitmap graphics can be very large but can be considerably reduced in size by converting them into different formats (such as JPEG or GIF). Some detail may be lost but usually this is not noticeable to the human eye.

If you create a website, the space you are allocated may be limited, so it is important that bitmap graphics are compressed into formats with smaller sizes.

Bitmap graphic files are large but can be compressed into other formats such as JPEG (.jpg) or GIF (.gif) (for example, for use on web pages), with little loss of quality.

Video files

Video files can be compressed by converting them into files that compare one frame to the next and only send data about the changes between them. (The standard format for compressed video files is MPEG.)

Sound files

Wave (.wav) files can be used to transfer sound files but these have become less popular as they cannot be compressed. Windows Media Audio (WMA) files can be compressed without loss of quality.

Sound files are usually compressed into MP3 format. The bit rate at which the sound is recorded can be chosen. The higher the bit rate, the better the quality of the recording but the larger the file. Small files with low bit rates will have poor sound quality.

Compressed MP3 sound files with low bit rates are poor in quality.

Small files allow people to download music files from the internet: even ones they are not supposed to! There is also a certain amount of controversy because it allows musicians to sell their music directly over the internet and bypass the large music recording companies.

ZIP files

There are general-purpose compression programs that can compress any file to a smaller size. This is commonly referred to as "zipping" a file and the file extension of the resulting smaller file is **.zip**. The process of decompressing the file is referred to as "unzipping" the file.

When files are archived, they are often saved in compressed format and many files can be compressed into a single archive file.

> Groups of files can be **zipped** into a single compressed file but it must be **unzipped** before the files can be used.

Activity

Graphics and compression formats

1 Find a bitmap graphic and save it as a .BMP file. This is uncompressed and the colour of every pixel of the image is stored.

2 Make a note of the size of the file.

3 Save the same picture in different formats (.JPG, .GIF, .TIF, .PNG, .CGM etc.).

4 Create a spreadsheet to record the sizes of the files and calculate the percentage of the original size.

5 Try this for different graphics. Choose some photographs and some graphics with large areas of the same colour (such as cartoons).

○ Web software

Tools and techniques for creating websites

We have already discussed briefly how to create web pages (short course Chapter 12). For the pages that have been created to appear on a website, a **host** has to be found. The host is a **web server** which is a computer with software capable of holding your web pages and which is linked to the internet so that HTTP requests can be received and HTTP responses sent out.

> HyperText Transfer Protocol (HTTP) is the set of rules for transferring web pages across the internet.

To create a website, you need to go through the following steps:

1 Choose your theme (what your website is about), for example, you and your family or a favourite hobby.

2 Plan the different web pages you are going to create.

3 Decide how the web pages are to be linked – you may want to create a **structure diagram**.

4 Choose a theme for colours, font size and style so that all the pages look as if they belong to the same site.

An internet protocol (IP) address is the actual address of the web server.

A uniform resource locator (URL) is the address for a web page on the internet.

5 Choose a **domain name**. This is the name of your website (such as google.co.uk or wjec.co.uk). This name must be unique and you can check your chosen name on many websites to see if it is already used by someone else. A registered domain name or IP address gives the destination location for the URL. The domain google.com (IP address 72.14.207.99) is the address of Google's website.

6 Create your web pages and test that all the links work.

7 Find a host – this could be your internet service provider (ISP) or your school, if it has a web server. There are also companies that specialise in hosting websites.

8 Upload the website to the host.

Issues with the hosting of websites

When choosing a host for your website, you should take into account the **security** of the web server. Because web servers are linked to the internet, they can be vulnerable to hacking. Firewalls are often used to prevent unauthorised access. Choose a host where the **speed of response** is fast and the **upload speeds** are good.

Web pages need **regular updates** and all links, internal and external, should be tested to ascertain whether they are still valid.

The **reliability** of the information is important. If you want your website to be taken seriously, you should be prepared to check everything you publish. Avoid breaking copyright regulations and don't write anything that would make people uncomfortable, such as racist remarks.

Internet browsers

In order to be able to retrieve information from the web, you need browser software, such as Internet Explorer or Firefox. It displays web page information and allows you to easily move from website to website.

A browser accesses resources when the user enters a URL that starts with the type of data to be retrieved:

- http: for normal websites
- https: for secure websites (e.g. online shops and banks)
- ftp: for transferring files
- file: for files on your own computer.

Figure 18.2 Internet Explorer

Browsers allow you to make **keyword searches** and to store **links** to favourite pages (bookmarks). Various **menus** allow the user to choose options for the way in which the browser displays information and its appearance.

Web browsers contain the following features:

● a **back** and a **forward button** to move back and forward between recently accessed pages

● a **refresh button** to reload or update the current resource

● a **stop button** to cancel loading a resource

● a **home button** to return to the user's home page

● an **address bar** to input the URL of the page required

● a **search bar** to input keywords

● a **zoom** facility to make the display larger.

Websites contain the following features:

● **navigation bars**, which have buttons or links to other areas of the site

● **banners**, which are boxes containing text, images or animations

● **icons**, which are commonly used visual representations, such as a shopping trolley for purchasing items.

When a user clicks on a banner, they may be taken to another area of the site or new web page. This is often used for advertising. A **leader board** is a type of banner advertisement placed across the top of a page.

Interactive features of websites

An interactive feature enables a "conversation" between the user and the computer. Often the user's input affects the output. For instance, when using **online forms**, if a user types in a postcode, the form automatically supplies the address. Other interactive features of websites are **email forms**, **games**, **quizzes** and **questionnaires**.

Figure 18.3 A "shopping trolley" web icon

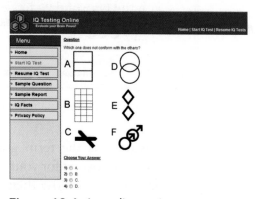

Figure 18.4 An online quiz

Creating web pages

It is important that all the pages of a website look similar. This ensures that the user feels just as comfortable using any of the pages. They can learn to use the website more quickly if the pages have a familiar look and are instantly recognisable as belonging to the same site.

To help achieve this, **master pages** can be created. A master page contains the general features of all the pages including background colour, position of buttons, logos and other features. The master page acts as a **template**. By using a template, it is possible to create new pages more quickly but using the same style as before. A person unfamiliar with the website would be able to produce a page in keeping with the rest of the site by using the template.

Every website should have a **home page**. The home page is the starting point for the site. It should contain buttons and menus to take the user to the rest of the pages on the site. The URL of the site should take you to the home page.

When studying the eye-scan movements of people looking at a web page for the first time, observers found that a triangular area in the upper left corner of the screen is where people look first. This is known as the **golden triangle** of the web page and designers try to place as much information in that triangle as possible. Look at any well-designed web page and you will find most of the buttons, links and important information on the left near the top. In Figure 18.4, the main menu for the site is in the upper left corner.

Figure 18.5 The golden triangle of the BBC GCSE Bitesize home page

Site navigation is the term given to exploring the pages of a website. It is important for your visitors to be able to work through your pages and never lose their way. Well-designed pages feature a home button so the user can jump back to first page. Many also duplicate the main menus on each page. Keeping the same

placement of important buttons and links on every page helps the new user to use the website easily.

There are various tools that can be used on pages to aid navigation:

- **Text hyperlinks** contain an address either to a web page on another site or to a page within the site currently being used. They are usually displayed with the link underlined such as **www.ict4wjecgcse.co.uk**. Sometimes the hyperlink is a word in the text you are reading but it can easily be recognised as it is underlined and in a different colour from the rest of the text. This type of hyperlink is also known as an **anchor**.

- **Graphical hyperlinks** are pictures (photos, clipart, etc.) that contain a hyperlink. When the user clicks on the picture, the hyperlink is followed to a new web page.

- **Hotspots** are used to give more information about an area on the web page. For instance, if you have a photograph of three people on the screen you can incorporate a hotspot over each of them. When a person is clicked, information about that person is displayed. In Facebook, for instance, people can be "tagged"; the tag is a hotspot.

- **Rollover buttons** are areas of the screen that change when a mouse is "rolled over" that area.

Graphics are **optimised** before they are placed on a web page to take up less space. The image is processed to use the smallest number of bytes without compromising the quality of the image. Images can end up 70 per cent "lighter" by using this technique and can therefore be downloaded faster, giving a more efficient process.

A **thumbnail** is a miniature version of an image that is hyperlinked to the full-sized image. Thumbnails load fast and if a user wishes to see the full-sized version, they can do so by following the link.

Search techniques

Search engines such as Google, Yahoo!, Ask and many others allow us to find information on the internet almost instantly. These search engines have huge databases of web pages and their contents; when we search, we are really searching the databases rather than the internet.

Once an address has been found, we can follow the link to the website that holds the full data. Once on the website, we can use other tools to search the page for the words we want. This is discussed in more detail in the short-course chapters.

Figure 18.6 Rollover button: when the mouse moves over the flower, it blooms (www. crawforddirect.com/roll.htm)

Analysing web pages

Analysing the effectiveness of a web page involves carefully considering the following questions:

- Does it meet the **original objective**? If it is a web page about dogs, does it provide information about dogs and not branch to other animals?

- Is it appropriate for the **target audience**? Some web pages are for children, others for adults; some are for beginners and easy to understand while some are for professionals and filled with jargon.

- Does it contain **accurate information**? Any information taken from web pages should be cross-referenced to make sure that it is correct. Some websites are more accurate than others.

- Does it provide the **correct information**? If you are looking for a page on healthy food to feed your dog, is that what you are getting or is it just advertising a particular dog food?

- Is the information **up to date**? You can often tell by looking at the bottom of the page to see when it was last updated.

- Is the page **unbiased**? Many websites are placed on the internet by people who have a particular axe to grind. What they put on the pages are just personal points of view and these not necessarily true or fair. Some may even be spoofs, that is, people trying to be funny by deliberately distorting the truth.

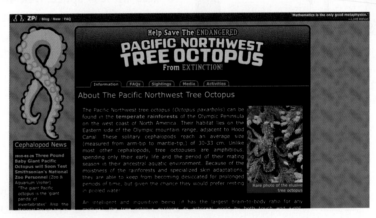

Figure 18.7 Watch out for spoof websites: some are funny but some pretend to be real and can be used by criminals

Finally when looking at websites and comparing them to each other, make comparisons of:

- **House style**: The pages should be recognisable and similar, perhaps with similar colour schemes, layouts and familiar logos. It should be possible to identify a site from any of its pages.

- **Audience**. Try to work out if the site is aimed at adults or children, beginners or experts, men or women, and so on.

- **Size**. Most good sites have a **site map** from which it is possible to check the number of pages and the way the site is organised.
- **Techniques used**. Look for the use of colour, pictures, sound, interesting hotspots, buttons, roll-overs, forms, searches, and so on.

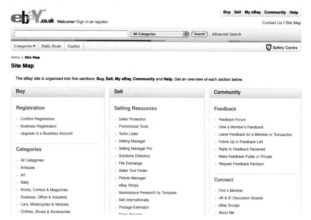

Figure 18.8 eBay site map link

Activity

A

Compare websites

Choose two websites and compare them using the criteria above. You might find it helpful to use a table to record your findings.

	Website 1	Website 2
House style		
Target audience		
Size		
Techniques used		
Accurate?		
Up to date?		
Unbiased?		

Colours

Colours used in web pages are based on the fact that any colour can be made from a mixture of red, green and blue light. It is known as the **RGB system**.

Colours are given numbers so they can be used in the code that makes up web pages. Each of the three colour components is given as a number in the range 0–255, so there are 256 shades of red, 256 shades of green and 256 shades of blue. This means that there are $256 \times 256 \times 256$, or over 16 million, different possible colours.

Computers handle data using a binary system. This is based on every number being made up of a combination of 0s and 1s. Some binary numbers and their decimal equivalents are shown in the table:

Decimal	Binary
0	0
1	1
2	10
4	100
255	11111111

Decimal numbers are awkward to use as there is not a simple conversion between decimal and binary. However, **hexadecimal** numbers are easy to form from binary numbers. Hexadecimal numbers are known as **base 16 numbers** and use the digits 0, 1, 2, 3, 4, 5, 6, 7, 8, 9, A, B, C, D, E, F to count. The digits are used in the same way as in base 10 from 0 to 9; the next object after 9 is given the digit A and so on until F, which means 15 objects.

The table shows how base 16 (hexadecimal) numbers match their base 2 (binary) equivalents:

Decimal	Binary	Hexadecimal	Decimal	Binary	Hexadecimal
0	0000	0	8	1000	8
1	0001	1	9	1001	9
2	0010	2	10	1010	A
3	0011	3	11	1011	B
4	0100	4	12	1100	C
5	0101	5	13	1101	D
6	0110	6	14	1110	E
7	0111	7	15	1111	F

Coming back to the RGB system, a single red component could be up to 255 which is 11111111 in binary and FF in hexadecimal. There are many conversion tables on the internet, so it is not necessary to know how to do the conversions but they are easy to do from the above chart.

Convert the binary number 00011111 to hexadecimal by following these steps:

1 Put a space after the first four digits and write it as 0001 1111.

2 Look at the table to find the hexadecimal value for 0001 is 1.

3 Look at the table to find the hexadecimal value for 1111 is F.

4 Write the individual digits to get the hexadecimal number 1F.

Activity A

Convert binary numbers to hexadecimal

Using the conversion chart on page 156 convert the following binary numbers to hexadecimal.

Binary	Hexadecimal
00101000	
11110011	
10101010	

The table below shows how some of the common colours are made up. These colours use the minimum and maximum amounts of red, green or blue and have names. It is impossible to think of 16 million different names so most colours are only known by their hexadecimal number.

Colour	Decimal (R,G,B)	Hexadecimal
Black	0,0,0	000000
White	255,255,255	FFFFFF
Red	255,0,0	FF0000
Green	0,255,0	00FF00
Blue	0,0,255	0000FF
Yellow	255,255,0	FFFF00
Cyan	0,255,255	00FFFF
Magenta	255,0,255	FF00FF

Summary

- A filename is a means of identifying a file.
- A file extension is a means of identifying the type of a file.
- Backing store is used to store data and programs that are not currently being used.
- Files can be compressed to make them smaller when stored and faster to transmit over a network but they need to be de-compressed before they can be used.
- Bitmap graphic files are large but can be compressed into other formats such as JPEG (.jpg) or GIF (.gif).
- Groups of files can be zipped into a single compressed file.
- A web server is a computer with software capable of holding your web pages.
- A domain name is the name of a website.
- HyperText Transfer Protocol (HTTP) is the set of rules for transferring web pages across the internet.
- An internet protocol (IP) address is the numerical address of the web server.
- A uniform resource locator (URL) is the address for a web page on the internet.
- When choosing a host for a website, you should consider the security of the web server, updates to the web pages, the reliability of the information and the speed of response.
- It is important that all the pages of a website look similar.
- Master pages act as templates. By using a template it is possible to create new pages more quickly but using the same style as before.
- Every website should have a home page, the starting point for the site.
- The golden triangle of a web page is the area of links and important information on the left side of a screen near the top.
- Site navigation is the term given to exploring the pages of a website.
- A hyperlink contains an address to another web page either on another site or within the site currently being used.
- A hyperlink disguised as a word is known as an anchor.
- Graphical hyperlinks are pictures that contain a hidden hyperlink.
- Hotspots are used to give more information about an area on the web page. An action occurs when a hotspot is clicked.
- Rollover buttons are areas of the screen that change when a mouse is "rolled over" them.
- Optimised graphics take up less memory and can be downloaded faster.
- Thumbnails are miniature versions of an image.
- Analysing web pages involves looking carefully at the objective, the target audience, whether it contains accurate and correct information.
- Websites should be up to date and unbiased.
- Websites should be compared for house style, audience, size and techniques used.
- Colours used in web pages are based on the fact that any colour can be made from a mixture of red, green and blue (the RGB system).
- Hexadecimal numbers are used to specify the colours in web page coding.

Practice questions 18

1 (a) Explain what is meant by the term **file extension**. [2]

   (b) Give examples of **three** file extensions and describe their use. [6]

2 Explain the difference between bitmap graphics and vector graphics. [4]

3 Discuss the main features of websites to look for when analysing their effectiveness. [5]

Animation

In this chapter, you will learn about how animation is created using a computer. You will look at claymation, rotoscoping, onion skinning, stop motion, tweening and much more. You will learn about storyboards, mood boards and pixilation.

Animation means making something move. When using presentation software, this may mean making the letters or words move, but it also may involve a moving cartoon image. All cartoons are animations, made up of many pictures, each one having a tiny difference. When the images are displayed rapidly one after another it appears that they are moving.

People have always tried to show stories using pictures and cartoons. Examples can be found in cave painting, in pharaohs' tombs, on ancient pottery and in the Bayeux tapestry. Making the pictures move or **animating** them did not occur until the 19th century. The first animated pictures were **flip books**. The drawing made on each page was slightly different from the drawing on the page before. As you flip the pages over, the pictures seem to move.

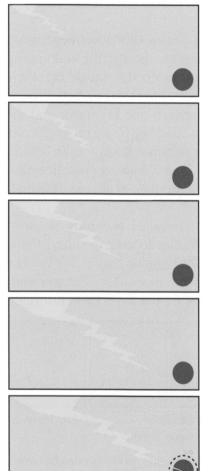

Figure 19.1 A series of images for animation

Activity

A

Create a flip book

1 Create some pictures similar to those in Figure 19.1.

2 Print each one onto a piece of stiff paper.

3 Staple them together to create your own "flip book".

At the start of the 20th century, cartoon films began to appear in cinemas. They were produced in the following way:

1 An artist drew a picture.

2 A photograph of the picture was taken.

3 The picture was altered slightly.

Steps 2 and 3 were repeated until the cartoon was finished. The photos were then displayed rapidly one after the other to make it seem as if the characters in the pictures were moving.

The process by which the eye is fooled into thinking that still pictures are moving is known as **persistence of vision**. Your eye is only able to "click" on one picture at a time. Your brain processes the image and then takes another mental snapshot. If you are shown the pictures fast enough then your brain thinks that they are a continuous process and that the images you are seeing are moving.

The speed at which images are displayed is measured in frames per second (fps). It is generally accepted that if you display images at 100 fps then the eye will perceive a smooth flow of graphics. The best way to create a moving image is to tune each frame until you get the effect you want.

In the traditional process of hand-drawn animation, **key frames** were drawn by the artist. Key frames are the starting and ending images. The background would probably stay much the same between the key frames. Lesser artists, known as **in-betweeners**, would create the drawings to go between one key frame and the next. To do this, they would place the first key frame on a light box and over it put a transparent sheet of paper known as an "onion skin". They would then copy the key-frame drawing onto the onion skin with a slight difference. After a number of altered drawings, the next key frame is produced.

Animation software uses a process called **tweening** to automatically create these in-between frames to save you the trouble of creating them yourself. Figure 19.2 shows how it works. The movement between the frames may not be exactly what you want so you often need to edit or **tweak** the frames to get them just right.

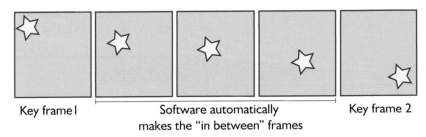

Key frame 1   Software automatically makes the "in between" frames   Key frame 2

Figure 19.2 Tweening: software automatically makes frames between the key frames

Another way of animating is known as **rotoscoping**. Here the animator draws round an image of an actor, animal or other moving object, frame by frame. These images can then be transferred into the animated film and changed so that the actor becomes a strange alien or a motorbike is transformed into a hover machine. The movements look authentic because they are copied from real life. Films such as *Lord of the Rings* and *Star Wars* use these techniques.

Stop-motion animation is where you build a model from Plasticine or clay, take a picture of it, make a small change, take another picture and so on. When you play the pictures back rapidly, it looks as if the models are moving. *Wallace & Gromit: Curse of the Were-Rabbit* is an example of animation produced using stop motion. This process is also called **claymation**. Along the same lines is the method known as **pixilation**. In this method, live actors take the place of the clay models. A picture is taken, the actor moves slightly and another picture is taken and so on. The actor becomes a kind of living puppet and the frames can be blended into an animation.

Using computers, it is possible to create animation in two dimensions (2D) or three dimensions (3D), which makes the images look three-dimensional. Older computers did not have the memory or processing power for this but nowadays most good computers can manage to create smooth animations in 3D.

When you produce animations, you often combine predefined shapes, clipart, photographed images and so on. When you move parts of an image from one place to another and preserve the compound shape, you don't want the separate components to become detached. To avoid this happening, you can **group** the parts you wish to keep together. They can then be placed in different positions on the **backdrop** to give the effect you require.

> A **backdrop** is the background to the film, picture, or stage. The word comes from a theatre curtain that is painted to represent a scene. It is kept rolled up in the ceiling of the stage. When the scene changes, the curtain is unrolled or dropped down to show the new picture.

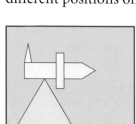 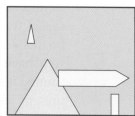 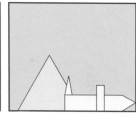

Figure 19.3 Grouping images: the yellow shape in the left picture is made of three parts; in the middle picture, the ungrouped shapes have been moved; in the right picture, the shapes were grouped before being moved

○ Vector and bitmap animation

You have already learned the difference between bitmap and vector images. You may remember that bitmap images are made up of thousands of pixels whereas a vector graphic has its lines defined by mathematical formulae. When using animation, the differences need to be taken into account. Imagine you have a background of trees and in front of the trees a bird is flying around. If the background was a vector graphic it would have to be redrawn in every frame, which would slow down the rendering process; bitmaps are already rendered.

> Rendering is a process of adding colour and shade so that an image looks real.

Planning an animation sequence

Before you produce any animation sequence, such as a film or cartoon, you need to plan carefully what it is you are going to do. You need to take into account:

- the intended audience – whether it is adult, child, learned or uninformed
- the subject matter you are presenting
- the length of the sequence
- any sounds you are adding in.

To help you do this, you probably want to use a number of tools. **Story boards** allow you to decide what is going to happen as you move through the sequence. The order in which the events unfold, the colour, shape and sound of each section need to be considered. In the film industry, talented artists spend hours creating story boards that are used by the crew to produce the finished film. Story boards are also used to plan websites and can show the relationship of the pages to each other.

Mood boarding is used in fashion, interior design, website planning and so on. A mood board is probably a collage or a collection of colours, pictures, ideas and font types which, in a very casual way, depicts the overall feel you are trying to create. Mood boards are often shown to prospective clients. For instance, if you were having a bedroom designed, you would have a good idea if you wanted it dark and dramatic or light and airy. A mood board could present you with a set of paint colours, fabrics, bedroom furniture style and pictures to "set the mood" for your new room.

Uses of animation in commercial environments

When films are made they often include exciting scenes such as explosions, space ships, robots, aliens, car chases and so on. In most cases, to try to shoot the real scene would be far too expensive or dangerous, or even impossible, so the film industry resorts to using special effects. Special effects industries can be sub-contracted to carry out the work on behalf of the film producers. They use many of the effects that have been discussed earlier in this chapter. **Computer-generated imagery (CGI)** is used to produce 3D films and exciting video games.

Web animations are used to make web pages more interesting and eye-catching. Designers use a variety of methods including:

- animated GIFs
- dynamic HTML

Figure 19.4 Films and computer games often use CGI

- Java
- Shockwave and Flash.

Standard banners for web pages often contain animated graphics. Logos are often used to create a **corporate identity** so that the public instantly recognise the site they are looking at.

The advantages of animation in commerce are that:

- Interesting interactive effects can be made on websites.
- Film makers can save money, produce films more safely and create "impossible" effects, such as bullets that turn corners.
- Successful films earn lots of money!

The disadvantages of animation in commerce are that:

- Pages can be slow to load.
- Some browsers may not be able to display the effects.
- Users with a dial-up connection may not be able to access them.
- Films become increasingly unbelievable; people may try the "impossible" stunts, such as trying to fly like Superman, at home and hurt themselves or others.

Uses of animation in learning environments

A virtual learning environment (VLE) is one in which the student is not confined to the classroom to study. By using smart boards, the internet, computer-based learning and so on it is possible to sit in your classroom but explore the world.

Imagine that you are studying Peru in a geography lesson. As well as listening to the teacher or reading a book, it is now possible to use Google Earth, for example, to virtually go to the place you are studying, look at the terrain and buildings, see photos taken by people living there and so on. There may be webcams you can look at or local newspapers you can read online. (Translating programs help you read foreign languages.)

You have already looked at the advantages and disadvantages of VLE in Chapter 5 so perhaps you should find that page and look at them again now.

Activity **A**

Produce a simple computerised animation

Ask your teacher if you can try to produce a simple animation sequence using a package such as Macromedia Flash.

Summary **S**

- Animation means making something move.
- Persistence of vision is a process by which the eye is fooled into thinking that still pictures are moving.
- The speed at which images are displayed is measured in frames per second (fps).
- A key frame is drawn by an artist to show where an image is at the start of a sequence and where it is at the end.
- In-betweeners create the drawings to go between one key frame and the next.
- An "onion skin" is a transparent piece of paper used for copying an image placed beneath it.
- Tweening automatically creates these in-between frames.
- Rotoscoping is where an animator draws round an image of an actor, animal or other moving object, frame by frame.
- Stop motion is where a model is made out of plasticine or clay, a picture is taken, small changes are made then another picture taken and so on. This process is also called claymation.
- Pixilation is a method where live actors take the place of the clay models.
- A backdrop is the background to the film, picture or stage.
- Rendering is a process of adding colour and shade so that an image looks real.
- Story boards allow you to decide what is going to happen as you move through the sequence.
- Mood boarding is a collage of colours, pictures, ideas and font types that depict the overall feel to what you are trying to create.
- Computer-generated imagery (CGI) is used to produce 3D films and exciting video games.
- Web animations are used to make web pages more interesting and eye-catching.
- Standard banners for web pages often contain animated graphics and create a corporate identity.
- A virtual learning environment (VLE) is one in which the student is not confined virtually to the classroom.

Practice questions 19 **P**

1 (a) Describe the differences between a bitmap graphic and a vector graphic. [2]

(b) Which of the input devices shown below could be used to draw a graphic? [1]

2 Describe what is meant by **key frames** and **tweening**. [4]

3 Explain the difference between **rotoscoping** and **stop motion**. [4]

Chapter 20

Networks

In this chapter, you will learn about how computers can be placed into networks and what advantages and disadvantages this creates. You will learn about the components used in computer networks and the differences between arrangements of computers in order to create a local area network (LAN) and how a LAN differs from a wide area network (WAN). You will look at data transmission in packets. You will also learn about stock control and some of the methods by which computers can capture data, such as using barcodes.

A computer that is not linked to a network is called a stand-alone computer.

When two or more computers are connected to allow them to exchange data, this is called a network. For example, an organisation might have a number of offices in different towns. If their computers are networked then a worker in one office can view and use the data that is stored on one of the computers in another office.

The advantages of networks are so great that nearly all businesses, schools and other organisations that have more than one computer use a network. Some networks consist of many thousands of linked computers but some, for example in a home, may only have two.

> Computers on a network are connected and can share hardware, software and data. It is also easier for them to communicate.

Overview

Each computer must have a network card and communications software installed in order for it to be able to use the network. A network interface card (NIC) looks like a small circuit board and generally slots into the main motherboard inside a computer. The card also has a slot into which a network cable can be attached. Once the computers are linked, they can share resources and communicate with each other.

Figure 20.1 A network interface card

A computer that has some shared resource that can be used by any computer on the network is known as a server.

Some networks connect computers in the same room, but some are much larger and may connect computers that are in different buildings or even in different countries. Computers on the same site may be connected by cable or wireless, but if the computers are distant from each other then the telephone system is used.

The largest network is the internet, which is really countless networks all connected together covering the entire world. It is now commonplace for computers to be connected to form a network.

A server is a computer on the network that has a resource that is shared and can therefore be used by any other computer on the network. There are different types of server:

- A file server has programs and data files stored on its backing storage. It probably has a large capacity hard disk.

- A print server has a printer that is shared. Jobs can be printed from any computer on the network.

- A database server stores a large database, which can be searched or maintained by any authorised user on the network.

- A mail server may manage the email traffic for all users on a network.

The resources may have permissions set so that only authorised users can access and use them.

Advantages of networks

- Hardware (peripheral devices) can be shared. For example, a printer on a network can be used by all the computers connected to that network. There is no need to buy a separate printer for each computer. The same applies to any other item of hardware on the network, such as a scanner or a high-capacity storage device.

- Software can be shared. A computer program may be installed on one computer on a network, but can be run on any of the other computers. This is generally not a good idea because the speed of running would be slowed down as many computers try to access the same software at the same time and a queue can form.

- Data can be shared. A database can be stored on one of the networked computers but can be accessed by a user on another computer. The computer where the database is stored is usually referred to as the file server. It is possible for several users to access the database at the same time. A number of office workers may wish to work on the same file. If it is saved on the file server's hard disk then each worker can load the file from there, make any changes or additions and then save it back.

- Networked computers can communicate. Messages or files can be speedily sent from one networked computer to another. Users can send messages, data files or emails to each other whether the network is a LAN in an office or a global WAN.

- The usage of computers on a network can be controlled by a network manager, who can allocate permissions to users to restrict their actions or limit the amount of storage space they can use.

- If data files accessed by users on a network are stored on a file server, then it is easier to make scheduled back-ups than if the files are stored on several different computers.

Disdvantages of networks

- The cost of cabling and setting up can be high.

- Computers on a network are liable to attacks from viruses if files are being sent between the computers. A virus can spread from one computer to another very quickly and precautions need to be taken to prevent this.

- Hackers may gain unauthorised access to files saved on a network server and use them for malicious purposes.

- Sometimes a network fails to work properly and this can cause havoc – work which relies on shared data, hardware and software cannot continue. Large networks can be very complex and need to be maintained by skilled IT staff.

The advantage of a stand-alone computer over a networked computer is that it is not as prone to attack by viruses or hackers.

Types of network

Networks can be simple, consisting of two computers linked together in a house, or they can be very complex. The design of a network is very important if it is to operate efficiently.

Peer-to-peer network

In a peer-to-peer network, all the computers are equal in status: no computer is more important than any other. The computers on a peer-to-peer network probably have similar specifications and are such as you might find in an office environment.

Client–server network

A client–server network is organised so that one computer acts as a server and all the other computers are clients that use the shared resources on the server. The server is probably a larger and more powerful computer with more memory and backing storage capacity than the client computers.

167

Local area network

Where all the networked computers are in the same building or on the same site, the network is called a local area network (LAN). Examples may be found in the home, in an office or even in several buildings of a school or college. There are direct links connecting the computers, using cabling or wireless.

> **Local area network (LAN):** The computers are on the same site and are linked by cable or wireless.

Wide area network

If the computers to be connected are geographically distant from each other, the network is called a wide area network (WAN). Computers anywhere in the world can be connected in a WAN. A business that has branch offices in a number of different countries around the world may link its computers using a WAN so that data can be exchanged between them. The connections are made using the telephone network and satellites. The most well-known example of a WAN is the internet.

> **Wide area network (WAN):** The computers are large distances apart and linked by phone or satellite connections.

○ Network topologies

The way in which a network is configured is called a **network topology**. There are three main types of network topology: bus, star and ring. Large networks are combinations of several of these topologies.

Bus network

The simplest type of network is where each computer is connected to the computers on either side of it.

Figure 20.2 A simple network

Such networks are cheap but if one computer in the line breaks down or one of the cables is damaged, the network is split into two parts that are unable to communicate.

A better way of setting up a network is to link each computer to a common cable called a **bus**. If this set-up is used then it does not matter if one computer breaks down. The rest of the network is unaffected.

The speed of data communication in a bus network is slow.

> A bus network is simple and cheap to install but data communication is relatively slow.

Figure 20.3 A bus network

Star network

All the computers in a star network are connected to a central hub, which directs the flow of data, or to a central computer that acts as the file server. Each computer has its own connection to the hub so, if one computer or cable breaks down, it does not affect the rest of the network. However, if the hub or file server at the centre of the network fails, then all the computers are affected.

Working on a computer in a star network is fast because of the direct link to the file server and each computer only one cable link to another computer. Star networks can be quite expensive to install because of the amount of cabling.

> A star network is more expensive than a bus network because of the amount of cabling but it is faster and more reliable.

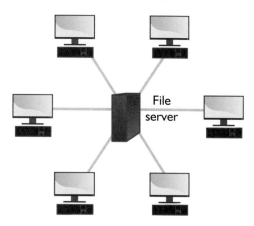

Figure 20.4 A star network with a file server

Ring network

The computers in a ring network are connected to each other in a loop. This topology is often used in a peer-to-peer network because there is no need for one computer to be more powerful than the rest, as there is in a star network.

Computers on a ring network communicate by sending data round the loop, always in the same direction, each one passing it on to the next, until it reaches the receiving computer.

A ring network is similar to a bus network but the last computer is linked back to the first, so it also has the problem that if one computer or cable breaks down the whole network is affected.

> Ring networks are often used in peer-to-peer networks. They are inexpensive but can be affected by breakdowns.

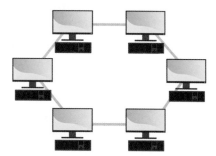

Figure 20.5 A ring network

Internets and intranets

The internet is a network of computers across the world using existing telecommunications such as telephone lines and satellite links. It allows the sharing of unlimited data and resources and such activities as messaging, shopping, banking, teaching and advertising to take place online. The coverage is world-wide and is generally unrestricted by governments or local conditions.

An intranet is a network providing similar services to the internet but within one company or school. Access is generally restricted to those who are part of a pre-defined group.

An extranet is a part of an intranet that is able to be accessed by authorised members of the public over the internet.

The World Wide Web (www) is the collection of multimedia information or resources available on the internet.

Network security

Security on networks is taken seriously. No organisation wants its data files damaged or deleted, and measures are taken to protect them from problems caused by accidents or malicious misuse. There may also be a problem if data is disclosed to the wrong people.

Threats to networks may include hackers, viruses, hardware breakdown or simple human error. A network security policy sets out what actions are allowed and the people who are authorised to perform them. The actions are:

- access: viewing the data stored
- modification: changing data in any of the files
- deletion: removing data or even whole files.

In order to try to protect the data from security threats, a number of actions are possible.

> Data and files stored on networked computers must be protected from damage or deletion, whether it is accidental or malicious.

Passwords

Every authorised user of a network is given a username and a password. These need to be entered whenever the user logs on to the network and the operating system only allows access to the network if the combination of username and password is correct. Networks are prone to hackers (people gaining unauthorised access to data and possibly causing damage) and passwords should make it more difficult for them to access files.

Access rights

There may be resources that are accessible only by some people and different levels of security may be used. It may be possible to

Figure 20.6 Encrypted data cannot be read by anyone without the key

It is easier to schedule regular back-ups if all files are stored on a file server.

A transaction log is a history of the actions that have occurred over a period of time. In a business, this is probably a record of what they are selling and buying.

limit the access rights to a file. This means that only certain people are allowed to access the data in that file. Permissions can be set on files or folders and may only apply to certain groups of users. A user may have:

● no right to access a file at all

● the right to view but not change a file

● full control so the file can be viewed and altered.

Encryption

If data stored on a computer is encrypted, then it is meaningless to someone who is not authorised to access it. Encryption means that the data is encoded using a special key known only to authorised people, who are able to decode it when it needs to be used.

Back-ups

It is essential that data stored on a network is backed up regularly. This is easier to do on a client–server network where all the files are stored on a file server. A back-up of all the files can be scheduled at regular times, such as every night. The back-up copy of the files is best stored in a different location to the original in case of a disaster, such as a fire. If there is a problem with the original data files then the back-up of the files is loaded and all changes made since the back-up was created need to be done again. This is why it is important to make regular, daily back-ups.

If there is a major problem with a computer, it is important that any lost files of data can be re-created. A back-up may have been made of all the files of data the previous night but all the transactions that a business has conducted on the following day need to be recorded so that they can be processed again on any restored back-up if necessary. This recording is known as a transaction log. All the transactions are recorded as they occur. Any action that caused a change in the data is added to the log.

Firewall

A firewall is software that runs on a computer to help prevent hackers from gaining access to the computer or a network of computers. The firewall monitors all data traffic going in and out of the computer or network.

Virus protection

Computers on a network connected to the internet may have a problem with viruses being introduced on downloaded files or on emails. To protect all the computers on the network, the internet server, the computer linked to the internet should run virus-protection software to prevent any attempted attack by viruses.

Data transmission

Data in a network can be transmitted by in various ways.

Cable

Each computer has a network card installed. On the card is a socket where the connecting cable is inserted. Network software (drivers) must be installed before the network card can be used. Speeds may vary according to the type of cabling.

There are two main types of cable: metal copper wire (twisted pair or coaxial) and fibre optic, which uses light.

Fibre-optic cables have a much higher capacity than copper wire cables and they can carry thousands of times more information with no electrical interference. They are also smaller and do not corrode like copper cables. Fibre-optic cables are more reliable.

Wireless (microwave, infrared, radio)

To avoid the inconvenience of a lot of cables, networks are sometimes set up using wireless technology. Each computer needs a wireless network card together with software drivers installed.

A wireless hub transmits radio signals that are received by the network cards in each of the computers. An example may be a home network where a wireless hub is connected to a broadband internet connection. The hub transmits radio signals to any other computer in the house fitted with a wireless network card. Laptops can be carried around and used anywhere in the house, or even sitting outside on the patio.

Businesses need to be aware that wireless networks present a potential security risk as hackers can "tune in" to the transmitted data.

Wireless networks do not need expensive and unsightly cabling but there is a limit to the distance the computers can be from the hub.

Satellite

Some networks incorporate satellites orbiting in space. Geosynchronous satellites orbit at the same speed as the spin of the Earth so they are stationary in relation to the Earth, allowing a constant signal to be transmitted. Networks using satellites can cover vast distances, but special satellite dishes are needed to receive the signals.

Bluetooth

Bluetooth allows devices, such as computers, PDAs, mobile phones, printers and cameras, to connect to each other wirelessly. This is over a small range – usually only a few metres – but it does make exchanging data very easy and eliminates the need for a lot of cables.

A home network might use wireless technology to beam data to laptops that can be used anywhere in the house.

Packet switching

When data is moved around a network it is split into manageable chunks known as packets. Each packet is composed of binary digits. It contains some control data (how many other packets there are in the transmission and where in the transmission it fits) and the address of where it is going, as well as the data it is carrying.

The advantage of packets is that they can find their way through the network to their destination. If one packet out of a transmission fails to arrive then only that one packet has to be sent again. Packet switching is the process by which network components check each packet, look at its address and direct it along the correct route. Packets from the same transmission can take different routes but when they all arrive at the destination computer, they are assembled into the original message before being used.

Network components

This table shows some of the common components used in creating networks of computers.

Component	Role and use
Switch	A device that filters data packets and forwards them between segments of the network.
Network interface card (NIC)	Computer hardware, generally installed inside the computer or peripheral, that allows devices to connect to a wired network.
Gateway	A system to allow a LAN to connect with a WAN such as the internet.
Router	A device that forwards data packets along a network. Routers are generally located at gateways (where two networks connect). They determine the best path for forwarding the packets, and they communicate with other routers to configure the best route between any two hosts.
Bridge	A bridge connects a LAN to another LAN that uses the same protocol.

Gateway: A computer that links two network segments.

Comparison of stand-alone and networked computers

Stand-alone	Networked
Less liable to virus attack and hacking	Needs extra protection, such as firewalls, against online intrusion
No communication with other computers	Potential for data sharing
Needs its own printer, scanner, software, etc.	Can share printers, scanners and software

ICT used by retail services

Figure 20.7 Point-of-sale (POS) terminal

Shops are major users of ICT. When you go to a supermarket to buy food or to a travel agent to book a holiday, you are probably served by someone using a complex computer system. Banks are another type of business that use computer systems to process your transactions, whether you are taking money out, paying in cheques or asking for a statement of your account. These businesses are almost certainly using networks for their stock control.

The checkout tills in a supermarket or other large store are usually all linked to a computer that monitors the sale of items. The main computer stores data about the prices of all the goods and how many of each item remain in the shop. The till is often called a point-of-sale (POS) terminal. The data is usually input with a barcode reader or a keypad. Items and prices are displayed on a small screen and a receipt is printed on paper using a small printer.

Stock is the name for all the goods a business has for sale or the items it uses in a manufacturing process. It is important that a shop does not have too many of any item. It may not be possible to sell them all and, in the case of supermarkets where items could be perishable, then they may go bad before they can be sold. Shops need to reduce this sort of wastage so they do not spend unnecessary money on goods they are unable to sell. If the shop has too few of any item then it may run out. A customer wanting to buy that item will be disappointed and may not return to that shop again. This is why stock control is so important.

Stock level is the quantity of a particular item in the shop or warehouse and stock control is the overall management of stock levels. It is important that there is enough of any item to meet demand, but not so many that some are wasted. The stock level of an item is the number of that item left in the shop. Each item has a re-order level set for it. When the stock level gets as low as the re-order level then more of that item is ordered from the supplier. When the new stock arrives the stock level of that item is re-adjusted.

When a customer buys an item in a shop that uses a POS terminal, the sequence of events is as follows:

1 The item being purchased is identified.

2 The data is sent to the main computer.

3 The computer looks up the item in its database and sends details such as the description and price of the item back to the POS terminal.

4 The description and price are displayed on a screen for the customer to see.

5 When all items have been processed, the total bill is calculated and an itemised receipt is printed for the customer.

6 The customer pays for the goods either with cash, by cheque or using a card.

> An itemised receipt is a sales receipt showing the time and date of purchase, a list of the names and prices of all the items bought, as well as a total amount, the amount paid and the change given.

○ Data capture

> Computers get their data for processing using some method of data capture.

All data processed by a computer comes from somewhere. The method of obtaining this data is called "data capture" and it can be done in many different ways. The next few sections look at the most commonly used methods of data capture.

Barcodes

A barcode is a pattern of parallel black and white lines of differing thickness which represent coded data. The code is usually 13 digits long and consists of four sections:

● a two-digit code for the country in which the item was made (e.g. 50 for the UK)

● a five-digit code for the manufacturer

● a five-digit code which identifies the product

● a check digit which is used to make sure that the barcode is read correctly.

Note that the price of the item is not coded as part of the barcode. This is because barcodes are usually printed onto tins, packets or books and so are virtually impossible to change. Prices may vary between shops and sometimes the price needs to be temporarily altered for a sale or a special offer.

A barcode reader scans the barcode using a low-power laser beam and senses the pattern of reflected light. Sometimes the

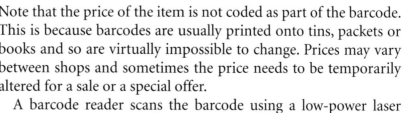

Barcodes are used to identify items, especially in shops. A series of lines is scanned by a barcode reader and the code number is sent to a computer.

A barcode system in a shop provides a faster service for customers with few mistakes made. The customer gets an itemised receipt.

The shop management can use the records of sales to analyse patterns of spending and make effective and productive management decisions.

reader is built into the surface of a terminal, and this is often called a **barcode scanner**. Handheld readers are sometimes referred to as **barcode wands**.

Advantages of a barcode system to the customer are that:

● The number of pricing mistakes made should be fewer than in the old system where prices had to be keyed in manually.

● The process of serving customers is faster so there should be less time spent in queues.

● The customer is given an itemised receipt so they can check their bill has been properly calculated.

Disadvantages of a barcode system to the customer are that:

● The price is not found on the item. If a customer has picked up an item, the customer cannot see how much it costs without going back to the shelf where it came from, unless a self-scanning station is available.

● Scratched or crumpled barcodes may cause hold-ups in the checkout queue as the barcode of the item may need to be entered manually.

Advantages of a barcode system to the shop are that:

● There is no need to put a price on every item for sale.

● Automatic stock control means that people do not have to be employed to count the numbers of each item left on the shelves.

● All sales are recorded by the computer so sales patterns can be analysed and better management decisions made about sales promotions, or which items to sell.

● Fraud is minimised. It is not possible for the checkout person to enter a lower price at the till and pocket the difference.

Barcodes are used in many different shops (e.g. supermarkets, newsagents and clothes shops, to name a few), but they are also used in other places. Libraries use them to identify and track books and they can also be found on the membership cards of the borrowers. You may also have seen barcodes on baggage labels at airports or on the shirts of marathon runners to identify them quickly at the finishing line. Hospital patients may have bracelet tags with barcodes printed on them. There are many other uses of barcodes but all have the same purpose: to quickly identify a single item.

A

Activity

Internet investigation

Biology researchers have managed to place very small barcodes on the backs of bees so they can study their flying and mating habits. A laser scanner reads the barcode every time a bee enters or leaves the hive. Find out more about this.

Optical mark recognition

Optical mark recognition (OMR) is a method used to detect the position of small marks on a sheet of paper. A pre-printed sheet is marked with small lines using a pencil or pen and then it is fed into an optical mark reader, a machine that uses reflected light to sense where on the sheet the marks have been made.

Some schools use OMR sheets to take daily registers of pupils. The sheets have a list of the pupils and a mark is drawn on the sheet against each pupil's name in one of two columns according to whether that pupil is present or absent. The National Lottery uses OMR to read the lottery tickets that players have filled in. Each of six numbers is marked with a line on the ticket. OMR is also used for multiple choice examinations. Each question has a number of different possible answers and the candidate has to put a mark on the correct one.

The advantages of OMR are that:

- It provides a fast method of filling in forms.
- It provides a fast method of reading the data on the forms. The data is usually input directly into a computer for processing.

The disadvantages of OMR are that:

- Forms can be large if they have to offer many options.
- People who are not used to filling in the OMR forms may not do it correctly and the reader may not be able to read the marks.

> Optical mark recognition (OMR) is a means of detecting marks made on a sheet of paper such as a form. The forms are easy to fill in and the reader can input data from the forms very quickly.

Figure 20.8 An OMR form used for a multiple choice examination

Optical character recognition

Optical character recognition (OCR) senses the patterns of light reflected from the surface of a sheet of paper with characters printed or written on it. The patterns are compared with stored data and the nearest match for each character is input to the computer. OCR software has to be able to recognise letters in a wide variety of fonts, sometimes including handwritten characters.

A scanner can be used to scan images of printed text into a computer. OCR software then converts these images into text that can be edited with word-processing software. OCR can also be used on handwritten characters provided they are carefully written.

> Optical character recognition (OCR): A means of reading text directly from paper using a scanner and placing it into a word-processing document. This can save a lot of time, as there is no need to type the text.

Electricity bills may be calculated and printed by a computer on special forms and sent out to the customers. There is a tear-off section of this form at the bottom that is sent back with a cheque payment for the bill. The details on this tear-off section are scanned and read using OCR and the computer then credits the customer's account with the amount paid.

The advantage of OCR is that it is faster to scan a document into a word processor than to type it. The disadvantage is that accuracy can be poor, especially if printed text is faint or the font is not a common one. Scanning handwritten characters may produce a lot of errors.

Machine-readable tags

> Machine-readable tags have data encoded on them that identify the item to which they are attached. A machine can automatically read these tags.

Sometimes in shops, items such as clothes have tags attached to them. These tags have coded data on them that identify the item and these are removed at the checkout and stored. At the end of the day, the tags are placed in a machine which automatically reads the data from the tags and records the sales on the computer. The data is processed and stock levels are automatically adjusted.

The data may be stored on the tag as printed characters, as a barcode or as patterns of holes.

The advantages of machine-readable tags are that:

● Stock control systems can by updated automatically.

● The tags provide a record of the day's sales.

The disadvantages of machine-readable tags are that:

● Too much handling by customers may damage the tags.

● The data is only updated at the end of the day, so data is not always up to date.

Activity

Internet investigation

Schemes are now in operation where pets can be tagged with small microchips placed just under the skin. If the lost pet is found, the tag can be scanned and the data from the tag can be looked up in a centralised database to find the owners. Find out more about this.

Portable data entry

A portable data entry terminal (PDET) may be carried around and used to enter data either by keying or using a built-in barcode reader. The PDET can later be connected to a computer and the data downloaded. Some portable data entry terminals use a wireless connection to download.

Figure 20.9 A portable data entry terminal

A PDET may be used:

- to gather data about items in a shop or a warehouse, such as the number of each item in stock
- to log data about packages sent out on vans or lorries from a depot
- by traffic wardens to enter data about parking tickets issued.

The advantage of a PDET is that it allows more flexible data collection. Users can walk round and collect data from different areas or buildings.

Touch-sensitive data entry devices

Some devices work by a user touching them. The position where the device is touched is sensed and used as data.

A touch screen might have a menu displayed on it. The user selects an option by touching the screen at one of a number of predefined positions. Touch screens are often used in places where devices such as a mouse or a keyboard may get stolen or damaged. There are no loose or detachable parts.

Touch screens are often situated in places where members of the public can use them. For example, they may be found in museums, banks or doctors' surgeries. The screen may offer information about a museum or explain to a customer the services the bank can offer. Some touch screens are used in doctors' surgeries to allow a patient to register their attendance without needing to see the receptionist. Touch screens can often be seen in restaurants or bars. Each item a customer buys is touched on the screen and the total bill is calculated and displayed.

The advantages of touch-sensitive devices are that:

- Only low-level ICT skills are needed.
- There is little possibility of damage or theft.

If a touch screen is used a lot it may become dirty or scratched and difficult to read.

> A touch screen is a user-friendly method of selecting options. The user does not need to be an expert in ICT.

Summary

- Two or more computers connected so they can exchange data is called a network.
- A server is a computer on a network that has a resource that can be used by other computers on the same network (e.g. a file server has shared files).
- In a peer-to-peer network all computers are of equal importance.
- A client–server network has a larger computer acting as a file server.
- A LAN is a local area network: computers on the same site are connected with cables.
- A WAN is a wide area network: geographically distant computers are connected using the telephone system or wireless technology.
- Network topologies may be bus, star or ring configurations.
- Files on a network must be protected from malicious or accidental damage. A network security policy lays down rules for what users are allowed to do.
- Users of a network have usernames and passwords which they must enter when logging on.
- Data files may be encrypted.
- Back-up copies of important data files must be regularly made.
- Firewalls protect computer networks from hackers
- Transaction logs record all changes made to data files.
- Virus-protection software protects computers from viruses.
- Computers on a network can share hardware, software and data. They can communicate with each other.
- Network cables can be copper or fibre-optic.
- Fibre-optic cables can transmit data much faster than copper cables.
- Wireless networks need no cables but use a wireless hub to transmit signals to network cards installed in other computers.
- Data in wireless networks is transmitted using radio, microwave or infrared signals.
- Stock control is the administration of stock levels to make sure there is no wastage and that nothing runs out.
- Some stock control systems operate as real-time transaction systems.
- A stock master file is updated using a file of recent transactions. The transaction file must be validated and sorted in the same order as the stock master file.

Practice questions 20

1 Many businesses use a computer network in their office.

   (a) Describe a computer network. [1]

   (b) Give **three** advantages of using a computer network rather than stand-alone computers. [3]

2 (a) Describe a LAN. [1]

   (b) Describe a WAN. [1]

   (c) Explain the difference between a LAN and a WAN. [2]

3 Security of a network is the responsibility of the network manager.

   (a) Give **two** ways in which the network could be protected from unauthorised access. [2]

   (b) Give **two** ways in which the network could be protected from viruses. [2]

4 Give brief descriptions of each of the following:

   (a) a file server [1]

   (b) a client–server network [1]

   (c) a peer-to-peer network. [1]

5 (a) Give the names of the **three** main network topologies. [3]

   (b) For each of the networks you have named, give a sketch. [3]

Chapter 21

Social and environmental impact

In this chapter, you will learn about how ICT has affected people and their jobs and how many old skills have become unnecessary while new skills are in demand. You will also learn about videoconferencing, codes of practice and computer-based crime.

ICT in the workplace

Nowhere has seen a greater impact from the use of ICT than the workplace. Offices and factories, shops and warehouses have all been affected by the development of ICT and the ways that people carry out their work have had to change. Most businesses have benefited from the change, but there are some people who have struggled to adapt to new practices.

The next few sections look at how the advancement of ICT has affected people in the workplace, what benefits have been achieved in the last 20 years or so and what problems have arisen.

Employment

Some types of job have disappeared, as they have become unnecessary or have been replaced by computers and automated machinery:

- **Boring, repetitive** jobs in factories have been lost because the people who used to do them have been replaced by robotic machines. For example, people used to be employed in factories to screw tops onto bottles of drinks as they passed slowly by on a conveyor belt; now, a robotic machine does this repetitive task.

- Jobs in **hostile environments** have been replaced by robots. There are some places that are unhealthy or uncomfortable for humans to work in, such as factories where paint spraying takes place. The fumes from paint are dangerous, so robots now spray paint onto the bodywork of cars in a car assembly plant, for example.

Figure 21.1 Welding robots have replaced humans in some factories

ICT has created many new jobs but it has caused some unemployment as old-style, boring and repetitive or dangerous jobs have been lost.

- **Old-style office** jobs, such as typist and filing clerk, are being replaced by computer systems that perform the same tasks more efficiently. For example, when a number of copies of the same document were needed, a team of typists would type them individually. Nowadays, a single worker can use a word processor to produce the copies in a fraction of the time.

- Fewer people work in shops. Supermarkets do not need to employ people to count the number of each item remaining on the shelf, as this is done nowadays using automatic stock control. People need fewer shops as online shopping becomes more widespread.

- Fewer people work in banks because of automated systems, such as ATMs, that perform many of the tasks of traditional bank staff.

Businesses generally have cut the number of staff working for them, mainly for economic reasons. By using ICT methods to carry out their business, they can do more work, increasing productivity and therefore the inflow of money, while being able to manage with fewer staff and cutting the outflow of money being paid as wages. The good news is that there are a large number of new jobs that have been created because of ICT.

Here is a list of jobs that did not exist before the introduction of computers:

- Computer programmer: The software that is used by computers or robots needs to be written by programmers (sometimes called "software engineers").

- Systems analyst: When a company wants to computerise its business or upgrade its existing system, then a systems analyst is called in to design the new system and start it working.

- ICT technician or network technician: Any school or organisation that has a large number of computers or a network needs a technician to manage the system and troubleshoot problems.

- Hardware designer: All new hardware must be designed, prototyped and tested.

- Website designer: Every web page displayed on the web needs to be designed and created; many also need to be kept constantly up to date. For example, a web page that displays news stories needs to be updated every few minutes.

- Database manager: If an organisation keeps a database of information, then it needs to be designed, created and kept up to date.

There are now large manufacturing companies that produce computer hardware, and they employ workers who carry out a wide range of jobs from production of the hardware to maintenance of the machinery used.

Retraining

We have seen that the introduction of ICT has caused some job losses but they were the more undesirable jobs, repetitive, boring or dangerous jobs. Many new jobs have been created, but they need different types of skill and therefore people have to be retrained so they can carry out these new jobs effectively.

ICT is constantly changing, so staff must be trained to use new equipment or new software, and they need to make sure that their ICT skills are up to date. This is not easy and companies must offer training to meet the needs of the staff, so their businesses can be more productive.

Training can be done using the internet or interactive CDs. Interactive CDs allow staff to learn at their own pace and not have to travel to a college. Some companies produce their own computer-assisted learning (CAL) software, which makes sure the staff learn exactly the right skills to be able to carry out their work.

> ICT has changed the way in which we work, making life at work easier and ensuring maximum productivity.

Changes in working practices

ICT has caused many changes in the way that work is carried out, particularly in the way that people communicate with each other. Here is a list of some of the changes that have taken place:

- Mobile phones are being used more often because they can be carried around and used anywhere. People can be contacted on the mobile phone at any time so they do not have to be in the office.

- Email is used to send messages. There is less need to write a letter and post it in a letter box. If copies of a document need to be sent to another office, they can be sent using a fax machine.

- The hours that people can work are extending because, for example, a laptop can be taken home or used on the train commuting to work, to catch up on unfinished tasks.

- Buying or ordering goods and materials can be done online over the internet instead of sending an order through the post or having to visit a shop or warehouse.

Teleworking

An increasing number of people are working from home and using ICT methods to communicate with their place of business. This is called **teleworking** and involves the use of email, the internet, and fax machines.

The advantages of teleworking are:

- no travel expenses
- no time wasted in travelling to work
- flexible hours: the teleworker has greater choice of when and how long to work
- less need for office space or facilities, such as a canteen.

183

Figure 21.2 You may easily be distracted working at home!

> Teleworking (literally "working at a distance") means working from home, using email and the internet for communication. A teleworker can choose when to work and for how long.

> Videoconferencing is a way of holding meetings between people who are not in the same room.

The disadvantages of teleworking are:

● less social interaction and more isolation for workers

● distractions (e.g. infants, domestic jobs and callers)

● difficulties for management in checking on whether work is being properly carried out.

Teleconferencing

In most workplaces, meetings need to be held to discuss business strategies or make decisions, but some employees may be many miles apart. They may even be in different countries around the world and this makes it difficult to hold a meeting at short notice. It can also be expensive, both in travel costs and time, to move staff between company locations.

Teleconferencing, sometimes called **videoconferencing** if it includes video links, solves this problem. Meetings are held using computers linked to the internet and the participants can communicate with each other using microphones and speakers to talk and cameras to see each other. Special videoconferencing software needs to be installed on all the computers being used.

The advantages of teleconferencing are:

● It is not necessary for people to travel to a meeting. This saves time and removes the need for expenses, such as buying tickets or hotel accommodation. People can attend the meeting from their home or office.

● Meetings can be called at short notice and it does not matter where in the world the people might be, as long as they have access to a videoconferencing computer.

The disadvantages of teleconferencing are:

● Many people prefer to meet face-to-face with others when important decisions need to be made. Meetings held on computers lack the personal touch.

● The videoconferencing equipment needs to be bought. Microphones, speakers and video cameras are required on each of the computers and the necessary software must be installed.

● Although it is improving, the technology is not yet perfect and the sound and pictures may not be completely synchronised and may appear a little "jerky".

○ Economic impact of ICT

Another effect that ICT has had on many businesses is that they have been able to offer their goods and services to people overseas. ICT has enabled them to advertise on websites, which can be viewed by anybody in any country in the world, provided they have a computer with internet access. It has also allowed people to buy goods from companies overseas by ordering them through a website.

This globalisation of business has expanded markets and allowed companies to streamline their operations so they can employ fewer people, decrease their expenses and therefore maximise their profits.

If people buy goods through a website, there is no need for the company to buy and equip as many shops, or employ managers and shop assistants to run them. Money is also saved on heating and lighting bills and property taxes. Goods can be shipped directly from a warehouse to the customer's doorstep.

Globalisation is not without its critics and some say that rich countries are gaining at the expense of poorer countries whose shares of the global market are extremely small.

> Companies that sell goods or services have increased their profitability by using e-commerce (i.e. buying and selling over the internet).

The environmental impact of ICT

The environmental impact of ICT is greater than we think. We must be careful about the use of ICT and the effect of this use on the environment. There are a number of ways to reduce the impact:

- Use recycled paper or store documents on a hard drive rather than using paper, to save forest resources.

- Manage the life-cycle of ICT equipment carefully by upgrading where possible rather than replacing the entire piece. Manufacturing of ICT equipment uses natural resources and generates carbon emissions.

- Dispose of old equipment carefully. Hardware contains a number of harmful elements. If the equipment is dumped in landfill, harmful chemicals can get into the water supply or contaminate growing things.

- Reduce the amount of energy consumed by switching off the computer or peripheral devices when not in use. Set up energy saving schemes on the computer.

- ICT equipment tends to generate heat; open a window rather than switch on air-conditioning.

- Businesses should consider using videoconferencing rather than sending delegates to meetings. This reduces the carbon footprint of meetings by cutting down on travelling.

More people are working from home, saving on expenditure of fuel and time but the home has to be heated and ICT equipment used. There is a balance between the energy saved by not heating and lighting offices and saving on travelling and having every worker heating and lighting their homes all day and having more time for leisure travel and trips to the shops.

Political impact of ICT

ICT is making it easier for governments to control people and to monitor what they are doing. CCTV cameras are everywhere. Communications from phone calls, emails and text messaging can be monitored. Satellites with cameras so powerful they are capable of seeing what you are reading or identifying a car number plate look down from above. Other cameras patrol the streets. Using Google Earth, anyone can see anywhere on earth, or even travel virtually the streets of unfamiliar towns. We can be tracked by mobile phone signals, debit and credit card use. We voluntarily leave our thoughts and pictures on Facebook, YouTube, blogs and Twitter. Most governments are creating databases of DNA and many have introduced identity cards and biometric passports. It is important that laws are passed to protect the individual from these threats to their privacy and a balance needs to be struck between what is beneficial (cutting down crime) and harmful (invasion of privacy).

ICT helps to form political opinion with survey groups such as YouGov allowing politicians and businesses to constantly monitor how people are thinking and to change the way they govern accordingly.

The internet allows the public to share experiences all over the world. This has meant that different groups can air their views to the world, and radio and TV broadcasts, especially news, can be seen and heard from anywhere in the world.

In the future, voting may be done from home using the internet.

Codes of practice

A code of practice makes sure that all customers are treated fairly and consistently.

A code of practice is a set of standards to which a business expects its employees to conform. It is not legally binding but the business may ask an employee to agree to it before starting their job, and so there can be grounds for dismissal if it were not obeyed. It is always in the best interests of a business to treat its customers fairly and with due consideration, or they will take their business elsewhere. A code ensures consistency of practice. All employees conduct their business in a similar way.

Legal issues

The development of ICT has created new types of crime. The problem of hackers gaining unauthorised access to sensitive or important data was tackled by the government when it introduced the **Computer Misuse Act** in 1990. This defined hacking as a crime; anybody caught accessing files that they are not entitled to on a network can expect to receive a fine or even a prison sentence. This act also makes the creation and spreading of viruses a criminal offence.

The increasing use of credit cards has led to an increase in computer fraud, where a criminal steals information about a person's card details and uses it (**identity theft**) to buy goods or withdraw cash from the owner's bank. Many people do not realise how easy it is for criminals to obtain personal data about us. They may watch us when we type a PIN at an ATM or listen to a conversation when we give our credit card number to a business. Receipts or statements that have our names, addresses or bank details can be retrieved from bins.

The internet has become a favourite place for trying to get personal details. Fraudulent emails may be sent asking for bank details. Criminals can then withdraw money from bank accounts, apply for credit cards and create enormous bills, or purchase goods online without the individual even knowing about it.

To prevent identity theft, you should:

- never give out bank details or passwords on emails
- not throw away receipts, bills or statements without tearing them up first or shredding them
- check your bank and credit card statements regularly to make sure that there are no unexplained transactions
- make sure nobody watches you when you enter a PIN at an ATM or other card authorisation device
- not write down passwords
- change passwords regularly.

There is also a law that makes it illegal to copy software without the permission of the holder of the copyright. Software companies usually issue a licence when you buy a piece of their software and include a special code number that has to be entered when the program is installed on your computer, to prove that it is a legal copy.

Businesses or schools may wish to run a software package on a number of their computers. They need to buy a "site licence", which allows them to install the program on a given number of computers on their premises.

Making illegal copies of software is called "software piracy". It is difficult to prevent. It is a common practice because it is easy to do and because of the high cost of software.

> It is a criminal offence to hack into a computer, create a virus, or copy software which is covered by copyright.

> Identity theft means pretending to be someone else by using stolen personal details.

It is illegal to run a copy of software that you have not paid for. You are breaching the Copyright, Designs and Patents Act. It is also illegal to download copies of music files that are not offered by the music companies.

It is also an offence to download copies of music files from the internet, unless they have been offered by the music company that owns the copyright. This practice, however, is widespread and difficult for music companies to trace.

Activity

Internet investigation

Many of the crimes mentioned in this section carry heavy penalties for people who are found guilty. These may include large fines or even prison sentences.

Use the internet to investigate the sentences that have been passed on people convicted of software piracy or copyright infringement in this country. What is the largest fine you can find for an individual? For a company?

Summary

- ICT has caused some jobs to be lost, but generally these are the boring, repetitive or dangerous jobs.
- Fewer people work in factories, offices, shops and banks.
- Many new ICT-related jobs have been created.
- The new jobs require new skills so people have had to be retrained.
- ICT changes very fast so people constantly need to be trained in new skills.
- The way people work has changed.
- Email and faxes have replaced letters in the post.
- Mobile phones are being used more for communication.
- Buying and selling is done over the internet instead of in shops.
- Teleworking means people can work from home using the internet and other ICT.
- Videoconferencing is a way of holding meetings between people who are not in the same room.
- Businesses can become global. They can expand their market to anywhere in the world by using e-commerce.
- Employees often are required to sign a code of practice, a set of rules stating how they are expected to work.
- Codes of practice ensure consistency: everybody is treated the same.
- The growth of ICT has created new crimes.
- It is illegal to:
  - hack or create viruses
  - steal software (i.e. use it without buying it or paying for a licence)
  - make copies of music or software. This is software piracy.
- Identity theft is a growing method of computer fraud. Guard against it!

Practice questions 21   P

1 Teleworking enables people to work at home by using the internet and other ICT.

  (a) Describe **two** advantages of teleworking to the employer. [2]

  (b) Describe **two** advantages of teleworking to the employee. [2]

  (c) Give **one** disadvantage of teleworking to the employee. [1]

2 Describe **three** ways in which the way people work in an office has changed with the introduction of computers and networks. [3]

3 The developments in ICT have caused some jobs to be lost but have also created new ones.

  (a) State **three** jobs that have been lost. [3]

  (b) State **three** new jobs that have been created. [3]

4 The developments in ICT have also created new types of crime. State **three** new crimes that have been caused by ICT. [3]

Chapter 22

The human–computer interface

In this chapter, you will learn about the way in which humans can interact with computers using an interface. You will study a number of interfaces and their characteristics. You will also learn about biometrics which is the use of physical characteristics, such as fingerprints, to identify a person. You will also study different types of operating system.

Interfaces

There have been changes in the ways that people use computers over the years. The **human–computer interface (HCI)** is the boundary where the user and the computer meet. It is commonly referred to as the **user interface** and it determines the way that the user interacts with the computer and gives instructions about what is wanted.

The design of the user interface of a piece of software takes into account the expected ICT skills of the users. Software companies

Figure 22.1 Windows 7

design user interfaces to make their programs as easy to use as possible, and they try to make the different programs they create as similar as possible, so that users are familiar with the way they work. For example, the Microsoft Office programs Word, Excel and PowerPoint always have the File menu first and the Print button always looks the same.

The main types of user interface are:

- **Command-line interface**: Users type instructions using a special set of words and symbols. This is the interface used in the early days of computing and is really only suitable for skilled ICT users, as the instructions need to be known.

- **Menu-driven interface**: A menu of options is displayed and the user selects one of them. This is more user-friendly than a command-line interface as the options do not have to be remembered.

- **Graphical user interface (GUI):** Small pictures are used to represent options that the user can select. Microsoft Windows uses a GUI (icons show the applications that can be run and programs use buttons with pictures on them).

- **Voice interface**: A microphone is used, into which the user speaks a command to the computer. Sophisticated software analyses the voice pattern and executes the instruction given.

- **Special devices:** There are a number of devices for people who have difficulties using a computer and for small children. These include Braille keyboards that use a limited number of keys to allow Braille input and "concept" keyboards with overlays placed on the keyboards. Touch-sensitive screens offer a non-keyboard method of selection. Puff–suck switches and foot switches allow input for people with no arm movement.

Command-line interface

The user types in a command at a prompt character. The operating system then executes this command. This way of telling a computer what to do was used in the early days of computing.

Some of the commands may have "switches" to provide options for the command. For example, in Microsoft operating systems, the command for listing the files in a folder called "DOCS" on drive C, is:

```
DIR C:\DOCS
```

A switch, **/W**, specifies that the filenames are to be printed across the screen instead of down and the instruction that needs to be entered at the command prompt is:

```
DIR C:\DOCS /W
```

Some instructions may have a number of switches and the commands can become quite complex.

> Human–computer interface (HCI) is the way a user gives instructions to the computer and the way the computer displays information back to the user. It depends on the **operating system** being used.

> Command-line interfaces operate fast but the instructions can be complex and need to be learned.

Activity A

Command-line interface

If you are unable to do this at school, try it at home. Perhaps your teacher can let you try it on a stand-alone computer. If you are using a computer with a Microsoft operating system, you can find the command-line interface by clicking on the START button. In the "Start search" box type C:\windows\system32\cmd.exe to see the command-line window.

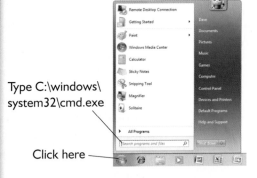

Type C:\windows\system32\cmd.exe

Click here

Figure 22.1 Finding the Windows 7 command-line interface

Figure 22.2 A command-line interface

At the prompt, type DIR C:\USERS. You should see all the user directories for the computer you are using.

The advantages of a command-line interface are that:

- The instructions execute quickly.
- The instructions are versatile. This means that the user can select a large number of options for each instruction.
- The operating system is smaller when loaded into memory.

The disadvantages of a command-line interface are that:

- You need to learn the special instructions used.
- If you mistype an instruction or spell it wrong, then it cannot be executed.
- Some commands and their options can be very complex, so high-level ICT skills are needed.

Menu-driven interface

A list of options available to the user is displayed and the user then selects one of them, usually by clicking the mouse button with the mouse pointer on the option required or by pressing a key on the keyboard. Some ATMs use a menu-driven interface.

Several menus may be available to the user and they are normally organised into groups of similar options. Selecting one menu option may open another menu (a sub-menu), and some sub-menus may have further sub-menus, etc.

The advantages of a menu-driven interface are that:

- Navigation to find the option required is simple.
- You do not need to learn what instructions are available. They are displayed for you in the menu.
- User input is validated as only the options shown can be used.

The disadvantages of a menu-driven interface are that:

- Some options in a menu may not mean anything to the user.
- It can be difficult to find options if there are many menus and sub-menus.

> Menus are easy to use but it is sometimes hard to find the option you want.

Graphical user interface

Most modern computer operating systems use a graphical user interface (GUI). Small meaningful pictures called icons represent instructions that are available to the user, and each one is selected by selecting it with a mouse pointer and clicking the mouse button. For example, an icon may be a small picture of a printer; when the user clicks on this icon, the file that is open is printed.

Modern operating systems use WIMP environments:

- **window:** a rectangular area of the screen within which an application is run
- **icon:** small meaningful picture
- **menu:** list of options
- **pointer:** an image moved across the screen by the mouse.

Figure 22.3 Applications running in Microsoft Windows use a WIMP interface

A graphical user interface (GUI) is an easy-to-use and intuitive interface that uses icons to allow the user to communicate with the computer. People with poor ICT skills should be able to use it with little difficulty.

The File menu (called the "Office Button") in Windows applications always has the Open, Save and Print options.

Most GUIs provide help if users have difficulty. The purpose of a command button is often displayed if the mouse pointer hovers over it and a help menu provides a searchable database that explains how to perform various tasks. Sometimes the help provided is a link to a website.

The advantages of a GUI are that:

● Only a low level of ICT skills is needed for the easy-to-use, intuitive interface.

● There is no need to learn any instructions.

● Pictures are more meaningful than words, so small children or people with reading problems can use this sort of interface.

The disadvantage of a GUI is that it is large and complex. It can use up a lot of a computer's resources and may run slowly.

It is helpful to the user if features that are common to different applications running within a GUI can be found in similar places or look the same. For example, a button that is used for printing should have the same icon and colour and be in a similar position in several applications.

Menus in all applications should have similar options so that users can become familiar with the layout and find options easily. This will make them more confident about using the computer.

You can alter the way in which a GUI displays data to suit your own circumstances. The background on the screen can be changed to a picture you like. The icons on the screen can be arranged and sized to your satisfaction. Often the colours and sizes of the fonts displayed can be changed too.

Sound and speech interfaces

Some user interfaces accept spoken commands. A microphone is used as an input device, the sound is analysed and the command is carried out.

This type of user interface is useful if the user has a disability or has no hands free to operate other input devices such as keyboards or mice. For example, a surgeon in an operating theatre may use a computer with a speech interface while performing an operation.

The advantage of a sound or speech interface is that it can be used without hands. The disadvantages are that:

● People speak differently (the pitch of the voice may be high or low; people speak at different speeds and in different accents) and the computer may have difficulty understanding different people.

● People in different countries speak different languages. The interface may only be able to understand one of them.

Touch-sensitive interface

Some devices work by a user touching them. The position where the device is touched is sensed and used as input data. A touch screen might have a menu displayed on it. The user selects an option by touching the screen at one of a number of predefined positions.

Touch screens are often used in places where devices such as a mouse or a keyboard may get stolen or damaged. There are no loose or detachable parts.

Touch screens are often situated in places where members of the public can use them. For example, they may be found in museums, banks or doctors' surgeries. The screen may offer information about a museum or explain to a customer the services the bank can offer. Some touch screens are used in doctors' surgeries to allow a patient to register their attendance without needing to see the receptionist.

Touch screens can often be seen in restaurants or bars. Each item a customer buys is touched on the screen and the total bill is calculated and displayed.

Touch screens are also found on iPods, mobile phones and palmtop computers.

The advantages of a touch screen are that:

- Only a low level of ICT skills is needed to use it.

- There is little possibility of damage or theft.

- They can be used in environments where gloves are necessary and so a keyboard cannot easily be used.

The disadvantage of a touch screen is that it may become dirty or scratched and difficult to read.

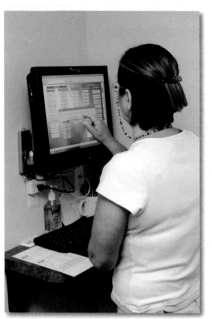

Figure 22.4 A touch screen being used in a doctor's surgery

On-screen help

Many interfaces provide assistance in the form of **on-screen help**. Most software has some way in which help can be obtained. Sometimes this is generalised help, sometimes it is known as **context-related** help as it gives you help about the part of the software you are using at that moment. In older versions of Microsoft Office, there was an Office Assistant which popped up to give **context-sensitive** help. After a while this could become annoying and it was often turned off.

Clicking the ? brings up a help menu

Figure 22.5 Accessing a help menu

An online tutorial guides you through a particular topic using animation and sound.

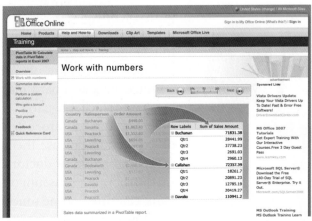

Figure 22.6 An online tutorial at work

Point-of-sale interface

The checkout tills in a supermarket or other large store are usually linked to a computer that monitors the sale of items. The main computer stores data about the prices of all the goods and how many of each item remain in the shop. The till is often called a point-of-sale (POS) terminal.

The data is usually input using a barcode reader or a keypad. Items and prices are displayed on a small monitor (screen) and a receipt is printed on paper using a small printer. A POS terminal uses a variety of sounds, buttons, touch screen entry and scanners. Many are also linked to scales on which items can be weighed and the results input directly to the computer for calculations to take place. Next time you are at a supermarket checkout, see how many aspects of the interface you can identify.

Biometric systems

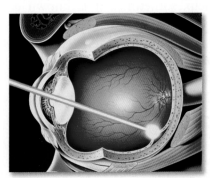

Figure 22.7 Retinal scanners project a low-power, infrared beam onto the pattern of blood vessels at the back of the eye

Biometric systems use physical characteristics such as finger-prints, voice, facial features and eye scans to identify people. These systems, although not yet foolproof, offer high levels of security but are expensive to buy and install. For example, a person may speak into a microphone and the computer analyses the voice pattern to see if it belongs to an authorised user.

The latest issue of passports in the United Kingdom are known as **biometric passports**. These passports contain an electronic chip which stores digitally coded measurements of passport holders' features, such as the distances between eyes, nose, mouth and ears. The information is taken from the applicant's passport photo and can be used to identify them.

Many laptops are now protected with fingerprint identification. Some people think we will soon be able to ask our front doors to let us in. We will not need a key: the door will check our biometric information to know if we are allowed in or not.

Computer programs have been developed which can analyse pictures form CCTV cameras and decide whether you are up to no good. These cameras can alert security guards at car parks, for instance, if it looks as if car thieves are at work. The system works by analysing the way people walk and move.

Computer software

> **Software** is the term given to programs (i.e. the instructions) that a computer executes.

A program is the set of instructions that tells a computer what to do. Software is defined as the programs that run on a computer system. Software is generally divided into two main types:

- Systems software: programs that help a computer system to work (e.g. operating system, disk defragmenter and compilers)

> **Generic programs** (such as spreadsheets) can be used for a wide variety of purposes.

- Applications software: programs that perform a specific task (e.g. a stock control program or computer game) and generic programs that can be used for general-purpose tasks (e.g. a word-processing program).

Operating systems

The most important program run on any computer is the operating system. A computer will not work without an operating system, as it is the program that controls the running of the computer. Every computer has one, from the smallest palmtop to the largest mainframe. Examples of operating systems include MS-DOS, Windows, Linux and UNIX.

When a computer is switched on, the first thing that happens is that the operating system is loaded into memory, usually from the hard drive. The computer is designed with a small amount of software on a ROM chip, which allows the computer to find the main part of the operating system on the hard drive. This process is called booting.

An operating system carries out the following functions:

- **It loads and runs programs**. For example, when an application icon is clicked on the desktop, the corresponding program is loaded from the hard drive and stored in memory. The operating system then starts the program running.

- **It maximises the use of memory** (RAM). For example, think of the operating system as a car park attendant showing a car where to park. The operating system makes sure that a program is stored in the best place in memory when it is loaded. It must not interfere with other programs and it must make efficient use of memory space.

- **It handles inputs and outputs** from peripheral devices. For example, when a key is pressed on a keyboard, a signal is sent to the operating system which outputs a signal to the monitor to display the character pressed.
- **If interrupts occur, then it deals with them**. An interrupt is a signal, for example, from a device that needs attention. A printer may run out of paper, so it sends an interrupt to the processor. The operating system outputs an error message to the monitor.
- **It maintains the security of the system**. For example, a user must log on to the computer using a name and password. The operating system only allows access if the password is correct.

Applications software is specific to a particular operating system and so cannot run under another one. For example, a Windows program cannot be run on a computer with a UNIX operating system.

There may be a number of utility programs stored separately that are only loaded into memory when they are run. Examples of utility programs are a virus scanning program, a disk defragmenter or a program that makes a back-up of a disk.

Many different types of computer system exist in schools, offices and organisations. Each different type of system needs an operating system and the characteristics of these vary, depending on how the computers operate.

Single-program systems

On some simple computers, the operating system only runs one program at a time. When one program has completed its processing, then the next program is loaded up and run. This sort of operating system is much slower than multi-programming systems and is not found much these days.

Batch-processing systems

> A **job** is a program and the data it needs. A batch is a number of similar jobs.
>
> **Batch processing** is usually done at off-peak times such as nights or weekends.

A program, together with any data it needs, is called a job. For example, a job may consist of an electricity bill program and the data about how many units of electricity a customer has used. In a batch-processing system, jobs that are waiting to be run are collected and stored in a job queue and then they are all processed together.

Batch-processing systems are often found in businesses where there is no urgency that jobs are processed. An example is a monthly payroll system for a company. The jobs are collected together at the end of each month and run at night to calculate the wages of each employee and produce pay slips.

The advantages of a batch-processing system are that:

- Processing can be done at off-peak times when the computer is not needed for other processing tasks. Batch processing is often done at night or at the weekend.
- No human intervention is required once the batch has been started.

Multi-programming systems

The computer holds more than one program in its memory and gives each one a small amount of processing time in turn. This happens so fast that it seems to the user that the computer is running more than one program at a time.

It is the job of the operating system to share the resources, such as processing time, so that each program is eventually completed successfully. The operating system decides the order in which to run the programs and makes sure that no program is ignored completely.

The advantage of multi-programming systems is that more programs are processed in less time than in an operating system that only processes one program at a time.

On a microcomputer, multi-programming is often called multi-tasking. Multi-tasking on a microcomputer gives the appearance that the computer is running more than one program at the same time.

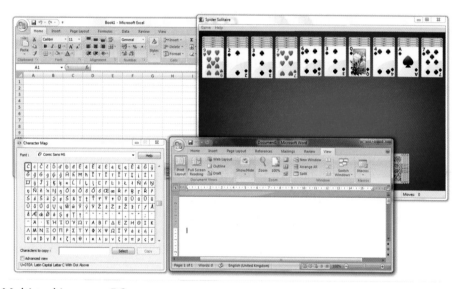

Figure 22.8 Multi-tasking on a PC

Multi-access systems

Multi-access system: Many users are able to work on the same computer at the same time.

A large mainframe computer may have a number of workstations connected directly to it. For example, hundreds of workstations may be spread out in different rooms and floors of a large office block and the mainframe may be in the basement.

The workstations consist of input devices, such as a keyboard and a mouse, and a monitor but there is no computer unit. This is because the user of the workstation is actually using the mainframe computer.

Each user works interactively, even though the computer they are using may not be nearby. The operating system of the mainframe has to organise the inputs from all the workstations and make sure the outputs go back to the right user. It also has to make sure that each user's program is processed quickly and it allocates resources,

Figure 22.9 A multi-access system

> In a **distributed system**, a user may not know which computers are being used to run a program.

> In a **real-time system**, input data is processed immediately.

> Even small embedded computers need an operating system.

Figure 22.10 A flight simulator uses a real-time operating system

such as processing time, to each user in turn. The speed of the processor gives the impression to each user that they are the only person using the computer.

Networks are now replacing many multi-access systems.

Distributed systems

In a distributed system, the processing and resources are shared between a number of different computers. It is the operating system that has to make sure that each of the computers in the system communicates properly. The user feels that a single computer is being used but, in reality, processing may be shared between several computers in the system and the user is unaware of which ones are being used.

For example, a user on computer A may run a program on computer B that uses data stored on computers C and D. The operating system makes sure that the correct connections are made and that processing is completed.

Real-time systems

Data is processed as soon as it is input into a real-time system. A **process control** system is an example of a real-time system. Sensors monitor a process by taking environmental measurements and sending them to the computer as input. The computer processes the data immediately and takes action if necessary. This system can react fast enough to be able to take actions in abnormal situations such as a machine breaking down or even a fire.

The computer monitoring a process control system is a dedicated computer (i.e. it is not used for anything else).

Another example of a real-time system is a flight simulator used to train pilots. If a rudder pedal is moved, a signal is input to the computer, which immediately analyses it and adjusts the attitude of the simulator accordingly.

Real-time operating systems can be found in embedded computers. The operating system is stored in a ROM chip and runs and manages a single program that operates a device such as a washing machine or a digital camera. It handles simple input and output and makes sure the controlling program runs without problems.

Real-time transaction processing

Another type of real-time system involves transactions. Every time an item is sold or bought, or a booking is made, the data from the user is processed immediately. This may involve updating some data held in a record of a database. The transactions are processed in the order they are received and each transaction is completed before the next one is processed.

An example of a real-time transaction processing system is a theatre-seat booking system. Each time a user makes a booking,

In a **real-time transaction processing** system, a sequence of transactions is processed in the order they are input and each one is completed before the next begins.

Large tasks are shared between several processors in **parallel-processing systems**, and so are completed faster.

the data is processed and the seats requested are marked as being taken. This system should make sure that no two people can book the same seat in the theatre at the same time! The important thing about a real-time system is that it is always up to date. If an enquiry is made, then current data is immediately available to be searched.

Parallel-processing systems

Some larger mainframe computers have more than one processor. There are large mainframes with hundreds or even thousands of processors. Large tasks are completed faster if they are shared between a number of processors (the more people digging a ditch, the faster it is finished!).

Special programming languages have been developed to write applications for parallel-processing systems and complex operating systems are needed to share out the tasks to the processors and coordinate their activities.

Computers that process large quantities of data, such as weather-forecasting systems, use parallel processing.

Interactive systems

A user inputs a command to a computer, which may then respond with a request for further input of data. This is interactive computing: it is similar to a conversation between a user and the computer.

An example of interactive computing can be found when you take cash out of an ATM. The first thing you need to do is enter your PIN and then the computer asks you what service you require. You select the option for withdrawing cash, it asks you how much you want and you enter the amount before it gives you the money.

System security

The operating system may put in place some security measures to protect files from damage.

One of the tasks of an operating system is to maintain security. This means protecting the system from malicious or accidental damage by users. Damage may involve changing a data file or even deleting it.

Security on single-user systems is different from security on multi-user systems. Single-user system security involves protecting files of data from accidental change or deletion and there is less need for protection from unauthorised users than there is on a multi-user system or a network.

Some of the security measures that might be taken by the operating system:

- On a multi-user system, the username and password are checked every time a user logs on to make sure that they are authorised.

- A log is kept of computer usage. The time when a user logged on and how long the user used the computer are recorded.

- The time and date when a file was last changed are recorded. This means that if a file has been deliberately changed, it may be possible to track down who was using the computer at the time.
- The attribute of a file can be set to "read only". This would make it impossible to accidentally change or delete an important file.
- If a file is deleted, it may be put into a "recycling bin" and if the user discovers that a mistake has been made then the file can be recovered.
- Tasks such as taking back-ups can be scheduled to occur at regular times.

Other software may be installed which protects the files on a computer from being changed by viruses.

In practice, a combination of security measures needs to be in place and it is worth remembering that the security of a system is only as strong as its weakest link. For example, it would be no good having really strong protection against viruses if the protection against hackers is weak.

Summary S

- The user interface is the way the user communicates with the computer.
- A command-line interface requires the user to type in instructions. The user needs to learn the instructions and what they do.
- A menu interface displays a list of options and the user selects one of them.
- A GUI uses icons (small pictures) to represent options to be selected.
- A GUI provides an easy-to-use and intuitive interface for people who have a low level of ICT skills or are not confident in using computers.
- A WIMP environment uses windows, icons, menus and pointers.
- Speech interfaces are useful for people who are unable to use keyboards or mice, but they may have problems if the user speaks with an accent or in a foreign language.
- A program is a sequence of instructions for a computer.
- The programs that run on a computer are called software.
- Systems programs help in the day-to-day running of a computer.
- Application programs perform a specific task.
- An operating system is a program that runs a computer.
- Booting a computer loads the operating system into the memory.
- Single-program systems load and run one program at a time.
- Batch-processing systems collect similar jobs together and run them at off-peak times.
- Multi-programming systems have more than one program loaded into memory. Each program is allocated a "slice" of processing time in turn.
- In a multi-access system, many users are directly connected to a single computer.
- A distributed system has resources on a number of different computers. The user is not aware of using more than one computer.
- Real-time systems process input data immediately.
- Process control systems are examples of real-time systems.
- In a real-time transaction processing system, the transactions are processed in the order they are input. Each transaction is completed before the next is processed.
- Data in a real-time system is always up to date.
- Parallel-processing systems share the processing between a number of processors.
- Interactive systems involve two-way communication between the user and the computer.
- An operating system puts in place some security measures to make sure data is not accidentally or maliciously changed or deleted.

Practice questions 22

1 Decide which of the following operating systems are most applicable for the applications listed: real-time; real-time transaction; batch-processing; multi-access. In each case, say why it is the most applicable.

  (a) An online theatre-booking system. [2]

  (b) A computer-controlled traffic light. [2]

  (c) Preparation and printing of electricity bills. [2]

2 Which of the following tasks are carried out by an operating system?

  (a) Load a computer game.

  (b) Display an error message about a printer running out of paper.

  (c) Put more paper in a printer.

  (d) Save a data record into a database stored on hard disk. [3]

3 If you were to design an integrated package of software that runs under a GUI, how would you make sure the programs were easy to use? [3]

4 Explain what an operating system is used for. [2]

5 What are the **two** main benefits of running a batch-processing system? [2]

6 What is the main advantage of parallel processing? [1]

7 Discuss what factors might influence your decision when deciding on a user interface. [5]

8 Give an example of where a speech interface may be used. [1]

9 Give **three** tasks an operating system might perform to maintain the security of a computer system. [3]

Chapter

Applications of ICT

In this chapter, you will learn how computers are used in banks and how payrolls are produced.

Banking systems and money

> Banks are some of the biggest users of ICT. Nearly all banking processes are performed by computers.

Banks are a major user of ICT technology. Computers now do nearly all the processing of money transactions, not only in this country but also all over the world. They were one of the first types of organisation to computerise their processes and banking systems are now global.

Here are some things a bank customer can do:

● open a new account; there are different types of account on offer with a variety of benefits

● deposit money into any of the accounts

● withdraw money from any of the accounts

● pay bills by cheque

● ask for a statement that shows the details of the most recent transactions

● buy items at shops or on the internet using a debit card.

There are many other services that banks offer, too many to list here, such as arranging overdrafts or lending money, changing money from one currency to another (e.g. pounds to euros), sending money overseas, and so on.

What part does ICT play in a banking system?

When a customer opens an account with a bank, their details are stored in the bank's large database. This database also stores details of all the transactions the customer makes. This allows the bank to print out statements at regular intervals and send them to customers to keep them informed about how much money they still have in their accounts.

Every time a customer uses a cheque or a card to pay a bill, the bank has to move money around from one account to another. This is all done automatically by computer these days and no actual money is involved.

A very important job that ICT has to undertake is that of making sure that there are no breaches of security. The computers need to check very carefully that no fraud or theft takes place in any parts of the system.

> One of the main tasks of a bank's computer system is to prevent or detect fraud.

Activity A

Discussion

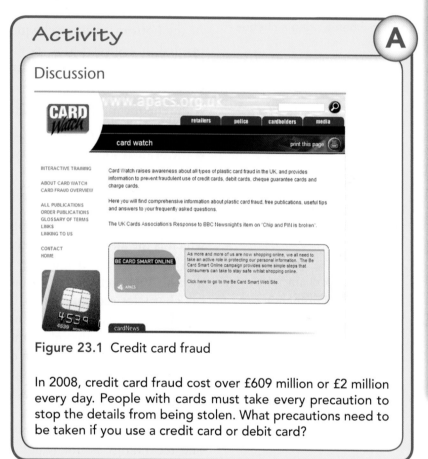

Figure 23.1 Credit card fraud

In 2008, credit card fraud cost over £609 million or £2 million every day. People with cards must take every precaution to stop the details from being stolen. What precautions need to be taken if you use a credit card or debit card?

Cheques

Even though a lot of people now use debit cards, cheques are still used to pay money to someone else, such as when paying a bill. Many older people rely on cheques as they find it difficult to remember a PIN but banks are threatening to stop using cheques as it is expensive for them. Usually a book of cheques is given to a customer by a bank when they open an account but this may change.

When payment is to be made, the cheque is filled in and given to the person being paid. They then give it to their bank for processing.

Figure 23.2 There are five things to fill in when writing a cheque

> Magnetic ink character recognition (MICR) is a method of input used by banks to read data from cheques. It is a fast method of processing cheques but the equipment is expensive to set up.

When a cheque is written, there are five items that need to be filled in:

- the date
- the name of the person (or business) being paid
- the amount in words
- the amount in figures
- the signature.

Magnetic ink character recognition

At the bottom of every cheque there are some special characters printed in a special font used by banks in ink that can be magnetised. Three items of data are encoded at the bottom of every cheque:

- the cheque number – each cheque for a customer has a different number
- the branch sort code – every branch of each bank has a unique number to identify it
- the customer's account number.

The bank prints a fourth number after it has received the cheque, which is the amount of money.

A bank may receive a large number of cheques in a day, and they all then get sent off to a central clearing house. **Magnetic ink character recognition** (MICR) is the process which reads the data from these cheques and inputs it to the computer. The MICR reader magnetises the ink as the cheques are fed into the machine and sensors detect the pattern of the electromagnetic field around them. Some clever science is at work here, but the machines can read a large number of cheques very quickly and provide automatic input for the computer system to process all the cheques.

MICR is really only used by banks to read data from cheques. The technology is not really appropriate for other applications mainly because of the high costs of setting up the system and buying the hardware needed.

The advantages of MICR are that:

- A large number of cheques can be read very quickly,
- Crumpled or dirty cheques can still be read – it makes no difference to the readability of a cheque if ink or coffee is spilled over it!
- The characters are difficult to forge.

The disadvantages of MICR are that:

- The equipment is expensive. MICR systems need special readers and printers that use the magnetic ink.
- Only a very limited number of characters can be used.

Electronic funds transfer

When a shopper pays for goods in a supermarket or shop, there are a number of different ways this can be done:

- cash
- cheque
- credit card
- debit card
- vouchers.

People are using cash less and less. There are now more convenient methods of making payments but we still need cash for things such as "pay and display" parking machines at car parks, vending machines or bus and taxi fares.

Some people do not trust other methods and still prefer to use cash. There are privacy issues here. Cash does not leave any trace of what has been bought or who bought it. Unscrupulous marketers cannot then use the information to send junk mail or make unwanted advertising phone calls.

Customers may write cheques to pay for goods but this can be a slow method and there may be a limit to the value a cheque can be written for, even with a guarantee card.

Electronic funds transfer at point of sale (EFTPOS) is a method of using cards at POS terminals to make payments for goods bought. The card may have a magnetic stripe embedded in it containing information about the customer's account. The checkout assistant swipes the card through a magnetic stripe reader that reads the data stored on the card.

The POS terminal is linked to the shop's main computer and sends it details of the customer's account and the amount to be paid. This computer contacts other computers, which then make the appropriate money transfers:

- **Credit card:** The money is transferred from the credit card company's account to the shop's bank account. The credit card company then bills the customer for the amount transferred and the customer arranges payment.

- **Debit card:** The money is transferred directly from the customer's bank account to the shop's bank account. The customer sees the payment on their next bank statement.

Some stores have their own cards and these operate in the same way as credit cards.

One major problem with using cards is that of card fraud. Magnetic stripes are easily copied and there have been many cases of criminals making copies of credit cards and using them to buy goods. This is why it is important to keep your cards safe and not let them out of your sight when using them in shops. Banks and credit card companies are often unwilling to admit to the full scale

> We are not yet ready for the cashless society; we still need money for small payments such as taxi fares or vending machines.

> Electronic funds transfer at point of sale (EFTPOS) is a system that allows payments to be made by swiping a card through a reader. Computers then automatically transfer money between bank accounts.

Figure 23.3 A card being swiped through a magnetic stripe reader

Figure 23.4 A chip and PIN payment device

A "chip and PIN" scheme cuts down on card fraud. Smart cards are used and customers have to verify payments by entering their personal identity number (PIN).

An automatic teller machine (ATM) is a device that allows customers to withdraw money (or use other services) without visiting a bank. A cash card is needed to use it.

Figure 23.5 An automatic teller machine (ATM)

Make sure nobody sees your PIN when you enter it at an ATM.

of the problem, as it affects people's willingness to open accounts if they think they may not be secure. To combat this fraud, the technology is moving on to smart cards.

A **smart card** has a very small microchip embedded in it. A large amount of data can be stored on this chip, much more than on a magnetic stripe. The card is also a lot more difficult to copy. Data about the customer's account may be stored on it but it can also be used to store details about how many points the customer has gained in a loyalty scheme.

Many stores now use "chip and PIN" schemes for card payments. The smart card stores details of a customer's personal identity number (PIN). The PIN is typed on a keypad to verify a card transaction instead of signing a receipt.

Automatic teller machine

Bank customers are given plastic cards when they open accounts. These cards have several purposes, such as guaranteeing cheques up to a certain value or being used as a debit card when buying goods. They may also be used in an **automatic teller machine** (ATM). These are devices that can often be seen in the walls outside banks, shops or petrol stations and are sometimes called "hole-in-the-wall" cash machines or "cash points". An ATM is simply a computer terminal that is linked directly to the bank's computer system.

There are a number of services that can be requested at an ATM. Here are some things you can do using an ATM:

- withdraw cash from your account
- print a balance (the amount of money left in your account)
- print a small statement that shows details of the last few transactions
- order a new cheque book
- change your personal identity number (PIN).

Here is the sequence of events that takes place when a customer wants to take money out of the ATM:

1 The customer pushes their cash card into the card reader slot. The card has a magnetic stripe that stores data about the customer's bank account.

2 The customer enters their PIN using a keypad. The ATM checks to make sure that the PIN is correct for the card. If the PIN is not correct, the card is rejected and no further action takes place.

3 The customer selects the option required, in this case "Withdraw cash".

4 The customer selects the amount of money to be withdrawn.

5 The money is dispensed through another slot. The hidden part of the ATM is a safe that stores large amounts of cash. Special sensors check the notes as they are issued to make sure they are not too worn or folded. The sensor can also measure the thickness in case two notes are stuck together.

6 A receipt is printed on a small printer, if it is requested.

Advantages to the customer of using an ATM:

- They are always open: 24 hours a day, every day.
- They are nearby: they can usually be found outside large supermarkets, petrol stations or banks; you are never very far away from one if you are in a town.
- The service is fast so there are never very long queues.

Disadvantages to the customer of using an ATM:

- Banks offer more services.
- The cash may run out at busy times, such as bank holidays.
- A card may be rejected if it is damaged and the card reader in the ATM cannot read it.
- A customer who forgets their PIN cannot use the ATM.

Advantages to the bank of ATMs:

- Fewer customers come into the bank so they do not need to employ so many staff to serve them.
- Checks can be made to prevent customers withdrawing cash if they do not have enough money in their account.

A disadvantage to the bank is that ATMs are expensive to buy and install.

◯ Home banking

> Home banking is an internet or telephone-based banking service. Transactions can be carried out at any time of day or night from the comfort of your own home.

As more and more people are becoming internet users, the number of people managing their financial affairs from home is increasing. It is now possible to do a wide range of bank transactions from home.

Many banks and building societies now have websites on the internet where customers can carry out basic banking tasks. You need to have an account with the bank and to register with them for use of their online services. They issue a password that must be entered whenever the site is used, to make sure that customers can access only their own bank account. You may also be asked to enter a personal identity number (PIN) for extra security.

Banks vary in their online services but the most common tasks which you can undertake are:

● View a statement of account. This displays the most recent transactions and gives a balance (i.e. how much money is remaining in the account).

● Transfer money from one account to another. For example, money can be transferred from a current account to a savings account.

● Bills can be paid. This is done by transferring money from your account to the account of the business whose bill is being paid.

● Set up or alter standing orders or direct debits. These are payments to be made regularly.

● Apply for loans or mortgages.

Other services may include ordering a new cheque book or applying for a credit card.

The advantages of home banking are:

● saving time and avoiding the need for travel

● banking activities can be done at any time on any day of the week

● greater control over financial matters: a customer can check the amount of money in an account every day.

The disadvantages of home banking are:

● Security: People are afraid that others may be able to hack into their account and transfer money but banks take security very seriously and put many safeguards in place to stop these sorts of problems.

● Lack of the personal touch: Sometimes people feel more comfortable discussing banking matters with people than with machines.

● There are some banking services which are not available online.

> Banks need dependable security measures.

○ The "cashless society"

For some time now there has been talk about the "cashless society": a time when people do not need to carry money around with them and all transactions use electronic means. All purchases will use credit or debit cards at EFTPOS terminals and all bills will be paid using a home-banking system.

The benefits of this would be enormous. Theft of money would immediately be eliminated. There would be no bank robberies. Attacks on shopkeepers and cashiers would stop and the streets would become safer as muggers would disappear and drugs would

no longer be sold on the streets. People would not have to carry cash around with them or go to the ATM or bank to withdraw more when they ran out.

You might be wondering why this has not happened yet. Well, the truth is that not everyone wants it to happen. People like to feel cash in their pockets or purses and it is certainly faster than using cards to pay for small-value items.

There are also privacy concerns that we have already mentioned. Cash payments leave no evidence, whereas payments by card can be traced to the person paying the card and where and when the payment was made.

It is not yet economically sensible for small payments to be made using cards. The equipment needed and the cost of setting up the system is too great for people such as taxi drivers or bus operators. Soft-drink-vending machines and car-parking machines would need to be altered to accept card payments and this would be an expensive operation.

E-commerce

Many businesses now operate websites on the internet that act like shop windows, allowing them to display details of the company and the goods they have for sale. E-commerce is the term used for "electronically" buying or selling goods or services over the internet and is becoming increasingly popular.

A buyer can navigate to the website of a business, browse the items offered for sale by looking at pictures and descriptions, and add the items they want to buy to a "shopping basket". When all items have been selected, the buyer then proceeds to a "check out" where the details of the purchase are confirmed and the method of payment is chosen. This usually involves giving details of a credit or debit card and information about the address where the goods are to be delivered. The goods are then sent, usually within a few days, and delivered to the buyer's home. Most companies add a charge for delivery, or postage and packing.

It is possible to buy almost any item over the internet these days, from books, CDs and DVDs to plants, insurance, computer equipment and even items you may buy at the chemist. The list is very large and increasing all the time as more and more companies set up e-commerce websites.

The advantages of e-commerce are that:

- The range of goods available is very large. Almost any item can be found for sale on an e-commerce site using search engines. Gone are the days when you might travel some distance to a shop to find that it does not stock the particular item you want.

- Shopping can be done from home, avoiding the need for the time and expense of travelling to the shops.

> Shopping can be done from the comfort of your own home using e-commerce websites as long as you pay by card. Extra charges are often made for packaging and delivery.

211

- Goods are delivered directly to the doorstep. Some items can be large, heavy or difficult to carry.

- A business operating an e-commerce website does not have to pay for premises such as an office or a shop.

- Businesses can easily expand their market to anywhere in the world. Any person with access to the internet can order an item from a website and have it sent to them.

The disadvantages of e-commerce are that:

- Sometimes there can be a wait of several days or weeks before an item purchased from an e-commerce site arrives. If you buy from a shop, you can have it immediately.

- You cannot touch or smell the goods you are buying. For example, it is sometimes not apparent from a picture what an item of clothing feels like (e.g. how soft or how heavy it is). Fresh food bought over the internet may not be exactly the same as the picture displayed and it would be impossible to feel how fresh an item of fruit is. There is no way of telling what a bottle of perfume or a bar of soap smells like.

- Some people are worried about giving their credit card details over the internet even though extensive precautions are taken by e-commerce companies to make sure the details are not inter-cepted. The details are usually encrypted (coded) before they are sent so they are meaningless to anyone else.

Figure 23.6 Buying goods is easy on the internet

Payroll

All companies need to make sure that the people who work for them get paid. Some people get paid a salary (this is normally a fixed amount each month). Some people get paid an hourly rate and the number of hours they have worked is recorded.

Some companies pay their employees at the end of every week, some at the end of every month. Whichever system is used, at the end of the pay period a payroll system is run on the computer, which calculates how much each employee should be paid. The hardware needed to run a payroll system depends on the size of the company and the number of employees needing to be paid. It is possible to run some payroll programs on PCs for small companies with only a few staff.

> A payroll database needs tight security measures, such as passwords, to prevent unauthorised access.

Input

The sources of data used as input for the payroll program may include:

- a database (the Employee master file) of the employees' details such as employee identity number, name, pay rate or salary, National Insurance number and tax code

- timesheets that provide data about the number of hours an employee has worked during the time period and whether any overtime has been done.

Timesheets used to be recorded on paper but it is more likely to be done on a computer now. Special timesheet software is available which is similar to a spreadsheet. There needs to be some validation of input data. For example, a range check on the number of hours worked by an employee should make sure that no number too large can be input.

Processing

The Employee master file is sorted in order of its key field. Before the timesheet file can be processed, it needs to be sorted into the same order as the Employee master file. This speeds up the processing.

The computer needs to calculate for each employee:

- the gross amount earned
- any bonuses or overtime earned
- deductions such as National Insurance, tax or pension scheme payments
- the net amount to be paid.

The gross amount may be a fixed monthly rate or it may be calculated by multiplying the number of hours worked by the hourly pay rate. The net amount is calculated as the gross payment and bonuses, with all the deductions taken away.

A payroll system is an example of a batch-processing system. All the timesheets and files are prepared and collected and the payroll system is run at an off-peak time such as at night or at the weekend. There is no human intervention required once the payroll program has been started; payslips are prepared and printed automatically.

A system flowchart is a visual way of illustrating how a system works. Different shaped boxes have different meanings and are labelled. Arrowed lines show the flow of data through the system. It is often easier to understand how a system works from a diagram than from a text description.

> A system flowchart makes it easy to understand how a system works.

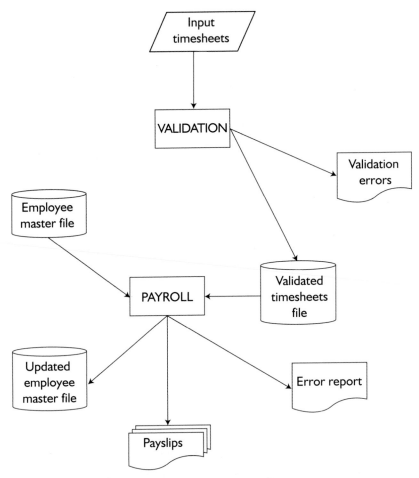

Figure 23.7 A system flowchart for a payroll system

Output

There will be some printed outputs from the payroll process, but also some of the fields in the employee database need to be updated with new values.

> Bankers' Automated Clearing System (BACS) is a system used to transfer money directly into employees' bank accounts.

- Printed **payslips** include a summary of the employee's pay and deductions for that period. They are given to the employee to advise how the pay has been calculated. They are normally printed on special pre-printed stationery.

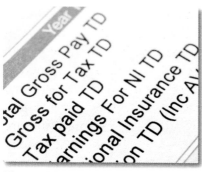

Figure 23.8 A payslip

- Updated fields, such as the "total amount of payments this year" or "total tax paid this year", need to be stored in the records of the employee database.
- Data needs to be sent to the BACS system so that money can be transferred to the bank accounts of the employees.
- Reports are output summarising the company's pay for the period. Accountants in the financial department use the data to update their accounting system.

Summary S

- Nearly all banking processes are performed by computers.
- One of the main tasks of a bank's computer system is to prevent or detect fraud.
- Usually a book of cheques is given to a customer by a bank when they open an account.
- Magnetic ink character recognition (MICR) is a method of input used by banks to read data from cheques.
- Electronic funds transfer (EFT) is used when a shopper pays for goods in a supermarket or shop using a credit or debit card.
- We are not yet ready for the cashless society; we still need money for small payments such as taxi fares or vending machines.
- Electronic funds transfer at point of sale (EFTPOS) is a system that allows payments to be made automatically between banks.
- A smart card has a very small microchip embedded in it that contains a large amount of data.
- A PIN is a personal identity number that is typed on a keypad to verify a card transaction.
- A "chip and PIN" scheme cuts down on card fraud.
- An automatic teller machine (ATM) is a device that allows customers to withdraw money without visiting a bank.
- Shopping can be done from the comfort of your own home using e-commerce.
- Payroll systems are batch-processing system that calculate pay for a company's employees.

Practice questions 23 P

1 A person is using an ATM (cash point) to withdraw some money.

   (a) What **two** data items must the person enter? [2]

   (b) Give **two** advantages of using an ATM to withdraw money rather than going into a bank. [2]

   (c) Give **two** problems that might occur when using an ATM to withdraw money. [2]

   (d) Give **one** advantage to the bank of using ATMs. [1]

   (e) Apart from withdrawing money, describe **two** other things a person can do at an ATM. [2]

2 MICR is used to read data from bank cheques and use it as computer input.

   (a) What does MICR stand for? [1]

   (b) What **three** items of data are pre-printed at the bottom of a cheque? [3]

   (c) Give **two** advantages of using MICR over other methods. [2]

3 Explain how batch processing is used in a payroll system. [4]

Process control in industry

In this chapter, you will learn about the way in which computers are used in industry and how they can be used as robots in a manufacturing process. A number of applications are explained, such as car manufacturing and glass production. You also learn about computer-aided design and manufacture (CAD/CAM) and, finally, how a computerised booking system works.

The number of factories producing goods in this country has declined in recent years, but there have been many changes in the way that industrial processes work. These processes have had to adapt to using ICT in many different ways.

The types of work that people do have changed from dangerous and monotonous jobs to those requiring ICT skills, such as programming or robot and machinery maintenance.

> Computer systems are often used to control manufacturing processes.

Manufacturing

One major change has occurred in the way a manufacturing process is controlled. You are less likely to see people standing around watching a process and taking measurements, such as temperature and weight, with portable instruments or timing with a clock, pushing buttons and pulling levers. Instead, you are more likely to see computerised control processes where the actions are carried out automatically by computer systems that are controlling all the operations.

Input data comes from sensors that measure quantities such as temperature, light, sound, weight or stress. Some sensors detect when an object moves in front of them and accurate clocks measure defined time intervals. The measurements from all sensors are taken at regular intervals and input to the controlling computer, which then analyses the data to decide if any actions need to be taken.

For many measurements, a range of values is defined within which the reading from the sensor should always lie. If the measured value

Figure 24.1 Many industrial processes are controlled by computer systems

Measurements from **sensors** provide the input for a control process.

A control program analyses the data input to it and may output control signals to devices operating machines.

A feedback system is a control system where the output actions affect the input data which affect the output actions, which affect the input data, etc.

lies outside that range then the controlling program decides that some action needs to be taken. If action is needed, the computer outputs a control signal to devices that operate the system. An actuator is a device that controls a motor, a switch or a tap. It receives a signal from the controlling computer, through a cable or possibly by means of a wireless signal, and activates a device.

An output signal may be in the form of a bit pattern, that is a number of binary digits (0s or 1s). Each bit may control a separate device. For example, a four-bit output signal is used to activate a heater, a fan, a ventilator and a sprinkler (0 means "switch off" and 1 means "switch on").

The output signal, 0110, switches on the fan and the ventilator and turns off the heater and the sprinkler.

Feedback is used in many control systems to maintain a stable environment for a process. Sensors input data and actions are taken which may influence subsequent readings from the sensors, which are input to the computer, and so on. This is sometimes called a **closed-loop system**.

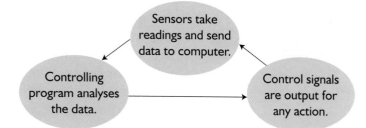

Figure 24.2 Feedback is used to control an environment

Process control is an example of a real-time system. Data received by the controlling computer is immediately analysed by the stored program and this allows the system to respond immediately to any variations in the processing.

The advantages of process control are that:

- Little human interaction is needed. This has implications about the number of people that need to be employed in a factory and workforces have been reduced as more control processes are used.

- The process can continue 24 hours a day, every day, resulting in greater output for manufacturing industries.

- Automatic and immediate response to problems can improve safety.

- People can be kept away from, and so are protected from, dangerous environments such as radiation or an atmosphere heavy in spray paint fumes.

The disadvantages of process control are that:

- Expensive equipment and computer hardware need to be purchased and installed.

- There has been some unemployment as fewer employees are needed to run the process.

- Some problems may arise which may need human decisions.

Case study: Glass manufacturing

When glass is manufactured, the raw ingredients of sand, soda ash, limestone and recycled glass are heated in a furnace up to 1500°C. It is important that the molten glass is allowed to cool at the proper rate. If it cools too slowly or too quickly, the glass will be of poor quality with visible defects or it may lack the proper strength.

"Annealing" of glass is the controlled cooling process and is normally done in a special oven. The glass is allowed to cool down to a certain point and then kept at that temperature for a while to allow stresses in the glass to relax, before the final cooling. Process control systems oversee this annealing process and control the cooling rate.

Sensors carefully monitor the temperature in the oven. If the glass is cooling too quickly in the annealing oven, the computer sends a signal to increase the heat. If the glass is cooling too slowly, the computer sends a signal to activate a cooling fan. The controlling program stored in the computer system receives the input data from the temperature sensors and compares the readings with maximum and minimum values stored on the computer. If the data lies outside the acceptable range, action is taken. The annealing process needs no human intervention and should result in perfect glass every time.

Figure 24.3 Process control is used in the manufacture of glass

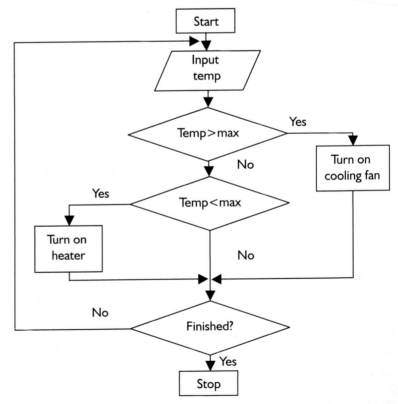

Figure 24.4 A flowchart for an annealing control system

○ Robotic control

A robot is a machine that can be programmed to perform a sequence of actions. Many robots are now used in industry, particularly in manufacturing where jobs are repetitive and boring for humans.

Many conveyor belt jobs are now performed by robot arms that have a number of "joints" (like elbows and wrists) which allow the arm to move in any direction. The arm may also have some sort of grip, which allows it to pick up an object or use a tool such as a drill. There are also robots that move around. A guidance system makes sure that the robot does not crash into solid objects.

Industrial robots do the following types of job:

- Repetitive, boring jobs that require the same sequence of movements over and over again; for example, a robot arm may place electronic components into a circuit board.

- Dangerous jobs in which humans may be at risk from handling toxic materials or unhealthy levels of toxic materials in the atmosphere; there may be radiation or extremes of heat and cold.

- Difficult jobs that a robot would find it easy to perform but in which a human hand might shake a bit!

- Heavy jobs; humans get tired of lifting and carrying heavy objects repeatedly but robots do not.

A computer program is an ordered sequence of instructions that a computer can execute. A robot needs a program to define and sequence its actions. This program runs continuously whenever the machine is switched on. Robots can be programmed in two ways:

- Instructions can be written using a special computer programming language.

- A human can guide the robot through the actions manually. The robot "remembers" the movements and is able to repeat them.

A robot may have sensors built into it, which are used to detect when an object passes in front of it. A moving robot would need sensors to detect the proximity of solid objects so that it does not crash into them. The data from these sensors acts as input for the controlling program. Robots that grip objects or turn them may have a sensor that measures the strength of the grip, or the torque.

Output from the robot's program consists of control signals that cause the machine to perform a number of actions.

Among many other things, industrial robots can:

- assemble parts

- weld or rivet

- spray paint

> Robots are used in hostile places, such as the surfaces of other planets where the temperatures are too extreme for humans.

> Humans use programs to give instructions to robots. Not the other way around as you sometimes see in films!

Figure 24.5 A robot can assemble complex electronic circuit boards accurately

Data from sensors provides input for the controlling program.

Torque is rotational force. Imagine you have a spanner on a nut you are trying to undo. You need to turn the nut round and round to undo it. The stiffer the nut, the harder you push. That's torque.

- lift and carry parts (robots can follow tracks on the floor and fetch parts from a warehouse)
- handle machine tools, such as drills or grinders
- turn objects such as tightening bolts to a specified torque.

There are even robots that can harvest fields of crops, detect and defuse bombs, explore the bottom of the ocean, or mow a lawn.

The advantages of using robots are that:

- Consistency can be ensured. A human performs a job less well if tired or distracted. A robot performs the job equally well all the time.
- Breaks or holidays are not required. A robot can repeat their programmed actions all day and every day.
- An hourly or weekly wage does not need to be paid.
- Boring or dangerous jobs do not need to be carried out by humans.
- New jobs, such as robot maintenance and programming, have been created.

The disadvantages of using robots are that:

- Initial installation and programming costs are high.
- Robots do not respond well to new situations. Some do not have the capacity to analyse a new situation and respond with the appropriate action. This could be a major problem if something goes wrong!
- Some unemployment has resulted in manufacturing industries as humans have been replaced by robots.

Case study: Car manufacture

The manufacturing of cars is based on a moving assembly line. The process starts with the basic chassis to which parts are added and a sequence of operations is performed on it as it moves along a conveyor belt. Some of the jobs are done by people, but many of the jobs are done by robotic machines.

Robots may do the following jobs (and others):

- Fetching and carrying parts from an automated warehouse. Robots can lift heavy objects and carry them along tracks embedded or painted in the floor. Sensors detect when the robot leaves the track and correct the direction of movement.
- Welding parts together. A robot arm can perform precision spot-welding.
- Applying adhesives or sealants.
- Spray-painting the body parts. Robots can achieve a more even coating than humans (and they do it perfectly every time!).

Figure 24.6 The assembly line in a car manufacturing plant

Robots are not worried about the amount of paint fumes in the air.

● Testing engines (sensors take measurements of timing and engine emissions).

The introduction of robots to the car assembly line has resulted in increased production (an assembly line produces cars 24 hours a day, every day). The quality of the finished cars is consistently good, which should impress customers who buy the cars, and satisfied customers are more likely to return!

Figure 24.7 Robots spray-painting bodies of cars

In an **embedded system**, a built-in programmed microprocessor controls devices. The microprocessor is dedicated to a particular task (unlike most computers which can be programmed at different times to perform many different tasks).

Embedded systems

An embedded system is a device that contains a ROM chip. Stored on this chip is a program that controls the functions of the device, which are dedicated to a particular job. It is not normally possible to program it to do another job.

You can find many examples of embedded systems in the home: washing machines, microwaves, televisions, cookers, etc. All of these have embedded chips that control their actions.

Bionics

Bionics is the attempt to link machines to living things. In medicine, this could be giving a person an artificial limb that can be controlled by the human brain. In some cases, the replacement is stronger and more durable that the original. Scientists are trying to advance medical treatment by creating more and more lifelike parts of the human body to help prolong life and to help people recover from accidents and disease.

If machines were developed that were capable of being controlled by the human mind this would eliminate costly and sometimes complicated input devices such as keyboards, mice and so on.

Computer control in hospitals

Computer systems are used for many different reasons in hospitals, but one of them is to control equipment. Important examples of this are controlling life-support systems in intensive care units or in premature baby units. Doctors and nurses are very busy people and computer-controlled systems remove some of their workload and allow them to carry out duties other than constantly monitoring a patient's condition.

Computers are used to control life-support equipment in hospitals because they are more dependable than humans.

The inputs are from sensors. The outputs are signals to alarms or large monitors.

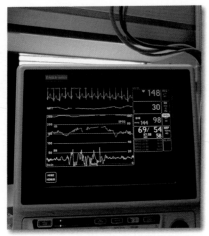

Figure 24.8 Output from the intensive care monitoring system is displayed on large monitors for easy viewing

Medical control systems are run by dedicated computers as they must not be affected by other applications.

Sensors attached to the patient measure:

● pulse rate

● temperature

● blood pressure

● blood gases (such as oxygen)

● breathing rate.

The readings are taken at regular intervals (fractions of a second) and are used as inputs to the computer system. If any of the readings falls outside an acceptable range, an alarm is sounded so that treatment can be immediately given.

The readings are output in the form of a graph displayed on a large monitor easily visible to nurses and doctors in attendance. Any changes are apparent and the state of the patient can be quickly assessed. Control signals may also be output to sound an alarm.

The advantages of medical control systems are:

● continuous monitoring of patients

● automatic alarm systems

● reduced chance of human error due to tiredness

● nursing staff freed to perform other duties.

The disadvantage of medical control systems are that the initial costs of buying and installing the systems are expensive.

The control system is an example of a real-time system. The computer processes the data as soon as it is received because it must check immediately whether an alarm needs to be sounded. The computers running a control system are **dedicated** computers. They constantly run the control program and cannot be used for anything else.

Power cuts are a serious problem to hospitals and could result in patient death, so back-up generators are used to make sure there is an uninterrupted power supply. Additionally, in case of breakdown, hospital administrators make sure there are always spares readily available.

CAD/CAM systems

Every object that is manufactured, from the smallest bottle top to the largest aircraft wing, must have been designed by somebody. The size, shape, colour and material must have been thought about and decided upon. It is easy to forget this when we are surrounded by so many material objects.

Computer-aided design

It is not only objects which have to be designed: designs are needed for kitchen layouts, motorway signs, housing estate plans and many other uses. There are software packages that help designers in their work. CAD stands for **computer-aided design** and CAD packages use computers to make the process of design simple and quick. CAD packages use vector graphics to create designs.

Designs are displayed on a monitor and can be edited using a mouse or a graphics tablet. Finished designs can be saved and printed out using a printer or, for larger designs, using a graph plotter. Some CAD packages use touch-screen monitors.

Figure 24.9 Complex designs are easier to draw using CAD software

Using a CAD package, a designer can:

- draw and edit shapes and lines
- work in two (2D) or three (3D) dimensions (and convert between them)
- render colours and textures onto shapes
- add pre-drawn shapes, components such as cogs, or clipart
- perform transformations, such as stretch and rotation
- zoom in to edit small details
- view 3D models from different angles.

Some CAD packages allow calculations. For example, you might design a building and be able to test the amount of stress at various key points. The model may then be coloured to show the high stress areas. Areas and volumes of shapes are easily calculated so the amount of material needed to make the model can be found. Some CAD software produces bills of materials so that production of the model can be costed. CAD packages for designing electronic circuits may allow you to test the circuits in advance of building the real thing.

The advantages of using CAD software are:

● Much faster development of designs: Pre-drawn components speed up creation of designs, as they do not have to be drawn from scratch.

● Three-dimensional views of models: 3D views cannot easily be drawn on paper. The angle of view can be changed so you can see the model from all sides.

● Easy editing: This allows for experimentation with the design as features can be tried out and edited if they are not appropriate.

● Designs or parts of designs can be saved and re-used in other projects.

● Fast and automatic calculation of quantities, such as stress in a building.

Once a design is finished it can be saved and printed on a printer. More usually, designs are output to a graph plotter which can draw on large pieces of paper. Designs can also be fed into a computer-aided manufacturing (CAM) process.

> Computer numerical control (CNC) machines receive instructions from CAD software as a sequence of numbers and can be used for CAM.

Computer-aided manufacturing

Output from a CAD design can be converted into a sequence of instructions for special types of computer numerical control (CNC) machine. The CNC machine then manufactures the item.

CNC machines include:

● lathes for turning metal or wood

● milling machines for cutting metal shapes

● drills for making circular holes

● welding machines

● soldering machines for creating electronic circuit boards

● knitting and sewing machines for manufacturing garments

● robots.

Figure 24.10 A milling machine may be used as part of the CAD/CAM process to shape a metal object

CAD/CAM is the term used for the whole process of using a computer to design an object and then outputting the finished design to a CNC machine, which manufactures it.

Computer-controlled machinery produces accurate results and minimises wastage. More importantly, it does the job consistently. The manufacturing process can be continuous and changes in design can be made with little interruption to the manufacturing process.

> CAD/CAM greatly speeds up the process of designing and manufacturing.

○ Booking systems

Whether booking a holiday in a Spanish villa, a flight to Paris, or a seat in a theatre, the chances are that a computerised booking system is used to make the reservation.

Case study: Theatre booking system

Theatregoers can reserve seats for performances of shows by telephoning the theatre or by using an online website. They can check whether seats are available on a particular day and where in the theatre they can sit.

The person booking the seats needs to input data about:

● the number of seats they want to reserve

● the time and date of the performance

● their details (e.g. name, address, telephone number, etc.)

● their card details for payment.

If suitable seats are available then they can be booked. Payment is normally made by credit or debit card. Tickets for the show can be mailed to the customer. The system also needs to cater for people who turn up on the day of the performance and buy tickets at the door.

Theatres may offer a service where customers can input their email addresses and have information sent to them about shows being performed in the future.

A large database needs to be stored on the theatre's computer, which has details about every seat in the theatre for every performance of every show that takes place. A typical record in this database may look similar to this:

Field	Field Value
SeatID	R32
Date	16/08/10
Time	19:30
Price	£12.00
Available	NO
CustomerID	JenkinsJD

This record shows that Mr Jenkins has booked seat number R32 for a 7.30 p.m. performance on 16/08/10.

When a customer contacts the theatre and wants to make a booking, the database is searched to find seats that are available for the requested performance. If the booking is confirmed, then the customer's details are entered into the record, those seats are shown as being no longer available, and the record is saved.

This needs to be done immediately in case somebody else wants to book the same seat for the same performance. The database must be updated as soon as the booking is made so that users of the system are always looking at up-to-date information about seat availability. The system is therefore a **real-time** system.

The advantages of a booking system are that:

● There should be no double-booking of seats, where two people book the same seat at the same performance on the same date.

● There can be a fast response to queries about seat availability from customers.

The disadvantage of a booking system is that the initial costs of buying and installing the system are high.

Online booking systems

Many booking systems are web-based and bookings can be made through the internet. A theatre may have information about its performances on a website where you can check if seats are available and what their prices are.

Some websites can look for seats in a number of different theatres, so if you cannot find what you want in one theatre, it may be available in another.

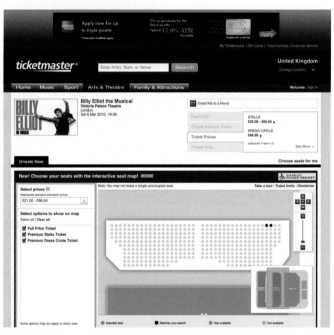

Figure 24.11 Many ticket agencies have websites where available seats can be searched for and bookings can be made

Multi-user systems

Some booking systems are operated as a multi-access system. For example, each branch of a travel agency may have workstations connected to a central computer. The agency branches may be all over the country and the main computer may be in London. Each branch computer has a network link directly to the main computer, which has a database storing the booking database.

Summary **S**

- Process control in industry has replaced humans in many repetitive or dangerous jobs.
- Input is from sensors and output is in the form of control signals to operate machines.
- Feedback provides a stable environment for a process.
- Process control provides uninterrupted processing with consistent results.
- Process control is an example of a real-time system.
- Robots have replaced humans in doing repetitive or dangerous jobs.
- Robots are programmed to repeatedly perform a sequence of tasks.
- Industrial robots can assemble, lift and carry, weld, spray paint, or handle tools such as drills or grinders.
- Robots allow uninterrupted production to a consistent standard.
- Embedded systems have programmed chips which carry out tasks.
- Computer systems control life-support machines in hospitals.
- CAD/CAM is the process of using computers to design and then manufacture objects.
- CAD is used to draw and edit a design in three dimensions using a vector graphics program.
- Completed designs are sent to CNC machines, such as milling machines or lathes, which manufacture the item.
- The whole process of design and manufacture is fast.

Practice questions 24 **P**

1 Robots are often used in car manufacturing to perform a number of different tasks when making cars.

(a) Describe **three** different jobs that robots can do. [3]

(b) Give **three** advantages of using robots. [3]

(c) Give **two** disadvantages of using robots. [2]

2 Life-support systems are used to monitor patients in hospitals.

(a) State **three** sensors used in a life-support system. [3]

(b) Give **three** advantages of using a computer-controlled life-support system. [3]

3 State what the following abbreviations stand for:

(a) CAD [1]

(b) CAM. [1]

25

Chapter

Stock control and order processing

In this chapter, you will learn more about stock control and the way in which computers can be used to bill customers. You will also learn about expert systems.

Figure 25.1 Stock control in a warehouse is important

Most large shops now have automatic stock control systems to make sure none of the items they sell runs out or is over-ordered. Customers will not be happy if the item they want to buy has run out and they will probably take their custom elsewhere. There is also a problem for the shop if they stock too many of an item. Unsold goods are a source of waste and unnecessary expense, as they may have to be removed from the shelves to be replaced by more desirable items. Supermarkets have a problem with perishable goods if they are not sold before their "sell-by date".

It is not just shops that have stock control systems. Factories need to keep stock of the raw materials they use, offices need to keep stock of their stationery and warehouses must keep control over the stock levels of their finished goods. An effective stock control system maximises the profitability of a business, minimises unnecessary expenditure and avoids wastage or supply problems. The stock level of an item is the number of that item remaining. Computers keep an up-to-date record of the stock level of every item. Stock control is the administration of stock levels.

A good stock control system will:

- keep track of the stock levels of all goods
- order more goods from the supplier if the stock level falls below the re-order level
- analyse which items are selling well and which are not; re-order levels may be adjusted on the basis of this information
- analyse sales patterns: there may be a need for seasonal adjustment for some items, for example, there may be more need for shops to stock umbrellas in the winter and sunglasses in the summer.

Stock control system

In a supermarket or large shop, input data is collected from a POS terminal, where barcodes or sales tags are read on each item sold.

Large stores or supermarkets may have a **real-time transaction** stock control system where every sale is processed immediately the data is input and stock levels are adjusted. Orders for new goods are automatically sent to the supplier without human intervention and goods are delivered the next day or as soon as possible.

Other shops may operate a **batch-processing system** where there is a stock master file holding details of all the goods the business either sells or buys. One record of the master stock file may look similar to this:

> A **stock master file** is a permanent file with details of all items sold or bought by the business, including the stock level (i.e. how many of the items are currently stored).

Field	Field Value
Stock ID	B67820
Description	T-Shirt (Blue) Large
Selling Price	£8.99
Stock Level	17
Reorder Level	10
Supplier	Casual Wear Ltd

This is a very simplified record and many more fields would be stored, such as the date of the last sale of the item and the amount usually ordered from the supplier. If the stock level falls below the re-order level, then an order for more of that stock needs to be sent to the supplier.

Whenever an item is sold, a record is created and stored in a transaction file. One record of a transaction file may look similar to this:

Field	Field Value
Order Number	32554
Customer ID	ThompsonJD
Transaction Type	Sale
Stock ID	B67820
Quantity	2
Date/Time	12/01/2010 11:32

> A transaction file is a temporary file of recent sales or purchases. The transaction file is used to update the master file.

Mrs Thompson bought two large blue T-shirts costing £8.99 each at 11.32 a.m. on 12 January 2010. After this transaction has been processed, the stock level for this item is reduced from 17 to 15.

For factories and warehouses, anything that causes a change in the stock level of an item is recorded as a transaction. This may be anything from using 50 kg of onions to make pickle or receiving a new consignment of 20 cm iron bolts.

At the end of each day, the transaction file is used to update the stock master file. The transaction file is first sorted into the same order as the stock master file and each record of the stock master file is input, adjusted if necessary and then stored on a new stock master file. Sales reports can be produced giving total sales figures or a list of the best-selling items. Most importantly, a report of all items that need re-ordering is output. Some companies may order new items over the internet using e-commerce websites.

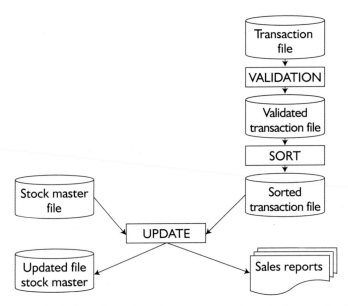

Figure 25.2 A flowchart for the process of updating a stock master file

Billing systems

From the smallest one-person business to the largest global companies, an accurate and reliable billing system is the lifeblood of a business. The survival of a business depends on customers paying their bills for goods or services, so they must be presented on time and they must be accurate. If customers are irritated by bills that are incorrect, they will take their business elsewhere.

A billing system produces bills for customers at regular intervals; possibly every month, or every quarter (three months). We do not get a bill for electricity every time we turn a light on in the house. Instead, the usage is measured and we receive a bill at the end of the

quarter. Similarly, regular customers of a retail business may receive a bill for all the goods they have bought over a given time period.

A billing system must perform the following main tasks:

- keep records of all goods or services purchased by customers
- keep accurate records of customer details
- produce accurate bills for customers at regular intervals
- print customer statements of all business transactions
- process payments received
- keep the company accounts updated.

Data capture

At the heart of a billing system, there is a database (master file) that consists of a number of different related files, for example:

- The **customer accounts file** contains all the details about customers, such as their account number, name, address, telephone number, amount of money billed this year and total amount of money paid.

- The **transactions file** contains records of all the purchases or services requiring billing.

The methods of data capture depend on the type of business that a company carries out. A retail business may receive orders online through emails or from a website. Public utilities such as telephone, water or electricity companies, have meters that monitor usage of their services. A **turnaround document**, such as an electricity meter reading form, with the customer's name and address printed on it is created by a computer to record a new meter reading. The form is fed into an OCR reader to input the data.

Other systems may be used, but whatever method is used, the data is recorded in a **transaction file**, which is needed at the end of the time period to produce the bills.

Validation checks are made on the data as it is entered to make sure that the data is sensible. It is important that customers do not receive extremely large bills because incorrect data has been input; if they do, the complaints line will be very busy!

Processing

The first part of the update process is to sort the transaction file into the same order as the master (customer accounts) file. The master file is updated using the transactions file at the end of the period. Invoices are printed and sent out to all the customers.

Reports are also printed to help the accounts department keep track of the company's finances. These include data on total payments made and how much is still owing from customers who have not made payments yet. The billing system is an example of a **batch-processing system**.

Bills to customers must be accurate and on time if a business is not going to lose customers.

A turnaround document is one that is output by a computer and then used as an input document using an OCR or OMR reader.

Data validation is used to check that data is sensible before it is processed. Typical validation checks are range checks, presence checks format checks and the use of check digits.

A billing system is an example of a batch-processing system. There is no immediacy for processing and no human intervention is required once the processing has started.

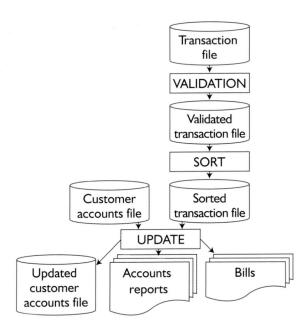

Figure 25.3 A flowchart for a billing process

Artificial intelligence

Artificial intelligence (AI) gives systems or machines the appearance of being intelligent. They behave in a way that in a human would be described as intelligent. Scientists hope that one day there will be intelligent robots to clean houses, repair machines, drive cars and so on but, except in films, this has not become a reality though many advances have been made. Various useful systems have been devised which could be called AI such as:

- chess-playing machines
- systems that can read handwriting or understand speech
- systems that can recognise objects or human faces
- systems that examine the way people walk and deduce their intentions.

One use of AI is in expert systems.

Expert systems

An expert system takes the place of a human expert. There are many expert systems around. They help miners to find metals or gold, astronauts to repair their spacecraft and computer owners to fix their computers. Another use of expert systems is in medicine.

An expert system simulates the knowledge and skill of an expert:

- It has a large database of knowledge.
- It allows the database of knowledge to be interrogated. Search tools can quickly find information.

An expert system takes the place of a human expert.

● It has an inference engine. This is a clever piece of software that allows the computer to make deductions based on the facts that have been input and the data in the knowledge database.

The program that runs the expert system is written using an artificial intelligence language such as Prolog.

Expert systems in medicine

Imagine discussing your medical problems with a computer instead of a doctor. The computer might suggest a diagnosis of your disorder, recommend a course of treatment and print a prescription for medicine. Is this a glimpse of the future? No, it is happening now, and not just in medicine! Computers are taking the place of experts in a variety of different fields. However, it is the intention that expert systems will help doctors rather than replace them. Computers have limitations!

In medicine, expert systems are being used to diagnose illnesses. A large database of diseases and their symptoms is stored in a database. A patient answers a sequence of simple questions by typing in the answers at a keyboard or possibly using a touch-screen device to select one of a number of options. The responses are analysed by the expert system and the inference engine uses a set of rules to make deductions about the probable illness. It may assign probabilities to each diagnosis and may also output recommendations about treatments or medicines.

Expert systems are not replacing doctors but are being used to help them. There are ethical and legal reasons for this: if a computerised diagnosis is wrong, who do you sue?

Figure 25.4 Web-based medical diagnosis expert systems are available

The advantages of an expert system are that:

- The knowledge in the database can be far more than a human is capable of remembering. New data can be added at any time as new medical research is undertaken. This is an advantage for the doctor as there is no need to learn as much information.

- The expert system should never get facts wrong. This is an advantage to the patient as humans make mistakes and may not be able to remember important facts correctly.

- Human experts retire when they get old. The expert system lives for ever, with no loss of knowledge, and may evolve into bigger and better hardware and software.

- Some people would prefer to enter personal data into a computer than discuss them with a doctor.

The disadvantages of an expert system are that:

- Some people may prefer the personal touch of discussing medical matters with a doctor. They may feel the doctor is more likely to understand their personal feelings and be more sympathetic.

- Expert systems are not cheap and considerable expenditure is needed to install one.

> An expert system can store far more information than a human and can "remember" all of it perfectly.

Summary

- Stock control is the administration of stock levels.
- Stock control makes sure there is no wastage and that nothing runs out.
- Some stock control systems operate as real-time transaction systems.
- Order processing is the administration of customer orders.
- Billing systems administer the sending of bills to customers and receipt of payments.
- A customer accounts file is updated using a file of recent transactions.
- A turnaround document is output by a computer and used as an input document with an OCR or OMR reader.
- Validation checks must be carried out to make sure data is correct.
- A billing system is an example of a batch-processing system.
- An expert system takes the place of a human expert.
- Expert systems are programmed using artificial intelligence languages.
- An expert system interrogates a large database of knowledge and makes deductions.
- An expert system can store more knowledge than a human and can remember all of it perfectly.

Practice questions 25

1 Give **two** benefits of using a computerised expert system instead of a human expert. [2]

2 For each of the following, state whether it is an example of a real-time, a batch-processing or an online real-time transaction system:

  (a) theatre booking system

  (b) billing system

  (c) process control in car manufacturing

  (d) payroll. [4]

26

Chapter

Safety in organisations

In this chapter, you will learn more about the various acts of parliament that have been made to help us live and work with computers with some confidence that our personal data is not being abused or exploited by someone. You will also look at ways of keeping data safe and secure.

Securing data

> Loss of important data is really bad news for businesses.

Security is a major issue with most businesses and organisations. The problems that arise with the loss of important data could have serious consequences for a business and may result in:

- loss of customers – unhappy customers will go elsewhere
- payments for goods may not be received
- bad publicity – a business relies on its good reputation
- cash-flow problems as the accounting system breaks down
- management unable to make decisions due to lack of information.

If data is secure then:

- It cannot be destroyed.
- It cannot be accidentally or maliciously altered.
- It cannot fall into the hands of unauthorised people.

Data is often stored on the hard drives of computers, so it is important that the computers themselves are safe. There are a number of physical methods of making sure that data on computers is secure and there are also some software methods.

Physical security methods

Computers need to be protected from natural disasters such as fire and flood, as well as from deliberate damage or theft. If a computer is damaged or stolen then so is the data stored on it.

Locks

Computer rooms should be locked and only authorised people with keys should be allowed to access them. Computer rooms should not be on the ground floor where people can see the equipment by looking through windows. It is also important to make sure that windows are locked.

Some computers have cases with locks which prevent them being switched on. Computers may also be bolted or attached by a strong steel cable (with a lock) to a desk so they cannot be stolen.

Figure 26.1 Computers can be attached to furniture by strong steel cables

Locking computer rooms and strong cabling makes it difficult to steal computers.

Alarms

Burglar alarm systems should be in place for computer rooms or rooms where important or valuable equipment is stored. Sensors should detect any attempt to enter the room and respond by sounding an alarm. Fire-protection systems should sense if a fire starts and attempt to control it by using non-water methods (possibly filling the room with a gas such as carbon dioxide).

Identification

A computer system sometimes needs to be able to identify the person trying to get access to the room or the computers.

To gain access to a room a user may have to swipe an identity card through a card reader. The card reader is connected to a computer system, which checks that the user is authorised to enter, before opening the door.

Biometric systems use physical characteristics, such as voice recognition, to identify a user.

Figure 26.2 An identity card may need to be swiped through a card reader to gain access to a room

Software security methods

Authentication means identifying a person and verifying that they are who they claim to be.

Password system

One way of identifying a user is a password system. Every authorised user of a computer system is given a username, which can be recognised by the system. Each user also has a password that must be entered every time they log in. The computer only allows access to a username and password that it recognises.

Single files can be password-protected. The user has to enter a password before being allowed to use the file.

Back-ups

> A back-up is a duplicate copy of a file kept in case the original is lost or corrupted.

Important data should be backed up regularly. This means making a second copy of the data. If a problem arises with the data file, then the back-up copy can be used instead.

Back-up copies of data files can be made locally (the back-up is saved on the same computer hard drive as the original) but there is no point keeping the back-up on the same computer if that computer is stolen!

Back-up copies can be made on removable media such as CD, DVD or tape cartridge. The back-up copy of the data should be kept in a secure place, such as a locked room or a fireproof safe, and preferably in a different location to the original.

Many organisations back up their data every working day. Computers can be scheduled to make back-ups at regular time intervals (possibly every night when the computers are less busy).

Encryption

Data can be changed into secret codes so that it is not readable by anyone who does not have authorisation. This is called **encryption** and it is a good way of making sure that sensitive or personal data accessed or intercepted on a network cannot be used.

> Encryption means encoding data to make it unreadable for anyone other than the intended user.

The intended user of the data must have a way of decoding the data. For example, credit card account numbers are encrypted when sent over the internet. If the data is intercepted by a hacker, it is meaningless.

File attributes

There are some characteristics of a file, called the file attributes, which the user can set. One of them is a "read-only" attribute. If this is set, then the file can be viewed but cannot be changed. Many data problems are caused by users accidentally changing or deleting files and the setting of the read-only attribute prevents this happening.

Figure 26.3 Setting a file's read-only attribute prevents it from being accidentally changed or deleted

Monitoring

Systems can be monitored to see what is going on. For instance, if you have a network then almost certainly the system keeps track of who is using what software, who is logged on and when and so on. The history of web pages accessed is almost certainly kept.

If something goes wrong then it is possible to track what was happening at the time. This helps the technicians to solve the problem and put the system right again. These files are known as **logs**.

> A **transaction log** is a history of actions executed since the log was turned on.

○ Legal and ethical issues

The progress of ICT has been rapid over the past 30 or 40 years and society has been forced to make many changes because of it. However, some of these changes happen slowly, such as the changes in the legal system and there are many areas in law that are rather vague when it comes to applying them to ICT systems. A number of notable UK laws apply to computer users.

As well as the laws discussed below, other laws have been introduced to help regulate the huge increase in the use of computers and the crimes that have followed. You have already looked at the Copyright, Designs and Patents Act (1988) (see Chapter 13) which makes it illegal to copy software without the permission of the owner. This means that copying games and downloading music and films is an offence unless you have paid or been given permission to do the copying.

The Data Protection Act

> The Data Protection Act states some obligations for organisations storing personal data and some rights of the data subject; there are some exemptions.

The first Data Protection Act was passed in 1984, but a revised version was introduced in 1998. The main provisions of this act came into force in 2000. The original act was introduced because so much data about people was being stored on computer systems and existing legislation was not appropriate.

The act deals with **personal data**: data held about a person. There are many organisations and businesses that may hold personal data on each of us. Here are some examples:

● the tax office

● a doctor or a dentist

● the Driver and Vehicle Licensing Agency (DVLA)

● the police.

The Data Protection Act states that the data subject (the person whose personal data is stored) has certain **rights** and the organisation that stores the data has certain **obligations**. When an organisation needs to store personal data, it needs to register with the Data Commissioner and state the purpose for which they need the information.

The obligations of the organisation storing the data are:

- to store and process data only for a lawful stated purpose
- to collect and process data fairly and lawfully
- to keep only adequate and relevant data, not excessive for the stated purpose
- to meet the rights of the data subject
- to keep accurate and up-to-date data
- to keep data no longer than necessary
- to keep data secure
- not to send data abroad, other than to EU countries.

The data subject has rights of:

- access: to view the personal data stored about them
- correction: to have incorrect data changed
- compensation: if unlawful processing of the data leads to damage or distress.

> Incorrect data can lead to you being refused a loan, not given a job or even arrested.

The act also defines **sensitive personal data**, which must not be disclosed or processed without the subject's knowledge and permission, unless it is necessary for other legal reasons. Sensitive personal data includes data about the subject's:

- racial or ethnic origin
- religious beliefs
- political opinions
- trade union membership
- physical or mental health
- offences and convictions.

Not all organisations have to register their use of personal data.

Exemptions from the Data Protection Act include:

- data held for purposes of national security
- data which helps in the detection of crime
- data for home use (household or recreational)
- data used for the calculation of wages, pensions or tax
- data used for the distribution of literature, information or advertisements.

Computer Misuse Act

> The Computer Misuse Act is legislation that makes hacking and creating or planting viruses illegal.

New laws have been necessary to combat new crimes that have emerged with the development of ICT. The Computer Misuse Act 1990 is a law that makes it illegal to:

- gain unauthorised access to files stored on a computer system, including viewing and copying the files – it is an offence to try to hack into a system even if you fail!
- gain unauthorised access to files and use them for criminal activities such as fraud or blackmail
- change or delete files unless authorised to do so –this includes creating or planting viruses as they may alter or delete files.

Electronic Communications Act (2000)

The Electronic Communications Act was introduced to set up a register of cryptographers, to help e-commerce and to recognise digital signatures as legal. This act has helped to build confidence in e-commerce.

A cryptographer helps to encrypt data so that it is meaningless unless you have a key to decode it. It is very useful in e-commerce as sensitive information such as people's credit card numbers and bank account information can be sent safely across the internet. Even if a hacker intercepts the data, it is meaningless.

Regulation of Investigatory Powers Act (2000)

The Regulation of Investigatory Powers Act makes it illegal to intercept emails, phone calls, letters and other communications without permission. This helps protect the individual from the state and means that groups, such as the police, cannot eavesdrop on conversations without special permission.

Health and safety legislation

You have already studied a number of health problems that can occur from using computers for a long time.

Health problems include:

- pain in the wrist caused by repetitive actions (RSI)
- pain caused by leaning on the elbow while using a mouse
- eyesight defects from staring at a screen all day
- deep-vein thrombosis (blood clots in the legs) from sitting still for too long
- general tiredness and stress from repeating the same activity over and over
- backache from incorrect posture and not using an adjustable chair.

Safety problems include:

- trailing wires which could trip you up or pull a computer off a table
- risk of fire or electrocution
- heavy equipment which might fall off a table or shelf and injure you
- food that lodges in keyboards and generates germs
- drinks that could spill onto equipment and cause electrocution
- proximity to water, such as having a computer near a water tap.

Legislation has been introduced to try to overcome these health and safety problems. The **Health and Safety at Work etc. Act (1974)** makes provision for:

- securing the health, safety and welfare of people at work
- protecting others against risks to health or safety in connection with the activities of people at work
- keeping and using dangerous substances
- controlling emissions into the atmosphere.

Computer crime

The increased use of computers and a general lack of knowledge about the computers being used have led to a number of crimes that might not have been considered before the widespread use of computers.

Almost everyone at some time or another will have received a **phishing** email. It pretends to have been sent by a bank, in which you may not be aware you have an account. The email asks you to send personal details to the bank. The purpose is to steal your identity. Once armed with your bank account details, your name and address, the phishers can apply for credit cards, buy goods, steal your money and so on. You must be as careful as you can with your data so that you do not become electronically cloned.

Personal data

As more and more data about us is held on computers, we need laws to govern that data and to try to prevent it falling into the wrong hands. The difficulties are that, with data held electronically, it is easy to search (and steal) enormous quantities of data in seconds and leave no trace.

Some people would like to know which famous people have health problems or convictions for crimes so that they can be blackmailed or so that the revelations can be sold to the newspapers. Our mobile phones and organisers are filled with information but if the phone should fall into someone else's hands all that information is now theirs.

Supermarkets and other organisations want to know all about us and our shopping habits so they use loyalty card schemes which allow them to record everything we buy. Our movements and purchases can be tracked using our credit card purchases and our mobile phone calls.

Hackers and computer viruses

The problems and possible threats posed by computer viruses and dangers from hackers have been discussed in earlier chapters.

In general, there will always be people who try to take advantage of someone else for their gain or gratification. Computer users and systems are always at risk. Good legislation and personal vigilance are needed to combat crimes associated with using computers.

Summary

- The Data Protection Act (DPA) deals with personal data.
- A data subject is a person who has data stored about them.
- Exemptions from the DPA include data used in national security, tax purposes or the prosecution of crime, household and recreational data, and data for the distribution of information, such as mail shots.
- Copyright law makes it an offence to copy a file without the permission of the owner or copyright holder.
- The Computer Misuse Act makes it illegal to hack into a computer system, use data files for purposes such as fraud or blackmail and create or plant viruses.
- The Electronic Communications Act set up a register of cryptographers and helped to build confidence in e-commerce.
- The Regulation of Investigatory Powers Act restricted the interception of communications.
- The Health and Safety at Work etc. Act makes provision for securing the health, safety and welfare of people at work.

Practice questions 26 (P)

1 A doctor's surgery stores personal information about its patients on its computer system.

(a) Name **three** fields of personal data other than name, address and telephone number that might be stored by the surgery. [3]

(b) Explain what the surgery would have to do to comply with the Data Protection Act. [2]

(c) Why could the surgery not pass on the data to an insurance company? [1]

(d) A patient is unhappy about the data stored about him on the surgery's computer and he demands to see it. The surgery refuses to show him. Who is in the right? [1]

(e) Name **three** types of data that are exempt from the Data Protection Act. [3]

2 What crimes are highlighted by the Computer Misuse Act? [3]

3 Complete the following table by placing a tick in the appropriate box to say whether the problem is an issue of health or safety. [6]

Problem	Health	Safety
Pain in the wrist		
Falling over trailing wires		
Electrocution		
Backache from playing computer games		
Failing eyesight from exposure to screens		
Stress		

4 Discus the various acts of parliament that have been introduced to help protect individuals and their work in the world of ICT. [6]

Introduction to the examinations

In this chapter, you will learn about the structure of the GCSE course and how the modules work together to create the GCSE qualification.

○ What is expected of you

The assessment of the GCSE is in two parts:

- The written exam is 40 per cent of the total mark.
- The controlled assessment element is 60 per cent of the total mark.

This applies to both the full and the short course.

> Coursework is the main part of the exam so you must make a good job of it!

○ Short course

Unit 1: Understanding ICT

This is the external assessment. It consists of one written paper which is 1 hour and 30 minutes long.

Unit 2: Solving problems with ICT

This is a controlled assignment that consists of a number of tasks for you to carry out based on a particular scenario. These tasks are worth 60 per cent of the total marks. The assignment tasks are set by WJEC.

The controlled assignment shows your attainment in:

- obtaining and interpreting different types of information
- using, developing and communicating information to meet a given purpose
- presenting the results of your work.

This assignment assesses the practical aspects of the functional elements of ICT.

○ Full course

For the full course, you take Unit 1 and Unit 2. In addition, you study and are examined in Unit 3 and Unit 4.

Unit 3: ICT in organisations

This is an additional external assessment. It consists of one written paper which is 1 hour and 30 minutes long.

Unit 4: Developing multimedia ICT solutions

This controlled assessment gives you the opportunity to develop a piece of work using multimedia software following a single task brief issued by WJEC.

Summary

	Short Course		Full Course	
Written exam paper	Unit 1	40%	Unit 1	20%
			Unit 3	20%
Controlled assessment	Portfolio of work (Unit 2)	60%	Portfolio of work (Unit 2)	30%
			Multimedia task (Unit 4)	30%
		100%		100%

Solving problems with ICT

In this chapter, you will learn about what is required to gain a good mark in Unit 2. You will find out exactly what you have to do and see examples of ways in which different types of evidence can be presented.

WJEC will set a different assignment each year.

This is a controlled assignment and should represent about 22.5 hours of practical work. WJEC will set a different assignment each year. There will be a number of tasks based around a given scenario.

You can see a sample task on the WJEC website. Go to www.wjec.co.uk and look for the ICT GCSE Sample Assessment Materials or ask your teacher if you can see an assignment from a previous year.

You will be assessed in the areas explained below.

○ Written communication

You are expected to use a high quality of written communication. This is assessed as an integral part of the marking so make sure all your written work is well done. Your written work is assessed under the following headings:

As you progress through the tasks of the assignment, you will make changes to your solution. It is a good idea to keep a log or diary of the changes you have made at the time that you make them, as this will help you in your evaluation.

- legibility of text: Your work must be neat and well presented. Most of your work will be word processed but where you annotate your work (for example, writing on it to show changes), you must make sure your handwriting is clear.

- accuracy of spelling, punctuation and grammar: Use the spell-checker of your word processor. If you are not sure how to spell a word, then ask!

- clarity of meaning: Make sure that what you have written is clearly explained and can be understood.

- selection of a form and style of writing: The way you present written work should be appropriate to the purpose and complexity of the subject matter and your audience. A party invitation is written in a different way from a letter ordering a new TV.

- use of specialist ICT vocabulary where appropriate.

○ Organisation of folders and files (*worth up to 5 marks*)

To gain these five marks, you should include evidence of the following:

● use of folders, subfolders and files with evidence of at least two different folder operations

● sensible naming of files and folders

● backing up work to an external device

● version management of your files

● organising emails, email groups and folders sensibly.

As you work, you will create a number of files. Each of these files should be given meaningful names and stored in sensibly named folders and subfolders. You should also be consistent with your names.

> You can see these three folders are subfolders of Healthy Eating

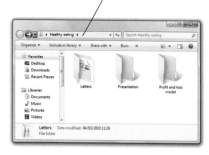

Be consistent!

If you have a file called "Letter to Mr Jones" then call a letter to Mr Evans "Letter to Mr Evans" not "Evanslet1".

Figure 28.1 Folders and subfolders with sensible names, containing files with sensible names

If you make a new version of a file then be careful to call the first one "version 1" or "v1", the next "v2" and so on.

Figure 28.2 Use version numbers on files you change

You need to provide evidence of at least two different folder operations, such as copying a folder, moving a folder to another place and renaming a folder. You should show that you have carried out some or all of these tasks by using screen dumps (see Figure 28.3).

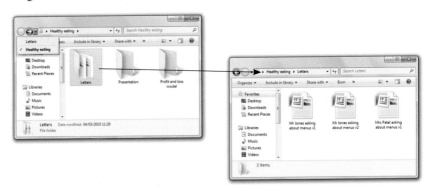

Figure 28.3 A method of showing evidence of your folders, sub-folders and files

As you have seen in the theory section of this book, it is very important to back up your work on a regular basis in case anything happens to the computer you usually work on. Using a memory stick or an external hard drive is best for this purpose. This is known as backing up to an external device.

○ Communicating information (*worth up to 16 marks*)

You need to create documents and presentations. To gain these marks, you need to include evidence of the following:

● a first draft of a document, annotated with comments

● a final version of the same document taking note of your annotated comments

● a presentation sequence showing a set of events using different sources of data

● use of appropriate page layout and formatting of data:

– fonts and font sizes and colours
– use of bold and text alignment
– word art or borders
– auto shapes
– simple tables or original templates
– bullets or numbering using internal facilities perhaps with sub-numbering

● inserting an image that is fit for purpose in a document and positioning, cropping or resizing it

- combining text with information in different forms from a library e.g. images, sound, video
- developing and formatting data, e.g.
  - enhancing tables with borders
  - merging cells
  - changing text direction or rotation
  - customised bullets
- using formulae in a document, such as an invoice
- using a different source for data such as a digital image, sound, an original graph or mail merge.

Creating documents or presentations

You should produce at least one draft and a final copy of each document or presentation. Use version numbers when saving; possibly include the word "final" in the last version, for example, **Mr Jones asking about menus final**.

> The audience referred to in ICT is the person or people who are to read your document or watch your presentation.

Take the example of writing a letter. The first time you do this, you will probably not get it exactly right. You may have phrased things badly, spelled words wrongly or even left out essential pieces of information. This is often referred to as your first draft. You may have to produce several drafts before you have a document or presentation that is fit for purpose. As you work, always bear in mind the audience you are writing for.

You should produce:

- at least one draft of each document or presentation
- copies of your documents or presentations showing comments made by reviewers

> All the evidence you produce must be accurate and believable!

- a final version of each document or presentation showing that you have responded to the comments made on the earlier versions.

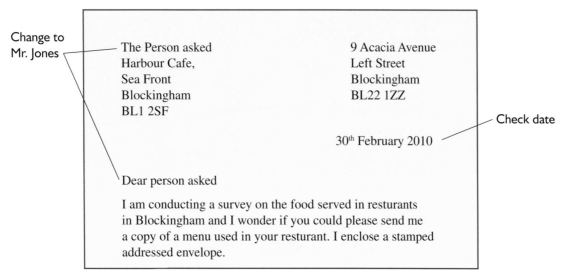

Change to Mr. Jones

The Person asked
Harbour Cafe,
Sea Front
Blockingham
BL1 2SF

9 Acacia Avenue
Left Street
Blockingham
BL22 1ZZ

30th February 2010 ⟶ Check date

Dear person asked

I am conducting a survey on the food served in resturants in Blockingham and I wonder if you could please send me a copy of a menu used in your resturant. I enclose a stamped addressed envelope.

Figure 28.4 This evidence is not accurate or believable!

You need to use appropriate page layout and formatting:

- page layout: make sure you fill the space provided and orient the page to landscape or portrait appropriately
- formatted data: take special care if the data involves numbers, currency or dates
- font styles and size of fonts: use sensibly and be consistent with fonts – too many different fonts just look a mess; use one style for headings and one for body text
- simple formatting techniques, e.g. bold, text alignment, colour, fonts
- WordArt, borders, auto shapes, simple tables or original templates
- bulleted lists or numbered lists.

You can gain extra marks by developing and formatting the data further using the following features:

- tables with borders, merged cells, vertical text direction or rotation
- images manipulated with cropping, sizing, flipping, or rotating (you do not have to use all of these)
- customised bullets (if you use numbered lists, try to produce some with sub-numbering)
- formulae in a document, for instance if you are producing an invoice
- headers and footers or page numbering.

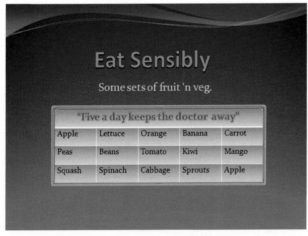

Figure 28.5 Some of the features that may gain extra marks: borders and merged cells within a table

Figure 28.6 A numbered list with sub-numbering

Using images, sound or video

Images, sound or video can enhance a presentation, help to keep the audience interested and draw attention to certain points.

However, you should be sparing in the use of any of these, so as not to confuse the audience. Make sure that the sounds and images you are using are fit for purpose.

You can insert:

● an image, positioning it carefully and cropping and resizing as necessary

● a sound and make it play automatically when a particular slide or image appears

● a video which can be set to play automatically or at the click of a button

● a graph which you have produced using a spreadsheet package or have found on the internet or some other source

● a macro which could be attached to a button.

Whatever you do to make your presentation more interesting, carefully build each slide with a combination of text and any of the above.

> A macro is a sequence of instructions that can be recorded, stored and given a name. The macro can then be run at any time. The instructions are executed in the given order. You can use the "record macro" feature to record and store a sequence of actions.

○ Modelling (*worth up to 16 marks*)

To gain these marks, you need to include evidence of the following:

● developing a model:
  – data entry
  – formatting data
  – a sensible number of decimal places
  – formulae
  – functions
  – relative and absolute referencing

● creating a chart or charts with appropriate title, legend, axis labels and formatting

● carrying out a "what if" investigation, changing data and formulae

● enhancing the layout and format of your spreadsheet by using:
  – borders
  – merged cells
  – text wrapping
  – headers or footers
  – forms

● using "goal seek"

● using pivot tables

● including macros

● testing your spreadsheet.

You may be asked to create and use a spreadsheet model. Spreadsheets are really useful for modelling as you have seen in the earlier chapters about spreadsheets. Now is the chance to use the knowledge you have gained. Remember, as with documents and presentations, your spreadsheet must be accurate and believable. Never make things up if you can do some research, ask some questions and use sensible data.

You should always remember to create your work with the audience in mind. As you develop and organise your data make sure that it is fit for purpose.

Data should be correctly formatted and you will be marked on your ability to use and format currency, percentages and decimal places.

Spreadsheets use formulae and you are expected to use formulae with single operators, though of course you can make the formulae as complicated as necessary to complete your task. You are also expected to use some of the built-in functions provided by the spreadsheet.

Operators you might use are:

```
plus, +
minus, -
divide, /
multiply, *
```

Functions you might use are:

```
SUM
AVERAGE
MAX
MIN
RAND
COUNT
LOOKUP
IF
```

Relative referencing and absolute referencing were explained in Chapter 10. If you are not sure about them then look back and see how they differ. For high marks, you need to include formulae with both types of referencing.

If you have to create charts, you must first decide which type of chart (pie, bar, line, etc.) shows clearly what you are trying to convey. Whichever chart you create, you must always use the following features when appropriate:

- title
- legend
- axis labels
- axis titles
- formatting.

If you are undertaking a "what if" investigation then, as well as changing data to see what effect that has on your spreadsheet, you should try appropriately changing one or more formulae. Whatever you change, you should give evidence of the before and after states of your spreadsheet and the results of making the changes.

Spreadsheets come with many built-in functions and you should try to incorporate some date and time functions. If you want to know what functions your spreadsheet has, use the "help" facility. Typing something such as "date function" into the help search box often gives references to other date and time functions and how to use them.

Make your spreadsheets attractive and also functional by using features such as

● borders

● merged cells

● text wrap

● headers or footers

● forms.

There is a wide variety of functions and advanced features which can be used in spreadsheets. You can get into the higher mark bands in this section if you use them. These include using IF or multiple IF functions, lookup functions, goal seek, pivot tables, macros, absolute referencing, multi-level sorts and so on.

○ Research and data collection (*worth up to 6 marks*)

To gain the marks in this section, you should include evidence of the following:

● using online information sources:
  – a specific URL used for a purpose
  – search engines
  – managing and using references to make it easier to find information again
  – downloading, organising and storing different types of information

● using other sources:
  – printed sources
  – other people.

You will almost certainly use the internet for research when carrying out your assignment. The important thing to remember is to record what you are doing using screen dumps and to keep the evidence you have collected, suitably named in a folder or folders, also suitably named, where you can find the information when you need it.

When showing your screen dump of evidence, make sure that the image shows the important information (see Figure 28.7). This is the evidence of your search and the results of the search.

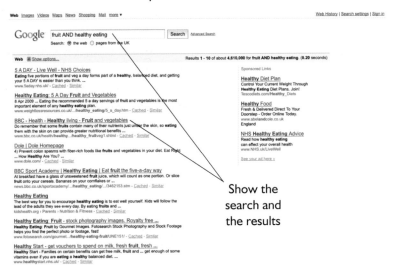

Show the search and the results

Figure 28.7 Evidence of a search

> Remember that **URL** stands for universal resource locator, the web page address.

Occasionally, you already know the address of the web page you wish to look up, in which case you already know its URL.

You may wish to include a link to a web page in a presentation. This is one way of using a URL for a purpose. When you provide your evidence make sure that it is clear what you have done. An example of evidence of using a link to a known URL is shown in Figure 28.8.

This is a hyperlink to http://blog.hotelclub. com/10-must-try- exotic-fruits/

Figure 28.8 Show your evidence clearly

You also need to use information sources other than the internet. These might be printed sources, such as books, magazines, menus or newspapers, and people (by interviewing or questionnaires). Whatever you do, keep notes of what or who you consult and provide the evidence that you did what you say you did. For books and other paperwork this could be in the form of noting the title, author, ISBN or other identifying information. For people, it might be the transcript or notes of an interview or a copy of a questionnaire used.

When you refer to a source of information in anything you are writing, make sure you acknowledge it.

○ Data handling (*worth up to 16 marks*)

To gain the marks in this section, you should include evidence of the following:

- importing data from a CSV file
- a range of basic skills, such as:
  - adding a key field
  - adding fields using suitable fieldnames
  - adding suitable data types
  - adding suitable data
  - editing and deleting a record
- obtaining information fit for purpose
- using a sort
- using a simple search
- a range of more advanced skills, such as:
  - creating an on-screen data entry form
  - adding a validation technique and testing that the validation works
  - using logical operators and at least one wild card
  - sorting on multiple fields (a complex sort)
  - using double searches (a search within a search)
  - using reports
  - using command buttons on forms
  - using macros
  - using Visual Basic enhancements.

If you have to use a database as part of your assignment, you may be provided with data as a CSV file by WJEC.

> In a CSV file, the data is provided as a number of comma-separated variables.

You will need to create a database file, give it a sensible name and import the CSV file into it. Whatever the assignment, you will be expected to carry out the following as a minimum:

● adding four extra fields, giving them suitable names and data

● choosing appropriate data types for each field

● choosing a key field

● making sure that all the data is accurate

● editing a field

● deleting a field.

Some of your data must be sorted to produce a list which is useful and meets some purpose in your assignment. You should also use simple searches to meet some useful purpose in the assignment.

To gain the top marks in this section you will also need to obtain information from the database using a double search (a search within a search), logical operators and wild cards.

Creating a database form which can be used to enter data into your database is a good way to gain extra marks. You should ensure that at least one of the fields has a validation rule attached to it and that it produces an error message if invalid data is entered. Remember to provide evidence to show all of this. One way of presenting this kind of evidence is shown in Figure 28.9.

> Use logical operators in your searches, such as **AND** and **OR**. Use wild cards, such as **LIKE** with *, # or **?**.

Figure 28.9 Evidence of a validation check

Email (*worth up to 6 marks*)

To gain the marks for this section, you should include evidence of the following where appropriate:

● opening an email

● saving emails efficiently

● creating and sending an email

● replying to an email

- sending an email to a group
- attaching a file to an email
- opening an attachment
- using a contacts list: adding amending and deleting entries
- forwarding an email
- adapting the style of the email to suit a particular purpose
- contributing to a blog or forum.

You will have an opportunity to create an email as part of the assignment. You should be familiar enough with emails by now, but of course you have to provide evidence that you know how to write and send an email. Show evidence of:

- opening, forwarding and replying to an email
- creating and editing groups of people from your address book and sending an email to a group
- attaching a file to an email and opening an attachment that you receive.

Make sure that any emails you write are written with an audience in mind. In this way, you will not upset anyone by appearing to be too casual with someone who needs a formal email or too formal with a friend. Always check the accuracy of any email you send and make sure that it appears plausible to anyone who reads it.

Don't forget that you get marks for organising your emails in folders.

You must show that you have a list of contacts and give evidence of adding, amending and deleting an entry in your contacts list (see Figure 28.10).

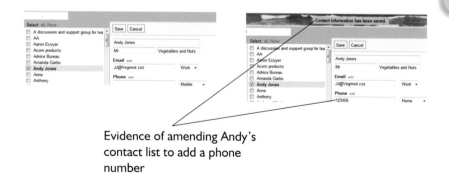

Evidence of amending Andy's
contact list to add a phone
number

Figure 28.10 Evidence of the use of a contacts list

You may be able to contribute to a blog or forum if it is relevant to your assignment. If you do so, then you should show evidence, probably using screen dumps.

○ Evaluation (*worth up to 15 marks*)

To gain the marks for evaluation, you should include the following:

- an evaluation of your working practices
- an analysis of the research methods you used and the data you collected
- comments on modifications you made as you developed the tasks
- an evaluation of any documents and presentations you produced
- an analysis of any data and information you used in modelling and data handling
- an evaluation of any other tools and techniques you used
- a review of feedback given and received
- any suggestions for improvements that you could make to anything you have completed for this assignment.

This section is where you discuss whether you think that what you have done is a suitable solution to the problems you were set and whether you think you have made a good solution. There are eight separate sections which you need to write about.

For any evaluation, you need to ask yourself a number of questions. These questions and answers form your evaluation. Be honest and sensible with your answers. There are no marks for just saying that you think you did everything perfectly. There is always room for improvement.

Since you need to comment on modifications you have made to your systems as you have progressed, keeping a log of changes you make as your assignments develop is useful.

Evaluation of working practices

This is where you analyse the way in which you carried out the assignment tasks. You think about what you did and then describe whether or not the method was successful or if you could have improved the way you worked. Here are some questions you might try to answer:

- Did you spend long enough on the tasks?
- Was the time between the tasks sensibly shared or did you spend too long on one task to the detriment of another?
- Did you work in a quiet place?
- Did you do all your research at school?
- Did you ask advice as often as you should or did you rely too heavily on advice?

- Did you use sensible file names and folders?

- Did you back up your work?

- Did you use sensible version numbers for files?

Remember that this is not a full list and you may think of other things to write about. If you have any criticisms of your working practice then try to describe how you could have improved. Write carefully and use full sentences.

Evaluation of my working practices

Generally, I felt that the way I carried out my tasks was good and worked well. Before I started the assignment, Mr Jones showed us how to draw up a plan where we assigned a certain amount of time to each task. I knew I had to spend about 22.5 hours on the tasks and there were six tasks in all. However, the tasks were not all worth the same number of marks. Also I knew that some tasks would be more difficult than others, so I gave more time to those.

. . .

I saved my work in folders with names associated with the tasks. After each name, I wrote the version number. Within the folder, I saved . . .

Figure 28.11 Evaluation of working practices

Analysis of research methods and data collected

You will probably be asked to collect data and to look for information about a number of things. This research can be carried out in a number of ways, such as looking in libraries, using the internet, talking to people and so on.

You will already have described how you carried out the research when you wrote up your tasks. Now is the chance to analyse how that research went. Here are some questions you might ask:

- Were your internet searches precise enough or did they produce millions of results? Could the searches have been refined?

- Did your questionnaires work and produce the answers you wanted? Was anything left out?

- Was the data collected sufficient for the purpose? Was it accurate and up to date?

- Did you plan interviews carefully enough?

- Would you change the way in which you collected data or information if you did the tasks again?

Don't forget that analysis includes what went wrong, what went right and how things could have been improved.

Comments on modifications made

As you worked, you will have made changes to whatever you were working on. Perhaps the data type of a file in a database or spreadsheet was changed or a question was added to a questionnaire.

You did these things for a reason. This is where you can look at the log you kept and comment on the modifications you made as you went along. For each change you can comment on:

● what the change was

● why the change was made

● whether the change worked or was helpful

● the consequences of the change.

Evaluation of documents and presentations produced

You will have produced at least one document and possibly a presentation. Whatever you have produced needs examining to decide whether it was appropriate and whether it worked.

For a document, such as a letter, a poster or a menu, you could ask such questions as:

● Did the information in the document convey the appropriate meaning?

● Did it work in relation to the audience?

● Was it accurate?

● Was the spelling and grammar correct?

● Did the layout and colour schemes work properly?

For a presentation, you could ask:

● Was the data in the presentation appropriate?

● Did the presentation slides have all the relevant information in them?

● Were the pictures or graphics used relevant?

● Was the presentation informative?

● Did it attract the attention of viewers?

● Was it easy to view the presentation from a distance (taking into account such factors as appropriate amount of text on slide, colour schemes, size and style of font, etc.)?

Analysis of data and information used in modelling and data handling

You will have used a database, a spreadsheet or possibly both. Some of the questions you could ask about a database are:

- Did the database allow you to find information easily and quickly?
- Was the data suitable and if so why?
- Were there any problems when using it and have they been sorted out?
- Was it easy to print out sorted lists?
- Did the database solve the problems asked?

Some of the questions you could ask about a spreadsheet are:

- Was the data used in the spreadsheet suitable?
- Have you made your spreadsheet so that it is easy to use?
- Did the spreadsheet produce accurate results?
- Did automatic calculations save work?
- Does it save time and if so, how?
- Did the spreadsheet solve the problems asked?

Evaluation of other tools and techniques used

If you have used any application packages or different techniques that are not listed above, you need to mention them here. You might have used email, or a graphics package to crop an image you produced using a digital camera. Base your questions and answers on those mentioned above so that you are critically examining what you did and whether what you did could have been improved in some way.

> I found the image of the banana on the internet but when I tried to enlarge it, it became highly pixellated. I think now I should have taken a picture of a banana using my digital camera. The quality of the image would have been much better and I could have edited the image without the pixellation.

Figure 28.12 Evaluation of other tools and techniques

Review of feedback given and received

While you were working on your tasks and after they were finished, you will have received feedback. Feedback consists of comments, written or spoken, that were made as a result of your work. Your response should be more than just "Mr Bloggs liked my menu"; it should include why he liked it or what he suggested could be improved.

> Mr Bloggs loved my letter. He said it was great!

✗

> Mr Bloggs loved my letter. He said that the way I had expressed the appeal in the second paragraph should certainly get me a number of favourable responses ...

✓

Figure 28.13 Evaluation of feedback

Suggestions for improvement

However good something is, there is always room for improvement and this is probably true of the way you have tackled the tasks in your assignment. Here are some possible questions to answer:

- Would any extra or different hardware be useful?
- Would any extra or different software be useful?
- Could you have made changes to the database, spreadsheet, documents or presentations, such as adding:
  - fields to the database
  - formulae to the spreadsheet
  - information to the presentation?
- Could you have followed up some of the feedback you received to improve your work?

Summary

S

Your work for this assignment is marked by the centre and moderated externally.

Section	Marks
File handling	5
Communicating information	16
Modelling	16
Research and data collection	6
Data handling	16
Email	6
Evaluation	15
Total	80

Remember that the quality of your written communication could affect your mark.

Chapter 29

Developing multimedia ICT solutions

In this chapter, you will learn about what is required to gain a good mark in Unit 4. As well as explaining exactly what you have to do to gain a good mark in this unit, this chapter also gives you some examples of ways to present your evidence.

WJEC will set a different assignment each year.

This is a controlled assignment and should represent about 22.5 hours of practical work.

You can see a sample assignment on the WJEC website. Go to www.wjec.co.uk and look for the ICT GCSE Sample Assessment Materials or ask your teacher if you can see an assignment from a previous year.

For the given task you will be expected to:

- research and analyse existing and contrasting websites or presentations
- analyse multimedia features used on existing websites or presentations
- design web pages or a presentation
- create navigation paths for six web pages or slides
- edit an existing template or slide style or design
- select and use a navigation bar or tool
- create two images and optimise and save them in an appropriate format for use in the web pages or presentation
- storyboard an animation or animated movie
- create an animation or animated movie
- create and manipulate sound or music.

You could gain extra marks using some of these additional techniques:

- web or presentation special effects
- animation effects

- movie effects
- sound effects
- interactive elements
- enhancement with original code.

You need to evaluate everything you have done, including:

- working practices
- the suitability and effectiveness of the features analysed
- tools and techniques used
- review of feedback given and received
- comments on modifications made
- suggestions for improvement
- effectiveness of final solution
- consideration of output to the web
- consideration of download times and file size
- justification of choice of image, sound and animation
- optimisation.

Your work will be marked using the sections outlined in the rest of this chapter. Some of it is very similar to the Unit 2 assignment and you should refer to Chapter 28 for reminders.

○ Quality of written communication

Everything you write is looked at for the quality of written communication.

The quality of written communication is assessed as an integral part of your evaluation and not as a standalone element. The following criteria are used:

- legibility of text: the accuracy of your spelling, punctuation and grammar and the clarity of meaning of what you have written
- selection of a form and style of writing appropriate to the purpose and to the complexity of the subject matter
- clear and coherent organisation of information
- use of specialist vocabulary where appropriate.

○ Efficient working practices (*worth up to 5 marks*)

You should include evidence of the following:

- use of folders, subfolders and files
- sensible naming of files and folders
- backing up of work to an external device
- version management
- a log of sources.

This section was discussed in detail in Chapter 28. If you are unsure about how to score these five marks, refer to Chapter 28.

In addition, you are expected to keep a log of sources. This is a record of the source of any data or other material you may use in your assignment. For instance, if you are using a page from a website, record the URL of the website and the reference to the page within the site. If you have used data collected from a book then record the book title, author and ISBN. A picture could be taken from a friend, the internet, scanned from a book or you might have taken it yourself but you should record where it came from.

○ Analysis and research (*worth up to 12 marks*)

You need to choose at least two websites to examine. These must be related to the subject matter of the controlled assignment that has been issued by WJEC. For example, if the task is to create a multimedia catalogue, you would need to look at two websites with multimedia catalogues.

You should include evidence of the following for each website or presentation:

- a description of:
  - the purpose
  - the house style
  - the target audience
- a comparison contrasting the design and layouts used in each website or presentation, including:
  - navigation
  - template design
  - hyperlinks or hotspots
  - anchors or bookmarks
  - rollover buttons

– pop-up comments

– mood colours

– number of pages

– interactive features

● a collection of the evidence of examples of multimedia features used on these websites or presentations including:

– banners or animations

– web icons

– digital images

– animations

– movies

– sound

● a description detailing the type and size of these features.

Your starting point is to go online and examine a number of sites with catalogues, looking for two that have contrasting features. Choose two contrasting sites and record the details of those sites.

I have chosen to compare the online catalogues of Amazon (www.Amazon.co.uk) and the New Modellers Shop (www.newmodellersshop.co.uk)

Figure 29.1 Contrasting online catalogues

Your analysis will probably take the form of an essay using images taken from the websites you are analysing.

The first section of the analysis will contrast the purpose, house style and target audience of the websites. It is important to choose two sites that are mostly different for these aspects or it will be difficult for you to find anything to write!

The two websites illustrated in Figure 29.1 are for Amazon, a general-purpose site that sells almost any type of goods, and the New Modellers Shop, which sells mainly to people who are interested in making models. In one, the target audience is all sections of the public, in the other the target audience is modellers.

For house style, look for:

● font style, sizes and colours for headings and body text

● the way bulleted or numbered lists are presented

● the justification of text in different areas

- the way illustrations are presented

- how the paragraphs are separated.

Companies like to have a corporate image so that people recognise pages belonging to that company. Colours and logos help with this as part of the house style.

Remember to illustrate your contrasts with images.

.... another way in which the sites are contrasted is with their use of logo and colour. The New Modeller Shop uses a complex logo which incorporates images of models:

The Amazon site uses a text-based image:

amazon.co.uk

Figure 29.2 Contrasting images

The second section of your analysis will consist of a contrast of the design and layouts used in each website including:

- navigation

- template design

- hyperlinks or hotspots

- anchors or bookmarks

- rollover buttons

- pop-up comments

- mood colours

- number of pages

- interactive features.

If you do not remember what all these terms mean, then refer to Chapters 12 and 18. Again, illustrate your answers where appropriate. If a site does not contain a particular feature, then say so.

The third section will consist of a collection of the evidence of examples of multimedia features used on these websites. This may include:

- banners and animations

- web icons

- digital images

- animations

- movies

- sound.

Some of these will be hard to illustrate – you cannot show a picture of a sound! You will need to use careful written descriptions when describing the features in this section and don't forget to detail the type and size of any features you are describing.

Design (*worth up to 5 marks*)

You should include evidence of the following in your design:

- identification of a solution to the multimedia task
- an explanation of how or why your solution is fit for purpose and audience
- a design of a master page style
- a design of mood colours.

You will have been set a multimedia task by WJEC and this is where you restate that task in your own words and identify your solution to the task. The contents of the solution are outlined below.

You are going to have to produce at least six web pages or multimedia slides. In this section, you describe the design of those web pages or slides. Your design should include sketches of the six slides or pages and an indication of what content is going on to each of these.

You need to show how the slides or pages are to be linked.

Think of who the multimedia presentation or web pages are for (the audience) and what is the purpose of these pages or slides and explain how or why your solution is fit for purpose and audience.

Design a master page which should include the following information about your slides or web pages:

- the theme (most packages provide a number of themes already set up and you could choose or adapt one of those)
- the general layout of the pages or slides
- the background style and colour
- fonts to be used for heading, body text and so on
- any special effects
- placeholder sizes for your headings, buttons and other items that will appear on every page and where on the page they will be positioned.

You need to design mood colours that depend on the purpose of your multimedia presentation and audience it is aimed at. When you have decided what colours to use, describe why you chose those colours and why you think they suit the mood of your presentation.

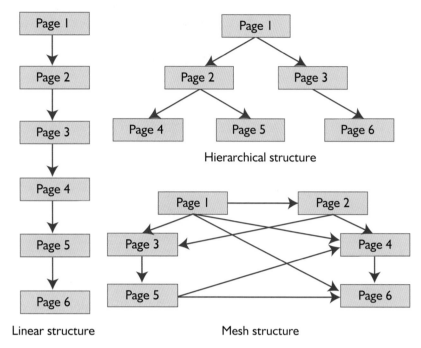

Linear structure   Mesh structure

Figure 29.3 Your layout will probably be like one of these (all pages will probably also contain a link to the home page)

○ Development – Template and navigation (*worth up to 12 marks*)

You will now start to develop pages or slides following the design you have created. You should include evidence of the following where appropriate:

● creation of navigation paths for six web pages or slides

● editing an existing template/slide style design

● use of house style colours

● selection and use of a navigation bar or tool

● use of navigation tools from a library of facilities provided by the software

● editing the standard navigation tool to include:
  – colour scheme
  – hyperlinks
  – icons
  – text fit for purpose.

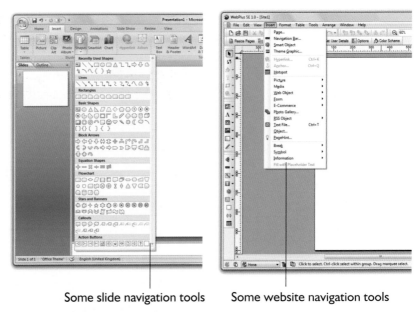

Some slide navigation tools   Some website navigation tools

Figure 29.4 Navigation tools

○ Development – Graphical images (*worth up to 10 marks*)

You should include evidence of the following:

- a logo or web icon that you have created
- a second image that you have created
- one of these images must be created with at least three layers
- both images should be optimised and saved in an appropriate format
- use of a range of software tools for example:
  - standard shapes and/or lines
  - fill tools
  - brush tools
  - text tools
  - selection tools
  - distortion tools
  - sizing or cropping tools
  - repeated patterning or cloning
  - transparency tools.

To score the marks in this section, you have to create a logo or web icon and a second image. Both of these need to appear somewhere in your multimedia presentation.

To show that you have created these images, it is not enough to just make them and insert them. You need to give evidence that you have used all or some of the tools and techniques listed above. You will find most of these tools in a good art or photo package.

The marks for this section are gained by your description of the development of your images.

One of your images must be created with at least three layers. Both of your images should be optimised and saved in an appropriate format.

Figure 29.5 Evidence of developing an image using layers

Development – Animation or animated movie (*worth up to 10 marks*)

You should include evidence of the following:

● a storyboard for an animation or animated movie

● an animation or animated movie that you have created:

    – an animation from clipart
    – a stop-frame animation
    – a Flash animation
    – an animated moving banner.

You need to include some kind of animation if you are to gain these 10 marks:

● You can create an animation from clipart using evidence of at least three different techniques (see Chapter 19). Use cloning, onion skinning or tweening and explain with examples when it is you are using each of these techniques. The moderator cannot guess which technique you are using.

> Don't forget to include your animation in your multimedia presentation and make sure it works. There should be a good reason for having this animation. The design should include where the animation appears.

● You could include a stop-frame animation. If you do, it should have at least three frames showing movement progressing.

● If you use a Flash animation, you should include at least three frames showing movement and an explanation of the timing or frame rate used.

● You can include an animated moving banner, which should combine both text and graphics, on a web page.

Whatever you decide to do, you should make sure that you describe what you did clearly and show evidence of producing what you have created. You should include a storyboard.

Development – Sound (*worth up to 3 marks*)

You should include evidence of the following:

● use of sound, music or narration

● editing of sound, music or narration to produce an original sound file.

An extra three marks can be gained by adding sound to your multimedia presentation. It could be sound effects, such as applause, jingles, appropriate noises to accompany images, or it could be a spoken narrative (commentary) to accompany the slides of a multimedia presentation.

Whatever you do, you need to describe what you did and how you edited the sound.

Development – Additional techniques (*worth up to 9 marks*)

You should include evidence of some of the following:

● web or presentation effects, such as:
  – rollover buttons or polygon hotspots
  – special effects added to objects, e.g. shadow, raised/outer glow
  – drop-down boxes or expanding and collapsing menus of at least two choices
  – hyperlinks in the form of text or graphics to external files
● animation effects, such as:
  – more complex animation of at least six frames or techniques
  – use of background or overlay frames
  – looping or repeating techniques

- movie effects, such as:
  - title or credits
  - video or transition effects
- sound effects, such as:
  - envelopes, echo, etc.
  - looping or repeating
  - overlay tracks
  - podcasting
- interactive elements from a library
- enhancement with original code, e.g. HTML or Visual Basic.

Other techniques or tools may be acceptable to WJEC, upon application.

You can gain up to nine marks with extra effects. Just remember that whatever you do to make your presentation or web page more interesting, you have to provide evidence so that your teacher and the external moderator know what you have done.

◯ Evaluation (*worth up to 14 marks*)

The controlled assignment may specify what should be evaluated but you could include the following:

- working practices
- the suitability and effectiveness of the features analysed
- tools and techniques used
- feedback given and received
- comments on modifications made
- suggestions for improvement
- effectiveness of final solution
- consideration of output to the web
- consideration of download times and file size
- justification of choice of image, sound and animation and optimisation.

When your pages and slides have been completed, you evaluate what you have done in a number of areas.

You are familiar with the process of evaluation as you undertook an evaluation at the end of your tasks for Unit 2. For Unit 4, the process is more detailed. You need to evaluate the items listed above if they are relevant to the solution you have produced.

Evaluation of working practices

You may be directed by the assignment to evaluate particular things.

This is where you describe the effectiveness and success (or not) of your file-saving techniques and back-up procedures. You should also include your log of sources here.

273

Look back to Chapter 28 for further information on the evaluation of working practices.

Description of the suitability and effectiveness of the features analysed

At the start of the assignment, you had to analyse two websites or presentations. Here is where you can describe whether or not the features you chose to analyse were useful and whether they helped you in the design of your own solution. Ask yourself questions and provide the answers. Did the websites you chose offer a variety of features? Were they sufficiently different to offer a reasonable comparison? How difficult did you find them to use?

Evaluation of tools and techniques used

Think of the tools and techniques you used to produce your solution. Were they easy to use? Did they produce an effective solution? Could you have used different software or tried something else?

"Tools" are usually thought of as the software applications you used, such as a web page editor or presentation software. "Tools" also include hardware such as a scanner or digital camera.

"Techniques" are the way you handled things within the tools you used. For instance if you produced an animation using an animation tool, did you use tweening? Was that technique useful or should you have used another technique?

Often these insights only come after you have created a solution and you can say to yourself, "If I did that again I would …"

Review of feedback given and received

While you were working on your tasks and after they were finished, you will have received feedback. Feedback consists of comments, written or spoken, that were made as a result of your work. Your response should be more than just "Mr Bloggs liked my website"; it should include why he liked it or what he suggested could be improved.

The assignment itself may give as an instruction, such as, "show your work to a friend and ask for their opinion". That opinion should be recorded here and you should comment on that feedback.

Comments on modifications made

As you worked, you will have made changes to whatever you were working on. Your web pages or slides will change from the original design as you find out what works or what does not. You may be dissatisfied with colour contrasts, for instance, when you implement your design and so you make modifications. The links you set up may no longer work to match your projected storyboard and you change them. For each change you should comment on:

- what the change was
- why the change was made
- whether the change worked or was helpful
- the consequences of that change.

Suggestions for improvement

However good something is, there is always room for improvement. Some suggestions will have come from the feedback you received from other people. You may not be satisfied with the final outcome and know that given more time or a different approach you could have made your pages or slides more interesting, better to look at or contain features such as sound or Visual Basic enhancements that you were not able to add because of lack of knowledge.

This is where you can allow yourself to imagine the wonderful pages you could have produced if only . . .!

Evaluation of effectiveness of final solution

When you have finished you need to step back, mentally, and ask yourself if your pages have effectively answered the original assignment. You will already have raised a number of points elsewhere in this evaluation section and here is a chance to summarise. Make sure that you do not give a facile answer to this section. If you think your solution was effective then say why it was and how you know it was. If you think that it could have been improved or changed then say why and how.

Consideration of output to the web

If you have created web pages you might have considered uploading them to a website. You could discuss here any difficulties you might have with that. Have you used copyright images, for instance, or opinions that might not stand international scrutiny? What are the difficulties of putting pages on a website? How will you achieve it?

Consideration of download times and file size

If you are going to place pages on the internet, what memory sizes are your pages? Have you used images which are very large (lots of megapixels) and so would take a long time to download? Will your users become frustrated waiting for your pages to load? What should you do to ensure that the pages you place in a website are a reasonable size and download quickly? Someone once said that more than two seconds waiting for an action to occur on a computer after a mouse click constitutes boredom!

Justification of choice of image, sound and animation, and optimisation

You should have included images and sound and you may have included some animation. This is a chance for you to explain why you chose those images and sound clips and why you chose a particular animation. You also need to say whether you think they are effective and, if so, why they are effective.

Don't fall into the trap of lumping all the images and sound together for this evaluation. Take each in turn and discuss it. Some images may have been effective and others may not have been.

With all of these things you should have reached a compromise between file size and quality of image or sound. This is known as optimisation and you should justify what you did here. For instance, if you want a web page to download quickly, you have to have reasonably small image sizes as opposed to using an image to produce an A3-sized family portrait to hang on a living-room wall.

Summary

Your work for this assignment is marked by the centre and moderated externally.

Section	Marks
Efficient working practices	5
Analysis and research	12
Design	5
Development – template and navigation	12
Development – graphical images	10
Development – animation or animated movie	10
Development – sound	3
Development – additional techniques	9
Evaluation and quality of written communication	14
Total	80

Remember that the quality of your written communication could affect your mark.

Chapter 30

Preparing for the examinations

In this chapter, you will learn about ways in which you can revise and prepare for the written examinations.

○ Revision

Have a revision plan and set yourself daily targets ... and rewards!

In the right atmosphere, revision can be fun!
Revise with a friend.
Set yourselves little tests.

Every chapter has a summary at the end. This could be a good revision starting point

It is impossible to remember everything you learn in lessons, and you will need to spend some time on revision: refreshing your memory on the topics that you have covered in the course. Revision for exams is your responsibility and it will not happen unless you make some effort!

The key to successful revision is planning and organisation. You will have other exams to sit and your ICT revision will need to be planned as a part of your revision for all of your exams. Make sure you do not run out of time or leave too much work to be done in the last few days.

First of all, get yourself a checklist of all the topics. Either make it yourself or download one from the website for this book. If you make your own, a spreadsheet is an ideal tool.

As you revise, you could try using the "colour code" technique. This involves shading a square alongside each topic, as shown in Figure 30.1.

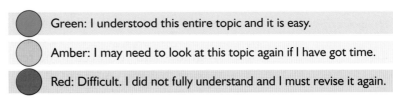

Green: I understood this entire topic and it is easy.

Amber: I may need to look at this topic again if I have got time.

Red: Difficult. I did not fully understand and I must revise it again.

Figure 30.1 The "colour code" technique

When you have read through all the topics, you will see the red and amber ones that need a second look. If you understand them better after a second revision, you can change the colour code.

If you are revising at home, do not work at it for too long at a time. Try to make revision an enjoyable task.

Revision tips

- Set yourself a time limit. About 20–30 minutes at a time is plenty. Several short sessions are better than one long one: "I will revise ICT for 20 minutes and have a break at 7.30 p.m."

- Give yourself rewards: "When I stop revising I will have a chocolate bar and a drink and sit and watch TV."

- If you are getting tired, take a break. Revision done when your brain is tired is not effective: you will think you have revised a topic but it has not really been absorbed.

- Set targets for your revision session and make a list of them. Cross them off when you achieve them. "I will learn this list of ten abbreviations and what they stand for."

- Find a quiet place. It can be unsettling at the start if you are used to blaring music, but you will get used to the calm. If you have to play music, use calming music without words and play it softly, just for the atmosphere.

Methods for revising

- Write out, or use a word processor, notes from a text book or copy out notes that you have made. You will learn them by writing them out. Short notes are easier to learn, so pick out the key points and write them down.

- Read your notes out loud.

- Make lists. It is easier to learn from lists than from a lot of text. Bullet points like the ones in this paragraph are handy for making lists of important points.

- Revise with someone else who is doing the same exam. Discuss topics you are revising and test each other . . . but you need to agree first that you are going to revise and not discuss next weekend's party! Some discipline is needed here!

- Try to do past exam papers. If you can get a copy of the answers then this will be useful, but if you are unable to answer a question or you are unsure of the correct answer, then ask your teacher.

The important thing is that you are as prepared as you can possibly be when you go into the exam. Not everybody is going to get top grades and you need to be realistic about your capabilities. Make sure that you come out of the exam and can say to yourself, "Well, I did the best that I could."

Before the exam

Hopefully, with a good revision plan, you have not left too much to do in the days leading up to the exam. It is important that you ease back and undertake light revision only.

One big mistake made by pupils is to spend a long time revising on the day before an exam. Don't! This tactic leads to mental exhaustion and you will not be able to perform your best on the day of the exam. It would be better to go out in the fresh air and take some light exercise, take the dog for a walk, get your football out and go down the park, or stroll along the beach with some friends.

A brief review of your notes in the evening and an early night is the recipe for success. Make sure you get a good night's sleep and you will wake up refreshed and ready to tackle the exam.

So remember:

- Late-night cramming sessions the night before the exam are definitely out!

- Blow the cobwebs away with some light exercise in the fresh air the day before an exam.

- Try not to get too stressed! It is important but it is not the end of the world.

There is one other important thing you need to do before the exam takes place. Find out exactly what time it starts and where you will be sitting it. You may be given a room and a seat number. It can be very stressful just before an exam, if you go to the wrong place at the wrong time!

○ Sitting the exam

You are sitting there with the exam paper in front of you and the invigilator tells you that you can start. Help!

You have done all the easy bits like filling in your name and exam number on the front cover and now the work begins.

You open the exam paper and see lots of questions and diagrams. You try to read the first question but you look up and see that everybody else seems to be writing already. You try reading it again. It makes no sense. Your mind is a blank. Panic begins to set in!

What you need are the three Golden Rules:

1 Read the question.

2 Read the question.

3 Answer the question.

○ Tips for success in ICT exams

- Do not rush. There is plenty of time for the written exam papers. It is not a race!

- Read the question. Read the question again … and keep on reading it until you fully understand the situation and what is being asked.

- Answer the question. Make sure you give an answer to the question written in the paper and not a question of your own!

- Cover up the other questions, if you have a spare sheet of paper, and leave visible only the question you are working on. The whole paper will seem much easier.

- Think before you write. Once you have read a question and know what is being asked, take time to stop and think, "What is the best way of explaining my answer?" Too many pupils rush through the written exams and fail to make their answers clear.

Banned words

Never use words such as "thing", "something" or "stuff".

BAD: A thing for reading stuff on shopping items.
☺ GOOD: A device for reading barcodes on shopping items.

Words such as "easier", "quicker", and "cheaper" usually only score marks if they are qualified.

BAD: An email is easier, quicker and cheaper.
☺ GOOD: An email is easier to send than taking a letter to the Post Office. It can be quicker to receive a reply as it arrives in a person's inbox almost instantly and it is cheaper than buying stamps.

Explain

Always make sure the examiner can understand your answer. Try to avoid using the word "it".

BAD: It is faster.
☺ GOOD: Serving customers is faster.

Answer all questions

- Blank paper does not score, so it is always worth having a guess: you never know, you just might be right.

- Avoid one-word answers (unless it is obviously needed). Use full sentences if space allows it.

- Use the mark scheme. The number of marks awarded to each question shows you how much to write. If a question has two marks, for example, then you need to write two points. Also keep an eye on how much space there is for the answer.

Above all, make sure you are properly prepared for the exam. Revise the work thoroughly and you enter the exam with confidence, but not too much!

You have reached the end of a lot of hard work, but hopefully you have found at least some of it enjoyable. Maybe you will go on to explore ICT in greater depths in the future or even make a career from it. Good luck with your results and your future!

Index